LIVING BIOGRAPHIES OF
Famous Women

By HENRY & DANA LEE THOMAS

Illustrations by GORDON ROSS

THE twenty famous women presented in this book have all played important roles in history. Some have ruled nations or led armies. Others have produced great literature and advanced the arts. A few have inspired revolutions and many have led the fight for human rights.

In this fascinating book are told the stories of the following women:

Cleopatra	Susan B. Anthony
Theodora	Frances E. Willard
Joan of Arc	Catherine Breshkovsky
Mary, Queen of Scots	Sarah Bernhardt
Queen Christina	Isadora Duncan
Madame de Maintenon	Schumann-Heink
Charlotte Brontë	Jane Addams
George Eliot	Evangeline Booth
Florence Nightingale	Helen Keller
Elizabeth Barrett Browning	Madame Chiang Kai-shek

Accompanying each of these biographies is a full-page portrait drawn by Gordon Ross, the distinguished artist, and reproduced in duotone gravure.

Florence Nightingale

LIVING BIOGRAPHIES OF
Famous Women

By HENRY THOMAS AND
DANA LEE THOMAS

Illustrations by
GORDON ROSS

Garden City Publishing Co., Inc.
GARDEN CITY, NEW YORK

CL

PRINTED IN THE UNITED STATES OF AMERICA

Contents

[*v*]

CONTENTS

NOTE. Additional sketches of *famous women* will be found in the following volumes of the LIVING BIOGRAPHIES series: Madame Curie —*Great Scientists;* Mary Baker Eddy—*Religious Leaders;* Queen Victoria, Queen Elizabeth, Catherine the Great—*Famous Rulers.*

Introduction

THE WORD *woman* comes from the Old English *wifmann,* and
it means *the wife-half of man.* This half of the human race—
many people would say the *better* half—was held in subjection
for thousands of years. "Day and night," we read in the ancient
code of Manu, "must females be kept in slavery under the domination of their males." Under the early Roman law a husband
could execute his wife, and a father his daughter, for adultery.
Even after the publication of the *Magna Carta,* many centuries
later, a woman could not legally accuse a man of murder. In
eighteenth-century France, the enlightened Rousseau could en-
vision the emancipation of the masculine but not of the feminine
half of humanity. "Women," he said, "are created only to please
men . . . Being incapable of judging for themselves, they must
always abide by the judgment of their fathers and their husbands." And in many parts of the United States, until the time
of the Revolution, women were fined and imprisoned for speaking in public. It was only the threat of a revolt on the part of
the *Mothers* of the Revolution that compelled the *Fathers* of the
Revolution to recognize them as something more than chattels.

INTRODUCTION

"I desire you would remember the ladies"—wrote Abigail Adams to her husband John Adams, who was sitting in the Continental Congress—"and be more generous and favorable to them than were your ancestors . . . If particular care and attention are not paid to the ladies, we are determined to foment a rebellion." It was not till a century and a half later, however, that the men really began to recognize the women as their equals.

Until the present generation, therefore, *the wife-half of man* was born under a handicap. Yet in spite of this handicap, she has presented an epic of achievement no less brilliant than that of her more tyrannical half. In the days of Cleopatra and of Theodora, when the great men were half brutes, the great women were no more brutal than their men. And today, when the great men are trying to be half gods, the great women are no less godly than their men. This volume of *Living Biographies of Famous Women* presents a group of human personages who can with dignity and without apology take their place side by side with their masculine peers.

H. T.
D. L. T.

CLEOPATRA

Important Dates in Life of Cleopatra

69 B.C.—Born at Alexandria, Egypt.

51 B.C.—Ascended throne.

49 B.C.—Deprived of her throne. Went to Syria to raise army for invasion of Egypt.

48 B.C.—Met Caesar and regained her throne.

46 B.C.—Visited Rome.

42 B.C.—Met Mark Antony at Tarsus.

32 B.C.—Induced Antony to divorce his wife.

31 B.C.—Deserted Antony at Battle of Actium. With Antony raised army to regain her lost cause.

30 B.C.—Met final defeat. Killed herself.

Cleopatra

Cleopatra

69 B.C.–30 B.C.

FLUSHED with his victory over Pompey, Caesar had just arrived in Alexandria. He settled down in the palace and proceeded to straighten out the chaotic tangle of Egyptian politics. King Auletes was dead; and two of his children, Ptolemy and Cleopatra, were trying to fight it out for the succession to the throne. At the time of Caesar's arrival Cleopatra was in exile. Her brother's adherents had succeeded in driving her off to Syria. Ptolemy, a child of fourteen, seemed to have the scepter safely grasped in his greedy little hands.

Such was the state of affairs in the fall of the year 48 B.C. It was about seven o'clock in the evening. Caesar, sitting on the balcony of the palace, was watching the busy traffic in the harbor of Eunostos (Happy Landing). Suddenly there was a commotion at the palace gate. An attendant hurried up to Caesar in the balcony. "A traveler, Sir, has just arrived from the Levant. He has a bundle of rare tapestries that he wishes to show you."

"Where is he?"

"The guard at the gate wouldn't let him in, Sir."

Caesar, a patron of the arts, was anxious to have a look at

[*3*]

those tapestries. They might make a good present to be sent to his wife, Calpurnia. "Tell the guard to let this man come to me at once," he said.

The traveler, with the bundle of rugs over his shoulder, was ushered into Caesar's presence. "I will show you something, Sir, the like of which you have never seen." Laying the bundle down carefully on the floor, he began to unroll it. He smiled at Caesar's look of amazement. "Was I right, Sir?"

But Caesar was speechless. For out of the rugs, with hair dishevelled and giggling like a school girl, stepped Cleopatra, daughter of the Egyptian king.

II

CLEOPATRA had the gift of dramatic timing. Throughout her life she played her role like a consummate actress. A woman of astonishing versatility, she could discuss painting, sculpture, poetry, theology, statecraft, philosophy and religion with the most learned men of the time. Her gorgeous personality was woven out of the threads of many colors. She was brilliant, charming, crafty, cruel, affectionate, frivolous, diplomatic, generous on occasion, yet always and completely consumed with a hunger for unlimited power. She had a passion for glory and a passion for men. In short, she was a genius in the fine art of living. Fighting against Destiny with no other weapons save her beauty and her wit, she almost succeeded—as we shall see—in turning Rome into a province of Egypt. Her life ended in tragedy. Yet what other end could the gods have devised for so spectacular a human adventure?

Cleopatra has been called the mistress of all the world's poets, and the hostess of all the world's revelers. Indeed, the age of Cleopatra may well be regarded as the High Carnival Season of the world's history.

[4]

III

The daughter of Ptolemy Auletes (the Flute Player) came by her ambition through a long line of Macedonian ancestors. (Cleopatra was not an Egyptian but a descendant of one of the Macedonian Greek generals who had come to Egypt in the army of Alexander the Great.) The Ptolemies who ruled over Egypt were a picturesque—and pitiless—race. Ptolemy I, called *Soter—the Savior of His People*—lived up to his name, an ancient inscription tells us, by "cutting off quantities of heads and shedding floods of blood." Ptolemy II, named *Philadelphus—Man of Brotherly Love,* murdered two of his brothers. He was fond, the historians tell us, of bad women and of good wine. Ptolemy IV killed his mother and his uncle. Ptolemy VII murdered his people at wholesale "to teach them respect for their king." This man's name, by the irony of the gods, was *Euergetes—the Benefactor*. Ptolemy XIII, nicknamed the *Flute Player—* the father of Cleopatra—murdered his daughter Berenice and then composed a dirge for her funeral.

Yet these Ptolemies were brilliant as well as bloodthirsty. Under their patronage the city of Alexandria became the center of the arts and the sciences of the ancient world. Painting, sculpture, music, literature, astronomy, mathematics, architecture, philosophy—all these refinements of society flourished in Alexandria side by side with the less refined arts of poisoning and the science of assassination. Ruling over the most cosmopolitan city of antiquity, the Ptolemies had acquired a great facility in linguistics. They could express their evil thoughts in many tongues.

Such was the semi-civilized, semi-savage heritage of the madcap princess who tumbled out of the rug to implore the aid of Caesar in the winning back of her throne. A whirlwind of tossing red hair, seductive smiles, supple restless motion, and glittering witticisms expressed in perfect Latin with a delightful Greek accent. There was no resisting this magnetic youngster of twenty Egyptian summers. Caesar, an old man long satiated with the excess of his passion—years ago he had been known as *Everywoman's Husband* (*Omnium Mulierum Vir*)—now found himself, at the age of fifty-two, an ardent young lover again. He restored her to her throne, and became a slave—this conqueror of the world—to Cleopatra's slightest whim.

IV

FIRST OF ALL, Cleopatra induced Caesar to stick his tainted fingers into the unsavory Egyptian pie. She persuaded him to kill Ptolemy, her young brother and rival to the Egyptian throne. And then she invited him to an excursion over the Nile in her royal barge of purple and gold. It was a love tryst between the twilight and the dawn. As they sat in their floating palace, propelled by the oars of fifty Nubian slaves, the epileptic old soldier and the ambitious young adventuress dreamed a golden dream of conquest. Caesar, with the help of Cleopatra, hoped to become the master of Egypt; and Cleopatra, with the help of Caesar, hoped to become the mistress of the world. In order to cement their love and to further her own aims, Cleopatra gave him a son and heir.

But while they were dallying away their time in passive dreams, the enemies of Caesar in Rome had become active and troublesome. They threatened to overthrow him. Even his friends had grown restive. It was not right of their general to languish in a foreign boudoir, they complained, while there were old conquests to be consolidated and new conquests to be made.

And so the "twilight bridegroom" tore himself reluctantly away from the arms of Cleopatra and set sail—not for Rome, but for Pontus in Asia Minor. It would be wise to return home as a triumphant soldier rather than as a triumphant lover. He must bring home a newly subjugated country as a present.

He succeeded in subjugating Pontus, and reported his victory in three swift and arrogant words: *Veni, vidi, vici* (*I came, I saw,*

I conquered). Under the coaching of Cleopatra he had learned to regard himself as a god, and to *boast* like a god.

On his return to Rome he sent for Cleopatra to share in his boastful triumph. He set her up in a palace across the Tiber and, egged on by this "Lady of the Nile," he began to lay plans for the overthrow of the Roman Republic. As soon as he became king, he promised, he would legally marry Cleopatra and make her his queen. And then they would remove the seat of their Empire from Rome to Alexandria, and from that centermost city of the Mediterranean they would rule the world.

Such was the dream of Caesar—or, rather, the dream of Cleopatra as reflected in the action of Caesar. For the cleverest man in Rome had become a mere tool in the hands of the cleverest woman in the world. He was like a man asleep and moving under an hypnotic spell. Under the relentless urging of Cleopatra, who used her own youth and Caesar's passion as a goad, he gradually moved closer and closer to a Roman throne. He made himself consul for ten years, then dictator for life, and finally Divine Son of Jupiter for all time. He ordered a temple to be built to himself and to Cleopatra, and he set up his own and Cleopatra's image in the shrine for public worship. His friends looked on with horror at this dissolution of a great man's character in the arms of an unprincipled woman. "I detest this woman," wrote the orator, Cicero, "and I have good cause for saying so . . . Her insolence I cannot recall without a pang." For this insolence was now threatening to destroy the liberty of the Roman Republic. Cicero and the other leaders of the Republic warned Caesar repeatedly against Cleopatra's machinations and against his own inordinate ambitions. But Caesar went heedlessly ahead with Cleopatra's plans. He caused a "divine bed" to be provided for him in the temple, and a golden throne to be built for him in the senate house. There was but one final step necessary for the consummation of Cleopatra's hopes—the official crowning of Caesar.

And then came the Ides of March, 44 B.C. Cleopatra's excitement was at the highest pitch. For on this day Caesar was to be officially crowned. Cleopatra was to become mistress of the world at last! In an effort to quiet her agitation, she ordered one of her slaves to be suspended head down from the ceiling. Somewhat relieved by this diversion—a favorite remedy for Cleopatra's overwrought nerves—she settled down impatiently to wait for the important news from the senate house.

In the afternoon she received the news. Caesar had been presented—not with a crown, but with a salute of twenty-three dagger stabs instead.

Cleopatra returned to Egypt with a great empty feeling in her heart.

V

CLEOPATRA had played for the highest stakes—and had lost. Yet before long she was ready once more to cast the loaded dice of her destiny. And this time her champion was another Roman soldier—Mark Antony—a younger, sturdier, handsomer, more passionate but equally reckless son of the fickle goddess, Ambition. Antony was a giant of a fighter with the mind of a child and the appetites of a god—a man born to dazzle for a while and to be consumed with the excess of his own ardor. He was full of pranks to amuse people and full of schemes to enslave them. Devoid of sober judgment, he was as intemperate in his generosity as in his cruelty. His soldiers idolized him. He was so much like themselves—a superhuman exaggeration of their own human virtues and weaknesses. Once, when driven with his legion out of Rome, "he gave"—in the words of Plutarch—"a most wonderful example to his soldiers. He who had just quitted so much luxury, made no difficulty now of drinking foul water and feeding on wild fruits and roots."

Life to Antony was a spicy jest, and he greeted it with gusts of laughter. He cared little for public opinion. "Your philosophers tell you how a man ought to live. But *I* show you how a man

[8]

ought *not* to live." Throughout his life he acted on impulse rather than on deliberation. Impulsively he presented his cook with a rich estate—another man's property, by the way, which he had acquired by force of arms—as a reward for a well-prepared supper. And impulsively, too, he ordered the massacre of two thousand Romans, including Cicero, because these men had opposed his political views.

At the time of this Roman massacre (43 B.C.) Antony, together with Octavian and Lepidus, formed a dictatorial triumvirate—an absolute rule of three glorified gangsters. These three men signed a bond of eternal friendship, and each of them made a mental note to stab the others in the back at the first possible opportunity. They divided the world, like a ripe melon, between themselves. In order to collect the funds for the perpetration of their crime—they euphemistically called it "the establishment of a Roman peace"—Antony was commissioned to journey to the countries of the Orient. And it was on this journey that Antony met Cleopatra and, like Caesar before him, became her devoted slave. This "colossal child, capable of conquering a world, incapable of resisting a pleasure," had just arrived in Tarsus. He summoned Cleopatra to come to that city in order that they might discuss "political and financial matters of mutual interest." Cleopatra set sail from Alexandria and anchored her fleet at the mouth of the Cydnus River. Antony took his seat upon the tribunal in the market place and waited for the arrival of his beautiful suppliant. But Cleopatra was in no suppliant mood. "If you want to see me," she sent word through a messenger, "you must come to my galley as my guest."

Antony accepted the invitation and found himself in an enchanted garden. Sea-nymphs and cupids and graces danced over a flower-strewn deck, while a company of flute girls played soft music and a cloud of incense showered a sweet forgetfulness over the senses.

And indeed Antony forgot everything when he saw Cleopatra

in this magical framework. Decked in the loose and semi-transparent robes of the goddess Venus, she sat under an awning bespangled with gold and greeted Antony with a smile of mischievous humility. After the customary exchange of formalities, she led him down to the salon where a sumptuous feast of Egyptian dainties had been prepared. A riotous vision of gold and silver dishes, of velvet embroideries, of goblets inlaid with precious stones. When Antony marveled at the splendor of the banquet, Cleopatra declared that it was only a trifle. And then, as if acting on a sudden impulse, she made him a present of the entire service —dishes, goblets, couches, embroideries and all.

And, in return, Antony made her a present of his heart and his hope and his life. But he did this with his usual abandon. A coarse soldier and a coarse lover, he knew nothing of the refinements of the royal court. At first he amazed Cleopatra with what Plutarch describes as his "rustic awkwardness." But after a while, superb little actress that she was, she adjusted her manner to that of Antony. "Perceiving that his raillery was broad and gross, and that it savored more of the soldier than of the courtier, she rejoined in the same taste and fell into that mood without any reluctance or reserve."

A succession of royal banquets, each of them more sumptuous than the last. Antony tried in vain to rival her magnificence. But the feasts to which he invited her were drab and poor and tasteless—the unimaginative concoctions of a prosaic Roman mind. One night, by way of apology, he remarked that his last banquet had cost him a hundred talents (about a hundred and twenty thousand dollars). "Surely no one can spend more than *that* on a single feast."

Cleopatra laughed. "Well, *I* can. My next feast will cost me a million dollars."

"You're pulling my leg, Cleopatra. Can't be done."

"Do you want to bet?"

"I certainly do."

Whereupon the queen offered him a wager that she would do this the very next day.

At the appointed hour Antony arrived on the queen's galley. The display was rather below the level of Cleopatra's customary splendor. "I guess I win the bet," exulted Antony to himself. Aloud he remarked: "I should say at a rough computation that this outlay—food, dishes and all—would come to about one-fiftieth your boasted sum."

"Wait," smiled Cleopatra. "This is only the beginning." And then, clapping her hands, she ordered her slaves to bring her a table with a little glass of vinegar upon it.

"I wonder what she's up to now?" thought Antony as he looked intently on.

But his wonder grew even more intense at what he saw. For the queen had detached one of the pearls that she wore at her ears and had remarked nonchalantly as she dropped it into the vinegar: "This trifle costs half a million." When the pearl was disintegrated, she let it trickle daintly down her royal throat. "And now," she said, "I am ready for the next pearl."

But Antony held her hand. "Enough," he cried. "You win the wager!"

VI

CLEOPATRA was no fool. There was a method to her madness. She had a practical reason for the lavish display of her wealth. She was anxious to impress Antony with the amplitude of her financial support in his struggle for the mastery of Rome. Her one desire, now that Caesar was dead, was to stir up a quarrel between Antony and Octavian—Lepidus, the third member of the triumvirate, was a man of no account. With Antony's generalship and with her own money they would overthrow Octavian and ascend to the Roman throne. Cleopatra would still be mistress of the world!

Buoyed up by the revival of her dream, she set sail for Alexandria and took back with her the promise of an early visit from Antony.

As for Antony himself, he was eager to see with his own eyes the fabulous wealth of Egypt—and to taste once more the kisses of that red-headed little enchantress of the Nile. And so he lost no time in following the queen to Alexandria. Received like a king, he plunged into a carnival of royal dissipations. "It would be trifling without end," writes Plutarch, "to give a particular account of Antony's and Cleopatra's follies at Alexandria." Mummeries, masquerades, carousals, picnics, excursions, dances, chariot races, and even occasional visits to the taverns disguised as peasants or as slaves. Sometimes at night, a little the worse but none the less merrier for wine, they would steal through the dark streets of the city, knock on the doors and the windows of unknown houses and giggle in the shadows as the owners came out to answer their knocks. Once or twice they were caught and received a severe drubbing, "though most of the people"— Plutarch informs us—"guessed who they were."

The light-hearted merriment of Cleopatra was a good foil for the heavy-witted boorishness of Antony. Once, when Antony had been fishing unsuccessfully in the harbor, he hired a diver to descend into the water and to put fresh fishes upon his hook. Great applause as Antony pulled up these fishes one after another. "What a superb angler you are!" And then suddenly, to everybody's amusement, he pulled up a pickled herring. This was Cleopatra's contribution. Having suspected Antony's trick, she had ordered a slave to dive under the surface and to pin this herring upon his hook. And then, turning to the disconcerted fisherman, she remarked sweetly: "Leave the fishes to us poor Egyptians. *Your* game is cities, provinces, empires."

But Antony, feeding greedily upon the lotus-flower of love, had forgotten his cities and provinces and empires. He was squandering not only his ambition and his strength, but "that most costly of all valuables—time." While Antony was languishing in his

Egyptian boudoir, Octavian was consolidating his own position in Rome.

And Octavian, the nephew of Caesar, was a political rival not to be despised. A physical weakling, he had a mind as inflexible as steel. His sallow complexion, his pockmarked face and his decayed teeth gave no hint of the monster that lay snarling under his skin. Owing to the numerous victims he had sent to their torture and crucifixion, he had come to be known as the "Executioner." Cruel and calculating and sagacious and morose, he hated the sunlight and rarely took a bath. A slimy creature living in a quagmire of physical and mental filth.

Such was the rival that had arisen against Antony in the struggle for the Roman throne. While Antony was a good-natured scoundrel, Octavian was an ill-natured sneak.

And little by little he was sneaking his way to the top. Anxious to seek a quarrel with Antony, he found the conditions ready made for such a quarrel. His sister, Octavia, was married to Antony. It was an easy matter—as indeed it was a matter of truth —to accuse Antony of neglect for his wife and of infatuation for a foreign woman. Octavian sent his sister—though he knew that he sent her in vain—to plead with her husband to return to his family. When Octavia came back empty-handed to Rome, her brother rushed into the senate house and denounced this "renegade and traitor, this drunken monster who has promised to the Egyptian prostitute the Roman Empire as the price of her love."

This sort of thing, agreed the Roman senators, was not to be endured. A fleet was fitted out to sail against Antony. And Antony, now that he was fully aroused, began to prepare a fleet against Octavian. He divorced Octavia, married Cleopatra, and proclaimed himself as the liberator of Rome. (Whenever two ancient gangsters started a civil war, each of them called himself the liberator of his country.)

So sure was Antony of winning the war that he celebrated his triumph even before the fighting had begun. The sailing of his fleet was like a pageant rather than an advance into battle. And it was in the selfsame spirit of pageantry that Cleopatra, with a contingent of her own, accompanied Antony into the battle of Actium. Their hopes were sky-high. A brief and exciting and victorious maneuver—their own fleet was bigger, stronger and better equipped than Octavian's fleet—and Antony and Cleopatra would emerge as the rulers of the world.

Antony prepared himself for the battle by plunging into a protracted drinking bout. In the early morning of the fight he was stupefied with wine. In the late afternoon of the same day he was stupefied with despair.

For the unexpected had happened. The superior ships of Antony had succumbed, one by one, to the inferior ships of Octavian. In the midst of the battle, finding the situation too hot for her comfort, Cleopatra had deserted with her entire contingent, leaving Antony to fight it out alone. And at that very moment Antony's courage, too, deserted him. The soldier had succumbed completely to the lover. As soon as he saw Cleopatra sailing away, he "abandoned all who were fighting and laying down their lives for him, and followed after her to Alexandria."

And to his doom. For the world was no longer a friendly host to Antony. He had outstayed his welcome at life's banquet. Everybody looked with disdain at the defeated champion who had "followed the flag of a woman's skirts." Even Cleopatra had come to despise him. She knew how to cheer with a victor, but not how to chafe with a victim. Antony, like Caesar, had failed her. She had no further use for him. His star had set.

But not her own star. Not yet. Her ambition to become the empress of Rome might still be fulfilled. If not as the wife of Caesar or of Antony, then as the wife of Octavian. Antony would probably kill himself—good riddance!—and Octavian would find her repentant and beautiful and ready to make amends. What matter who sat beside her, provided she occupied the throne as mistress of the world?

In this her final reckoning there were but two flaws—her own waning beauty and Octavian's unresponsive heart. Antony killed himself, and Octavian came to see her. He came, he saw, and remained unconquered. He offered indeed to take her back to Rome—not, however, as his wife but as his slave. To him she was nothing but a woman captured in war, and not a princess fit to rule by his side. She smiled as he spoke to her, promised that she would acquiesce in his wishes, and made up her mind to submit to the sting of an asp rather than to the tender mercies of Octavian. Though Octavian's prisoner, she managed to have the snake smuggled into her apartment in a basket of fruit.

And thus the over-hungry princess, the mortal who would rule the world, received her full final share of mortal glory. She supplied a royal banquet to the hungry worms.

THEODORA

Important Dates in Life of Theodora

508—Born at Constantinople.
520—Entered professional career on stage.
523—Married Prince Justinian.
527—Became co-ruler, with Justinian, of Roman Empire.
529—Helped her husband to formulate the famous Justinian Code of legal reform.
532—Quelled, through her courageous refusal to flee, the Nika insurrection.
548—Died.

Theodora

Theodora

508–548

Her life began dismally enough. Her father, the trainer of
the wild beasts at the Constantinople Arena, had been hugged
to death by a bear. Her mother, left with three little daughters
on her hands, hired them out at first to the menial tasks of the
circus. Later, when they became older and prettier, she introduced
them to the more profitable but none the less degrading duties of
the brothel. Theodora was only ten when she became acquainted
with the "dishonorable profession"—not, however, as a partici-
pant but as an assistant. She followed her older sister Comito
from house to house, with a stool on her head, and waited until
her sister was ready to start for her next assignment.

At twelve, Theodora was considered old enough and sophisticated enough to assume the full duties of the profession. And
then she was graduated from the stews to the stage. But this
meant no elevation in her social rank. For actresses and courtesans
and race horses were regarded as of equal rank—the sub-human
instruments of public and private entertainment.

But Theodora soon came to be known as an entertainer of
unusual gifts. She had a way of puffing out her cheeks, and screw-

ing up her face, and writhing with imaginary pain at imaginary blows. She could send the entire circus into gales of laughter. A likely bit of baggage for the tired businessmen of Constantinople.

And a toothsome little morsel for the aristocratic young blades at their private dinners. At one of these dinners—our authority for this is the historian Procopius—she entertained in turn ten guests and thirty slaves. "And when the dawn came, she was the least tired of the lot."

She was the delight of all the young men and the contempt of all the old women of Constantinople. Seductive, talented, cunning, beautiful and avaricious, she was ready to sell her charms to patricians and plebeians alike. She showed little interest in the tincture of a man's blood. All she cared for was the color of his coin. She was as empty of graciousness as she was full of grace. A woman to be caressed but not to be trusted. For her bond was as bad as her word. Again and again she would sell one of her "nights" to a high bidder and then drive him out of her house if a higher bidder happened to present himself. "One of these days," her mother warned her, "you'll get an awful jolt."

"Yes," nodded her sister Comito, "or a lucky strike."

"I'm ready to take them both," smiled Theodora. But she was quite unaware at the time how prophetically she spoke. For her entire future was to be a dramatic succession of blessings and blows.

II

HER FIRST GREAT BLESSING came in the guise of a Tyrian nobleman by the name of Hekebolus. This man had just been appointed governor of the African province of Pentapolis (Bengasi). To celebrate his good fortune, he invited a number of his friends to a banquet and hired Theodora to entertain them. Her performance was so delightful that Hekebolus, in a fit of drunken inspiration, asked her to accompany him to Africa.

"As your wife?"

"Sorry, but that is impossible. The law against the marriage of a patrician to an actress, you know."

"Very well," she said, "I'll go as your mistress."

It was quite a step for the daughter of the animal trainer. From the circus to the governor's mansion. Yet it was not exactly what Theodora had wanted. Africa was a dull country full of "barbarians." She missed the glittering night life of Constantinople. Hekebolus, to be sure, was quite pleased with her. But she was not at all pleased with Hekebolus. The governor had placed her away, for safe keeping, in the *gynaeceum* (the women's quarter of the palace). No fun to be sitting there alone, her only pastime a snatch of spicy gossip with the eunuch who had been set up as her guardian. But she got even with Hekebolus. She bribed her eunuch to admit an occasional young gentleman of leisure when the governor was busy with his administrative duties.

An indiscreet thing to do. And this indiscretion brought about her first great blow. One day Hekebolus came unexpectedly into her apartment, discovered her infidelity, and sent her packing into the desert.

Desolate stretches of sand before her. Hot and trackless and hopeless days. From town to town and from village to village she wandered—a bedraggled peddler of love. Poverty-stricken communities, poverty-stricken louts. Just a few crumbs of bread to keep skin and bones together. A rag of a tunic over an exhausted body, a ragged pair of sandals over swollen feet. A swirling dust-storm overhead, a swirling despair within.

Little by little she dragged her way to Alexandria. For an admission ticket within the gates, she greeted the guard with a lascivious gesture. He understood her business and let her go in. In a city of a hundred thousand courtesans and five hundred thousand men, Theodora would find toleration if not prosperity.

Yet shortly after her arrival in the "Paris of the ancient world" she was arrested—some street brawl or other—and her back was branded with a red-hot iron. She was to retain this "beauty spot" to the end of her days.

A succession of aimless street-walking in quest of trade, and then another liaison with a rich man. And another desertion. This last lover was a merchant of Antioch. When his business in Alexandria was over, he left her unceremoniously in spite of the fact that she was about to become a mother.

Barely eighteen, and she had already drained bitterness to the dregs. There were but two ways out of her difficulty—suicide or a convent. She chose the latter.

For a while she yielded to the shelter of the convent; and then, when her son was born, her restlessness drove her on. She sailed to Antioch, only to find that the father of the child had died. Leaving the babe on the doorstep of its grandmother, she peddled her way back to Constantinople. "Perhaps with the return to my country, I will have a return of my luck."

And now the historians give us two versions of the next stage in her career. One school would have it that she settled down in an out-of-the-way cottage, plying the loom and praying to the saints, until Justinian, the "Prince Charming," learned of her pious ways and removed her from her Cinderella-like poverty to the splendor of his palace. The other school, less romantic but more realistic, declares that the incorrigible adventuress literally danced her way into the royal bed.

We shall here adopt the second version, since it is more in keeping with the character of Theodora. In accordance with this version, an old actress-friend of Theodora's gave her a letter of introduction to Justinian. "I knew him in the days when his blood was younger," said the actress Macedonia. "Perhaps with my recommendation, you can induce him to send you back to the circus. That is," she added, "if you can ever get to see him."

"At least I can try," said Theodora.

She tried, and she succeeded. One night, as Justinian sat poring over his state papers and sipping his favorite mutton-broth, there was a stir behind the tapestries at the window, and Theodora stepped into the room. Justinian looked up with a frown. "I am busy," he growled, "and I don't want to be disturbed."

He was about to ring for an attendant, when something in her face stopped him. A familiar look. He had seen it somewhere . . . Oh, yes, in the circus, several years ago. That droll smile of hers, half comical, half pathetic. How *could* you resist it! "But how did you get past the guards?" he asked.

"I came in through the back, scrambled up the vines, almost fell down and broke my silly little neck—and, here I am!"

The hem of her dress was slit, showing the turn of an exquisite ankle. He rather liked this daring tomboy of a slut. "And what," he asked, "do you want of me?"

"Your friendship," she replied simply, as she handed him Macedonia's letter.

He read it, and then ran his fingers through the fringe of his grizzled curls. "So you want to return to the circus?"

"If I must, your Excellency. But I would far rather not."

She looked at him provocatively, and his eyes met hers in an understanding smile. "You shall not go back to the circus."

III

JUSTINIAN, the heir to the Eastern empire, was a Bulgarian peasant by birth. His uncle Justin, an illiterate Hercules of a lout, had started as a soldier of fortune and had fought his way to the throne. Sixty-eight when he was crowned emperor, he adopted Justinian as his son and heir. Justinian had the body of a clown, the mind of a sage, and the tastes of a parvenu. Though scholarly and saturnine and generally aloof, he loved to surround himself with fabulous grandeur on his few public appearances. His pomposity became him like a diadem on the brow of a bull. He was a civilized savage. And he found in Theodora a gaudy adornment for the Byzantine splendor of his palace.

Yet an adornment which even the easy-going inhabitants of Constantinople were reluctant to accept. To turn a peasant into a king was well enough. But a courtesan into a queen? That was too much! "Down with the harlot!" they shouted. "Her name is not Theodora, the gift of God, but Demonodora, the gift of the Devil!"

More serious even than the displeasure of the multitude was the disapproval of the Empress Lupicina, the wife of the Emperor Justin. A woman of rustic manners and of rigorous morals, Lupicina refused to accept a courtesan for her niece. But Justinian waited patiently for Lupicina's death—a very old creature by now—and then he induced his uncle to liberalize the marriage laws as affecting the various social classes. "A glorious repentance"—so ran the new edict—"is left open for the unfortunate females who have been compelled to demean their persons in the theater; and henceforth they are permitted to contract a legal union with the most illustrious citizens of the Empire."

And so Justinian married Theodora, and forbade the people to cast any further aspersions upon her. "Let greatness own her, and she's mean no more."

At the beginning of their reign, Theodora was known as the wife of the king. Before long, however, Justinian came to be known as the husband of the queen. For Theodora's personality had completely subjugated the personality of Justinian. No princess of the royal blood ever wore her crown more arrogantly than did this daughter of the circus bear-keeper. When the nobles, after a long and dreary attendance in the anteroom, were finally admitted to kiss her feet, she dismissed them with a kick or a biting jest. Sensitive about her past, she hired a host of spies to report any slurring remarks they might hear about her. A single hasty word even on the part of a senator meant the loss of his head—or of his tongue at the very least. And when the executioner was too laggard in the performance of his duty, she spurred him on in the name of Christ but with a most un-Christlike threat: "If you fail in the execution of my commands, I swear by Him who liveth forever that I will have you flayed alive!"

She was as avaricious as she was vicious. She took away the money from the wealthiest citizens; and then, "out of pity for their bitter destitution," she took away their lives.

Born actress that she was, she knew how to dramatize the death of her victims. One day Justinian got word that the Gothic chieftain, Vitalian, had designs upon his kingdom. At Theodora's advice, he invited Vitalian, together with his retinue, to visit him at Constantinople. "I wish to discuss the matter of a military alliance between us." Had Vitalian been on his guard, he would have treated Justinian's letter in his customary manner. That is, he would have lopped off the messenger's ear and sent it back to Justinian as a sign that he paid no heed to his message. Suspecting nothing, however, or fearing perhaps to come out into open rebellion, he accepted Justinian's invitation and arrived in Constantinople with a company of his most trusted followers.

"Welcome to our palace!" The emperor and the empress were all blandishments and smiles. They took them to the chariot races and the theaters and the gladiatorial fights. And then they regaled them with an entertainment prepared especially in their honor—the execution of a hundred criminals who were thrown into the amphitheater as the sport of twenty lions and thirty leopards.

"We shall have much to tell our friends when we return home," said Vitalian.

"Yes, indeed," replied Theodora gaily. "But the best of your entertainment is yet to come." That evening they were to be tendered a farewell banquet at the palace. "I hope it will be a memorable occasion."

"I am sure it will."

The feast was one of the most extravagant even in that most extravagant of ages. It was held in the famous Hall of the Nineteen Couches—golden roof, gold-fringed draperies, three hundred crescent-shaped tables inlaid with ivory and studded with precious stones. The guests arrived in all their barbarian glitter. The royal pair met them with honey-dripping cordiality. "We shall be so desolate when you are gone!"

And what a sumptuous assortment of appetizing dishes! And garlands and wines! And flute-girls and dancers and jugglers and mummers and clowns! Late into the night they sat and emptied their cups and bawled out their none-too-delicate sallies of barbaric wit. At last Justinian and Theodora begged leave to depart. "The Empress is tired. Has had a busy day . . . But don't disturb yourselves, please. You're welcome to stay here forever."

A gracious king. And a generous queen. Vitalian and his retainers settled down again to their wine-cups and their flute-girls and their jests. They stayed on long after the torches had been extinguished. And the gray of the dawn came in through the windows and fell upon a ghastly sight. A banquet of the dead. Under every couch, a puddle of wine mingled with a pool of blood. The royal couple had ordered the slaves to stab their guests when they had grown too intoxicated to fight back.

IV

THEODORA had no regard for anybody save one class—the "professional" class out of which she had sprung. She understood these ill-fated derelicts, she knew their hardships, and she pitied them for their helplessness. These poor harridans were compelled to sell their bodies so frequently in their youth that they were swept in their middle years, like so many outworn rags, into the gutter. And so the harlot-empress turned one of her palaces into an asylum for her less fortunate sisters. Five hundred of her co-professionals found a refuge in this *Repentatory-on-the-Sea;* and the picture of their rescue drew many a tear from the sentimentalists but brought an occasional snicker to the cynics. For some of these women were so disgusted with their enforced virtue that they threw themselves headlong into the sea. They wanted nobody, not even an empress, to interfere with their "legitimate" business.

Theodora was a busybody. She insisted on sticking her dainty finger not only into the domestic pie but into the pudding of foreign affairs. She inspected the silk factories, the dye works and the shipyards, and she directed important changes in their management. She took a hand in matchmaking—often to the inconvenience of the young people involved—in order to secure the stability of her throne. She helped her husband in the formulation of the Justinian Code. She instituted laws which restricted the freedom of men and furthered the interests of women. (Theodora was the first militant feminist in history.) She dethroned a pope and set up another in his place. And she insisted on presiding, along with Justinian, at the trials and the petitions of her people. Indeed, her domination over Justinian had become the subject of a popular ditty that was being sung in the taverns:

> *Justinian was strong and real,*
> *Justinian was made of steel.*
> *And now Justinian the brave*
> *Is turned into a woman's slave.*

But, even her enemies confessed, Justinian was the slave of a brilliant woman. In spite of her lowly origin, she acted the queen with consummate skill. A glittering heroine in the drama of a barbaric age.

Theodora was all-powerful. And yet she was unhappy. For Justinian was unable to give her a son. An heir to the throne of her eastern Empire. To be sure there was a "natural" heir, the illegitimate son she had borne to Hekebolus. But this young man—he was now full grown—represented a phase of her life she was only too eager to forget. He had committed the unpardonable rashness to visit her on one occasion. It was the last visit he ever paid to her. Indeed, it was the last time anybody ever heard of him. Theodora knew how to deal with unwelcome guests, even if these guests happened to be her own flesh and blood.

And so she continued her career of unhappy splendor—a woman despised for her cruelty yet admired for the flashes of her brilliant statesmanship. The people despised and admired —and starved. Increasing taxes, protracted wars, excessive cost of living, widespread unemployment, sickness, despondency, death. The daily ration of corn had been reduced by two-thirds. Hungry people in crowds stood around the palace, wondering what new extravagance was going on within. Little by little their wondering grew into a murmur, and then into a sullen roar. One morning the officers of the palace were amazed to find that during the night the two royal statues had been plastered with mud. And finally the aspersions were turned from the statues to the royal personages themselves.

It was in the hippodrome that the revolt took final shape. Sunday, January the eleventh. The audience facing the *kathisma* —royal box—were singing the national hymn to the emperor. Theodora was not present at the time—she had remained behind to pray at the Church of Saint Stephen. It was a lucky thing perhaps that she wasn't at the hippodrome. For suddenly the audience got out of hand. A scattering of hisses, a handful of catcalls, and then thousands of voices began to shout:

"Down with the extravagant king!"

"And his murderous queen!"

"Away with the strumpet! Back to where she belongs!"

Justinian, his face the color of wax, slipped out of the hippodrome and made his way through a covered passage to the palace. He gave immediate orders for the execution of the ring-leaders. It was a grave mistake. Seven men were beheaded, and seven hundred sprang up in their place. The rebellion had now spread throughout the city. Shops were closed, the market was deserted, all business had stopped. An infuriated mob, armed with knives and stones and pickaxes, was descending upon the palace. "Burn down that gilded brothel! . . . Death to the tyrants! . . . Victory!"

They stormed the cellar, staved in the wine-barrels, and wallowed in a red river of frenzy. "Where are those murderers? Lead us to them!"

In an inner room of the palace cowered Justinian, his body quaking with an unkingly tremor. In another room lay Theodora, dangerously ill. For some months now she had been suffering from an incurable cancer. She had dropped into a fitful doze. A beautiful dream. No pain, no rebellion, no opposition to her imperial will. Nothing but a host of marching soldiers, shouting the battle-cry of victory . . .

The shouting woke her from her sleep. She gasped as she tried to catch her breath. That excruciating thorn in the flesh. And that ominous din. They were beating at the doors of the imperial suite.

So *that* was the end of her triumph? Not if she could help it! Painfully raising herself on her elbow, she rang for her lady-in-waiting. "Dress me in my robe of state—the Tyrian purple gown and the mantle of gold."

They dressed her and put her upon her feet. She bit her lip to suppress the twisting torture in her flesh. "Draw aside the curtains."

"But your Majesty, it would mean certain death."

"I told you to draw aside the curtains!"

"Yes, your Majesty."

The sky was a crimson flame. The mob had set fire to the city during the night. The conflagration, like a hungry beast, was

[29]

licking at the charred houses with a thousand tongues. Theodora turned once more to her attendant. "Unbolt the window."

As the window came open, a stone flew into the room and barely missed Theodora's head. But she paid no attention to it. Supported on the arm of her lady-in-waiting, she stepped out upon the balcony.

Involuntarily the leaders of the mob started back. They hadn't expected this courage on her part.

"She's got plenty of nerve, all right."

"Yes, and they say she's sick."

"She sure *is* sick. Look at that white face of hers."

"Poor thing! She was one of us, you know."

"And she is still one of us, even if she *is* a queen."

Theodora raised her hand for silence. "Tell me what you want."

"Bread, Basilissa, nothing more!"

"You shall have bread," she said, "and something besides. A special performance at the circus. The most exciting spectacle Constantinople has ever seen."

Her promise passed from mouth to mouth. "Hail, Basilissa! Long live the Queen Theodora!"

January the eighteenth. The fires in the city had not as yet subsided. But the people, heedless of their homes, had flocked to the hippodrome. A hundred thousand spectators, to see the free show. The imperial couple—Theodora had just barely managed to get out of her bed—were being ushered into the kathisma. The emperor was dressed in black, the empress in white satin. The spectators stood up, and shouted their greeting: "God save Justinian! God save Theodora!"

And now the spectacle begins—a festivity of races and gymnastics and dances that will continue from early morning until late in the afternoon. The spectators have brought their lunches along with them. They like their food highly spiced—blood-puddings, pickled olives, sausages seasoned with garlic, boiled peas and lentils, goat's cheese mixed with mustard, sour wine. All this food has been supplied at the personal expense of Theodora. A red letter day in Constantinople.

Before the day is over, the royal couple have left the arena. They always manage to leave just before the climax.

The final chariot race, and then—a surprise. An act not announced on the program. Belisarius, the imperial general, marches into the arena with his German battalion of armed soldiers. The spectators greet them with loud cheers. A battle maneuver, no doubt, arranged for their special benefit. It must have been Theodora's idea. Wonderful basilissa!

But this is no maneuver. It is the real thing. "Ready, aim, fire!" A volley of arrows flies straight into the crowded ranks of the arena. It *was* Theodora's idea.

A cry of consternation—"we are betrayed!"—and a stampede for the exits in the back. Here, however, they are met by another battalion of armed men. A four-deep phalanx of barbarian peasants intent upon ploughing a furrow of blood. "We are ready, General Belisarius!"

There was no escape for the entrapped audience. The clangor of metal, the twang of the bowstrings, the shrieks of the dying, the rattle of death. The slaughter continued well into the sunset —a huge red disk reflected in a huge red pool of blood. Thirty thousand men lay massacred in the arena.

And Theodora, her lips twisted with agony, smiled a bitter smile of triumph. She had conquered the rebels.

V

BUT there was one rebel against whom neither Belisarius nor his German cohorts could protect Theodora. Her fate. In her effort to escape from this antagonist, she fled to the hot springs of Brusa. A surrounding shield of four thousand men went along to guard her. She tried the medicine of prayers and the salve of charity. But to no avail. That constant, terrifying, ominous stab in the side. Like an expert duelist playing with his victim and tantalizingly putting off his final blow. Theodora expressed but a single wish now—that she might die before her body would become disfigured.

She had her wish. Her face, as it relaxed in death, was still unwrinkled with age. She left a simple request. "Have my body bathed in oil of roses and sprinkled with Phrygian perfume." Fastidious voluptuary to the end, she wanted to be fresh and fragrant when she came to her final rendezvous with death.

JOAN OF ARC

Important Dates in Life of Joan of Arc

1412—Born at Domremy-on-the-Meuse.

1424—Heard "voice of God" for the first time.

1428—Started on her crusade to save "the pity that was France."

1429—Raised the siege of Orleans. July 16—Brought about coronation of Dauphin Charles at Reims. December 29—Raised to noble rank.

1430—May 23—Captured at Compiègne.

1431—January 3—Handed over to her judge, Pierre Cauchon. February 31—New trial begun at Rouen. May 23—Signed abjuration. May 30—Burned at the stake in the Old Market Square of Rouen.

Joan of Arc

Joan of Arc
1412–1431

Once, on a holy day in midsummer, when all the pious folk were fasting and heaven and earth seemed to be closer than ever to each other, a little peasant girl of Domremy heard a voice speaking to her out of the silence. It was the voice of the archangel Michael, and it said, "Be a good girl, Joan. Go to church often."

She was frightened, but not altogether surprised. The angels, her parents had informed her, were known on occasion to speak to mortals. Why not to her as well as to another? Saint Michael was far from being a stranger to her. She had learned his story at her mother's knee, and she had often seen his picture on the wall of the church. It was quite natural that he should tell her, just as the priest of the village might have told her, to be a good girl and to attend to her prayers.

But she kept her secret to herself. People might laugh at her, and her parents might scold her. After all, she was only a little bit of a girl, too young perhaps to understand the language of the angels.

And so she held her peace and continued to live in her fairy world of heavenly communication. Before long the archangel Michael was joined by Saint Marguerite and Saint Catherine. They, too, were familiar figures to Joan. When she saw them in the air above her, she recognized them at once from their pictures.

Joan was twelve years old when she first met the angels. They came to speak to her every day, and frequently several times a day. She saw them most clearly, and heard their voices most distinctly, when the church bells were ringing. At first they spoke to her of ordinary matters, but one day Saint Michael told her of the pity that he had for the kingdom of France. "Daughter of God," he said—for this was the name he had given her—"the time has come when you must leave your village and go to the aid of France."

There was no doubt of it in her mind now. God had appointed her to deliver her country from the English invader—the terrible ogre that infested the fairyland of her dreams.

II

IN THE FIFTEENTH CENTURY almost everybody "talked with the angels or knew somebody who talked with them." A certain Brother Richard, interpreting—as he said—the direct voices of heaven, stirred the whole city of Paris into a frenzy of superstitious evangelism. The Carmelite friar, Thomas Conecta, taking his cue (as he declared) from the saints in heaven, preached in Belgium and in France to audiences of fifteen and twenty thousand at a time. In Brittany, a young woman by the name of Pierrette startled her compatriots by telling them that she was in constant communication with Jesus himself. A French shepherd boy was reported to have sweated blood in the holy days. Every province had its hysterical men and women who believed, and who made others believe, that they saw and conversed with the spirits in heaven.

It was these miraculous tales of heavenly visions that nourished little Joan's imagination throughout her childhood. She was never taught to read or to write. Her education consisted almost exclusively of myths and fables which she was brought up to believe as true. "Born under the very walls of the church"—we are quoting the French historian, Michelet—"rocked to sleep by the sound of the bells and nurtured on legends, she came to be a living legend to herself." Not far from her father's house was a forest in which fairies were believed to dwell. Above, in the flying clouds, she saw the angels riding in their chariots. Far away on the horizon, the Vosges Mountains towered even above the clouds up to the very throne of God. If only she were old enough to climb those peaks that led the way to heaven! Oftentimes, when her father was away in the fields and her mother was working in the house, she sat dreaming on the doorstep and listening to the sounds of the village. A confused, drowsy, exquisite murmur—wasn't it the very voice of the angels talking to her? The dividing line between this world and the next was very vague. Angels and men, to her childish imagination, could mingle and talk together as naturally as two next-door neighbors meeting on the street. To hear an angel call you from above was no more surprising than to hear your mother call you from the kitchen. There was no miracle in this. On the contrary, Joan would have regarded it as a miracle if you had told her that the angels did *not* speak to God's children on earth.

In short, she lived in a world in which it was impossible for her to distinguish between the unreal and the real. The angels could come down to her on earth; and she, on occasion, could be lifted up to meet them in heaven.

A beautiful and heavenly existence was hers—or rather, *might have been* hers were it not for the ogre of that invading army. The English "Goddams"—the French called them "Goddons" —were overrunning the kingdom of France. The English soldiers were reaping the harvests of the French peasants. They were burning their homes and carrying off their cattle. Sometimes, in the middle of the night, Joan would be awakened by the cries of the fugitives from other villages. Once her own parents were obliged to flee from the invader. When the family returned home they found the village sacked, their house plundered, and the church in flames.

The goodness of the saints in heaven, and the pitiable plight of the kingdom of France—these were the two outstanding facts in the life of the little peasant girl of Domremy. France was dear to the saints—her mother had impressed this thought upon her mind again and again—and they would do everything in their power to drive the "English robbers" away from its sacred soil. It was prophesied that a young virgin would become the Savior of France. Merlin the Magician, and Marie of Avignon, a holy woman who regularly conversed with the angels, had both foretold this. And, little by little, the conviction had grown upon Joan of Arc that *she* was the virgin—*la Pucelle*—appointed by heaven for the salvation of France. The time had come for her to speak to her parents. "Tell them," Saint Michael had admonished her, " that you must leave your home and your beloved, and go to the aid of your king."

III

WHEN Joan informed her parents about her decision, her father insisted that she must remain at home. He had had a number of disturbing dreams about her—a succession of nocturnal warnings that his daughter would go away in the company of soldiers. And to his rude and masculine mind, familiar with the ways of fighting men, this proposed adventure on the part of Joan could mean only one thing—a life of shame. "If you dare to leave this house," he threatened, "I will drown you with my own hands!"

As a further obstacle to her departure, her father attempted to marry her off to one of the local peasants. He even conspired with her suitor to trump up a breach of promise case against her. But she defied her father and rejected her suitor and convinced the judges that she had never given her promise to anybody. "In obedience to the heavenly voices, I have dedicated myself to a life of chastity and to the task of delivering my country."

Yet how to go about this task? She went with her perplexity to her protecting saints. "I am only a poor girl. I can neither ride nor fight. How, then, can I come to the aid of France?"

Whereupon Saint Michael advised her to go to Robert de Baudricourt, the lord of the township of Vaucouleurs and of the village of Domremy. This man, the archangel assured her, would supply her with the men and the means for the journey to Chinon, where the Dauphin Charles, heir apparent to the French throne, lived timidly in the palace—an uncrowned king in a conquered land.

Joan left for Vaucouleurs under the guidance of an elderly cousin, a certain Durand Lassois—the only member of her family who trusted in her. The others were too close to her to know her. You'd never suspect that an angel would be peeling potatoes in your kitchen. Her parents and her brothers saw nothing divine in Joan. To them she was merely a kitchen drudge carried away by a foolish dream of adventure.

And to Baudricourt, too, she appeared to be nothing but a foolish little adventuress. He had no faith in her self-appointed mission. Ridiculous to regard this homely, awkward farm girl, with the heavy features and the rustic speech, as the Savior of the French people!

But the rank and file of the people thought otherwise. Nothing strange about a Savior coming out of a lowly position. Good medieval Christians that they were, they believed in her story about the angels just because it was so unbelievable. They bought her a horse and a soldier's uniform, and gave her a small escort of armed men. Baudricourt, carried away at last by the enthusiasm of the people, presented her with a sword.

And thus, early in the spring of 1429, the seventeen-year-old Joan of Arc, accompanied by her escort and dressed in male attire, was off on her strange errand to heal "the sad pity that was France."

IV

HER FIRST OBJECTIVE was to reach the Dauphin's palace at Chinon. The Dauphin Charles was a vacillating, weak-kneed, credulous, stupid and superstitious clown. When Joan of Arc was admitted into his presence he was surrounded by a group of courtiers. She had no difficulty, however, in singling him out, for he was by far the ugliest man in the palace. She presented herself humbly, as befitted a woman of her station. "Gentle Dauphin," she said, as she embraced his knees, "my name is Jehanne la Pucelle. The King of Heaven has commanded you, through me, to be crowned as the King of France."

The Dauphin gave ready ear to the story of Joan of Arc. For he was a devout believer in the miracles and the magic of the fifteenth century. He, too, had been inspired by the prophecy of Merlin and of Marie of Avignon. A virgin was to be the Savior of France. And here the promised Savior actually stood before him, armed with the command of the Lord and ready to lead him to victory and a crown!

The ardent wish of the peasant girl became the will of the Dauphin Charles.

In accordance with the plans of the angels, declared Joan, she was now commissioned to perform two solemn duties. She must deliver the city of Orleans from the English Goddons; and she must lead the Dauphin to the city of Reims and anoint him with the sacred oil which had been used in the coronation of King Clovis, the Christian founder of the royal line of France.

The Dauphin accepted her mission and appointed her commander-in-chief of the little army that he had been able to gather around his standard. In those days it was not unusual for women to fight side by side with the men. There were thirty women wounded in the battle of Amiens. A number of women soldiers fought among the followers of Johannes Huss in Bohemia. There was hardly a medieval siege in which some woman was not conspicuous for heroism. It was, therefore, quite natural for Charles to accept the military services of Joan of Arc. He remembered the heroines of the Old Testament—Deborah and Judith and Jael—who, with the help of Heaven, had conquered the enemies of Israel. Here, now, was a new prophetess, summoned also by the messengers of Heaven, to conquer the enemies of France. With Saint Michael leading the way, and with Saint Catherine and Saint Marguerite on either side of her, this inspired maid of Domremy would enable him to drive the Goddams forever out of his kingdom!

Raising an army of 8,000 men, a considerable force for those days, she set out against the English who were besieging the city of Orleans. See her now launched upon her "holy adventure," this unschooled and inspired country girl, dressed in her snow-white armor, and riding at the head of her column upon a coal-black horse. At her side she has buckled on a battleaxe and a sword, and in her hand she carries a white standard with God and the angels painted upon it against a background of fleur-de-lis. The people, the soldiers, "and even the animals," as one of her contemporaries quaintly expressed it, acknowledged her as the messenger of God. "I saw her mount her great black charger," wrote Gui de Laval. "The horse, which was making a great fuss before the door of her lodging, would not allow her to mount. So she said, 'Lead him to the cross,' which was in front of the neighboring church. And then she mounted, *and the horse stirred no more than if he had been enchanted.*"

Joan of Arc possessed the magic spell of a warrior-angel descended from Heaven. Yet she was not warlike by nature. She preferred, if possible, to drive the English out of France without any fighting. For herself, she vowed that she would never use her sword in the killing of anybody. When she arrived at Orleans, she dictated to the English a letter in which she asked them, simply and bluntly, to get out. "I call upon you, in the name of the King of Heaven, to take yourselves off. *Allez-vous en.*"

The English, naturally, paid no attention to her ultimatum and awaited her attack, which developed into the historic Battle of Orleans. The final victory of Joan of Arc over the English was no miracle. The English army, under the brave but unintelligent Talbot, numbered only 2,000 or 3,000 men in all, and quite a few of them were Frenchmen. This small force was dispersed over several strongholds that surrounded the city. There was practically no communication between these scattered units of the besieging force, and it was an easy matter for Joan to enter the city with her "army of Saviors." This army was regarded, both by the French and by the English, as heaven-sent. Their leader was not Joan of Arc, but the Archangel Michael. It was a foregone conclusion that the English would fall before the onslaught of this terrible warrior who had descended from the very skies to drive them out of France.

The French troops, like the English troops, were a horde of scoundrels. Soldiering in the fifteenth century was no profession for gentle souls. The soldiers of that period had no romantic illusions about the glory of war. They looked upon it as a pleasurable and profitable business, like piracy or highway robbery. Frankly brutal in their attitude toward their profession, they admitted that it was impossible for a soldier ever to be a respectably decent man. La Hire, the captain of Joan's army at Orleans, once remarked that "God Himself, if ever He enlisted in the army, would become a brigand." But the presence of Joan, accompanied by her invisible saints, had turned the French troops into *consecrated* brigands. Every last soldier in the French army devoutly believed that battalions of angels were fighting on his side. And this belief was shared by the English. Some of the English, to be sure, were of the opinion that the so-called celestial auxiliaries of the French troops were demons rather than angels. But of one thing the English were certain: they were fighting against insuperable odds. They were quite able to cope with the powers of the earth; but against the powers of heaven or of hell, even a medieval soldier felt rather helpless.

The English soldiers, in short, were driven out of Orleans by their own fear of the supernatural, as well as by the superior numbers of the French. "There fell upon us," wrote the Duke of Bedford, "a terrible stroke by the hand of God."

V

THE Battle of Orleans was over. Joan of Arc had been wounded on the final day of the fighting. But the wound was not serious— "a mere piercing of the shoulder," as she nonchalantly put it, to a depth of six inches.

And now the shouting has died away. The flames have subsided. The soldiers, French and English alike, are plunged in a sleep of exhaustion after their strenuous ordeal. But there is no sleep for the restless *Pucelle*. Her wound dressed, "she refreshes herself with a slice of bread dipped in wine mixed with a great deal of water—the only thing she has eaten or drunk during the whole day—" and then she lies down on her couch, wide-eyed, alert, planning the next step of her heaven-appointed journey.

This next step took her back to the Dauphin Charles. Her army had now increased to 12,000 men. Everywhere she was looked upon either as a saint or as a sorceress, depending upon whether one espoused the French or the English cause. She met the Dauphin at Tours and together they advanced along the banks of the Loire to the city of Reims. Impatient as the Dauphin was to receive the crown, Joan of Arc was even more impatient to bestow it. "Gentle Dauphin, do not hold such long and wordy councils, but hurry to your coronation at Reims . . . The voices have said to me, 'Daughter of God, go, go, go!' "

It was as if she knew that her days were numbered. She must fulfill her mission before it was too late. And so she advanced in feverish haste toward Reims. And the English army, driven into a frenzy of terror, fled before her. Now and then, to be sure—at Jargeau, at Patay, at Troyes—they made a half-hearted attempt at resistance. But the inspired soldiers of Joan of Arc swept them out of their path. Joan tried to avoid fighting as much as possible. She wanted the English to depart from France, but she did not hate them. She sickened at the sight of blood. She mourned at the sufferings of her enemies as much as she mourned at the sufferings of her own men. A wounded soldier, whether English or French, was to her a Christian brother in distress. After the battle of Patay she wept to see so many of the enemy's soldiers lying dead on the ground. One of her own comrades brutally struck down an English prisoner. Dismounting from her horse, she knelt down at the side of the dying Englishman, took his head in her hands and spoke gentle words to him as he breathed out his life.

But her devoted brigands, ready to fight and to die for her, were unable to understand her spirit of mercy. In spite of her protests, they killed most of their prisoners in their battles with the English.

The victorious French army arrived at Reims on July 15, 1429. Two days later Charles VII was crowned by the archbishop in the magnificent cathedral. Many of his courtiers—and not a few of his courtesans—were present at the coronation. But his queen, Marie d'Anjou, had been left behind at Chinon, "in order to save the expense of the journey." Charles VII was not only a penniless king, but one of the most penurious of men.

The preliminary mission of Joan of Arc was completed. She had raised the siege of Orleans, and she had brought about the coronation of King Charles. "If Heaven would only permit me now to return to my sheep!" - .

But Heaven would not permit. The holy voices informed her that she must go on. She had reached the peak of her triumph, and now she must shoulder the burden of her cross. "If I should die," she said to the cheering multitude at Reims, "it is here that I would want to be buried."

Yet there was further work to be done before she was ready to die. The English must be *completely* driven out of France. A hopeless task. The edge of her popularity, in spite of her triumph, had begun to wear off. Her soldiers, like her parents, were too close to her now to worship her. "When the gods draw near, their haloes disappear." Accustomed now to her daily communication with the angels, her comrades-in-arms were no longer carried away by the miracle. The splendor of her heavenly visions had faded into the light of common day. The longer she stayed with her soldiers, the more impatient they became with her. She kept them away from their plunder, she deprived them of the pleasure of their profanity, and she condemned them to a life of unaccustomed chastity. "What sort of a leader is this, who makes us go to the chapel when we'd rather be in a brothel?" She was trying, they said, to make mere women out of them. Many of her soldiers rebelled, and some of them deserted.

In the meantime, her enemies were laying plans for her destruction. There were four distinct groups that wanted her out of the way: the English invaders, the French partisans of these English invaders, the courtiers of Charles who were envious of her popularity with the king, and the more fanatical of the clergy who were jealous of her familiarity with the angels.

The English, as a result of the battle of Agincourt (1415), were in possession of most of the French provinces north of the Loire. They were anxious to extend their dominions over the entire kingdom of France. But Joan of Arc, the "devil-inspired witch of Domremy," was not only checking their further progress, but was threatening to wrest away from them the territory which they had already won at the cost of so much toil and blood. They were determined to stop her at any price.

Allied with them were some of the French nobility who hoped to advance their own interests through the victory of the English over King Charles. Chief among them was the Duke of Burgundy, Philip the Good—whose real name should have been Philip the Not-so-good. (He was the father of eighteen illegitimate children.) The coronation of Charles VII was a great blow to Philip. Richer, abler, and far more powerful than the Dauphin, he had expected, under the protection of England, to become the master of France. But the advent of Joan of Arc nipped his plans in the bud. Together with the English, he was determined to punish her for her meddlesomeness.

More dangerous even than her outspoken enemies were her avowed friends. The insincere courtiers of Charles VII, and particularly his councilor-chamberlain, Georges de la Tremoille, feared the frankness and the forthright honesty of Joan of Arc. The Duc de la Tremoille was forceful, domineering and treacherous. He had deserted his first wife, and he had married another whose husband he had killed. He had insinuated himself into the king's good graces by means of falsehoods and flatteries. He was a hypocrite of the worst type. Ready at all times to betray his king —for he was secretly in league with the English—he did his best to get rid of the peasant girl who could see right through him and who at any moment might open the king's eyes to his treachery. True to his character, therefore, he treated Joan with every show of respect and secretly plotted her downfall.

But of all the enemies that were arrayed against her the most dangerous were the fanatical officials of the French Church. The Archbishop of Reims, the Bishop of Beauvais, and the entire clerical faculty of the University of Paris were determined to bring about her death. She had dared, without the permission of the Church, to communicate "what she was pleased to regard as the plans of God." Presuming to speak directly with the angels, she had violated the sanctity of the clergy. For the clergy alone, by virtue of their office, were allowed to interpret the will of God. The Church stood as the sole intermediary between Heaven and earth. The revelations of Joan of Arc, they believed—and they were quite sincere in their belief—could have come only from the Devil, since they did not come through the Church. She was a heretic, a traitor to Heaven, and a source of danger to the clergy. And therefore she must be put to death.

And thus the four-fold net of her destiny was being rapidly tightened around her. At the Battle of Compiègne she was trapped by the maneuvers of her own countrymen. Her French captors, at the instigation of Tremoille, sold her to the English for 10,000 pounds of gold. The English, in turn, in order to make sure of her death, delivered her into the hands of the Inquisition. And this is how, though a prisoner of war, Joan of Arc was tried and condemned as a heretic.

The man who presided at her trial was Pierre Cauchon, the Bishop of Beauvais—a Pharisee of the most bigoted type. "The flesh of burning heretics was sweet in his nostrils." He it was who, at the Council of Constance which brought about the death of Huss, had defended the thesis that it was "permissible on certain occasions to condemn a sinner to death without the formality of a trial."

In the trial of Joan of Arc the bishop had a personal as well as an ecclesiastical interest. Having espoused the cause of the English in their invasion of France, he had lost his bishopric at Beauvais as a result of Joan's military successes. It was in a spirit of revengeful satisfaction, therefore, that he accepted his commission "to try this heretic and dangerous enemy of the Church."

When the English delivered Joan of Arc into the hands of Pierre Cauchon, they really signed her death warrant. They had no intention to let her get off alive. It was agreed before the trial that if the Inquisition failed to condemn her as a heretic, the civil courts would convict her as a traitor. If she slipped out of the hands of the French, she would slip directly into the hands of the English. It was a case of "heads you lose, tails I win." At the beginning of the trial, two of the priests who sat among her judges denounced the whole procedure as illegal. One of these priests was promptly removed from the trial and jailed by Cauchon. The other had the good fortune to escape before his superiors were able to arrest him.

As for Joan, she was hardly aware of the intricate tangle of enmities she had aroused. She knew that the English were anxious to persecute her. But why should her own beloved Church have entered into this persecution? Had not God the Father spoken to her through the angels and the saints of the Church? "I have come from God," she said to her judges. "I have no business here. Send me back to God, from whom I have come."

But the judges tried to convince her—as they themselves were very likely convinced—that she had come from the Devil. There were sixty-three of these judges headed by Cauchon, and they spent nearly four months in their vain attempt to prove to her that she was a sorceress. But always she gave them the selfsame answer. "The voices I have heard are from above, and not from below."

Finally she began to realize that her doom was sealed. Yet she retained her composure and her sense of humor to the very end. At one of the sittings, when several of the judges began to upbraid her at the same time, she replied sweetly, "Please, good fathers, do not speak all at once. You are liable to confuse yourselves."

The tragi-comedy came to an end on May 30. Joan of Arc was found guilty of having "trafficked with the Devil," and Pierre Cauchon was congratulated by the University of Paris for the "great solemnity and the just and holy spirit" in which he had conducted the trial.

The judges of the Church condemned her to be burned; and then, in accordance with the ecclesiastical custom of the day, they turned her over to the executioners of the state for the burning. And thus legally, if not morally, the Bishop of Beauvais could wash his hands of the entire business.

But Joan of Arc knew better. Pointing to Pierre Cauchon as the flames began to rise about her, she cried, "Bishop, I die through you!"

And then, as the flames rose still higher, she whispered: "It *was* God who sent me. And now I am going back to Him."

VI

Now AND THEN the heavenly powers send us an angel for our instruction. And it is only after we have driven him out of our midst that we recognize him for what he was. In 1431 Joan of Arc was officially executed as a sorceress. In 1920 she was officially canonized as a saint.

MARY, QUEEN OF SCOTS

Important Dates in Life of Mary, Queen of Scots

1542—Born at Linlithgow.
1548—Betrothed to the French Dauphin, Francis; taken to France.
1558—Married the Dauphin.
1560—Became Queen of France. Lost husband, Francis II.
1561—Returned to Scotland.
1565—Married Henry Darnley.
1566—Gave birth to son, James.
1567—Her husband was murdered at the instigation of Bothwell. She married Bothwell. A month after their marriage, they were defeated at the Battle of Carberry Hill. Made prisoner at Lochleven Castle. Compelled to abdicate in favor of her son, James.
1568—Escaped from Lochleven. Came to England.
1569—Imprisoned at Sheffield Castle.
1585—Accused of plotting against the life of Queen Elizabeth.
1586—Placed on trial.
1587—February 1—Condemned to death by Queen Elizabeth. February 8—Executed.

Mary, Queen of Scots

Mary, Queen of Scots

1542–1587

Unable to play in her childhood, she began her playtime in the maturity of her full-grown years. And that was what brought about her destruction.

The daughter of King James V, she lost her father on the day of her birth. On the sixth day of her life she became the queen of Scotland. From the very first she was used as a pawn in the royal checker-game of destiny. And the players that moved this pretty little pawn in her swaddling clothes were the Scottish lords of whom the French ambassador had written: "Money and personal advantage are the only sirens to whose voices this pack of scoundrels will lend an ear. To try and bring them to a sense of their duty toward their sovereign, to talk to them of honor, justice, virtue, decent and reliable negotiations, merely incites them to laughter." Helpless in the hands of these "noble brigands," the wee lassie remembered her childhood as a series of kidnapings and hushed whispers and sudden journeys from castle to castle. First of all, a group of lairds tried to sell her to King Henry VIII of England as the bride of his son, Edward. But another group attempted to sell her to Henry II of France as

[53]

the bride of his son, Francis. Whereupon her mother spirited
her away from both factions and hid her in the castle of Stirling.
But the English king was impatient. He had paid for his prize
and he insisted upon its delivery. He was interested not so much
in acquiring Mary as in annexing Scotland to the British crown.
When the child-queen was not forthcoming, his army invaded
Scotland and killed ten thousand men at the Battle of Pinkie.
Mary was not quite five when her country received its first
drenching of blood in her behalf.

And then another secret journey and the royal little refugee
was smuggled to an island in the Lake of Monteith. It was now
the French turn to send out an expeditionary force in search of
Mary. This time her mother surrendered her precious bit of
merchandise; and on August 7, 1548, the diminutive queen of
Scotland—she was now five years and eight months old—was
bundled off to Brest, to marry the heir to the French throne.
Her bridegroom-to-be had just reached the age of four and a
half years.

They received her with overwhelming pomp. They gave her
everything she wanted—except a chance to play. They educated
her in Greek and in Latin; they taught her to write poetry; they
schooled her in the fine art of pleasing but not in the finer art of
being pleased. "Your daughter," wrote the Cardinal of Lorraine
to Mary's mother, "is so perfect and accomplished in all things
. . . that the like of her is not to be seen in this realm." True
words. In all France there was not another unhappy creature
like Mary of Scotland—an adolescent girl who had never been
a child. A queen begrudged the pleasures of a peasant. Even the
ordinary satisfaction of married life was denied her. For her
royal husband was a sickly lad who fawned upon her and who
wilted in the sunlight of her beauty, but who was never able to
give her his love. Queen of Scotland, queen of France, satiated
with glory, starving for life. For several years she dutifully
watched his recurrent paroxysms of fever, and then one day

[54]

she dutifully laid him to rest and put on the widow's weeds.

For forty days, in accordance with the etiquette of the royal house of France, she remained secluded in her apartment and kept her shades drawn against the intrusion of the sun. Her bedroom, lighted day and night by candles, was like a crypt.

And then, when the period of mourning was over, she emerged from the gloom of her crypt and returned to the gloomy fogs of Scotland. She was by now an old woman of eighteen.

II

SUDDENLY the old woman blossomed into a young girl. She had found an exquisite plaything—her own warm and beautiful body. Time to make up for her dreary childhood, to reach out not only for power but for passion as well. A "suitable" marriage *this* time—with a man of vigor and of rank. A nobleman of royal descent whose ambition would embrace the English throne. Mary of Scotland wanted to become also the queen of England. Why not? Elizabeth, she believed, was an interloper. The daughter of a common hussy, Anne Boleyn. She, Mary, was a much fitter ornament for the throne of England. Like Elizabeth, she was the great-granddaughter of Henry VII. But unlike Elizabeth, she could boast a royal bloodstream that was pure and unstained. She would ally herself with a man of equally pure blood—a man full of laughter and of love, a husband fit to be king. Together they would overthrow this "bastard" queen of England, assume the English crown and rule supreme over the British Isles.

But was there such a young man to be found? Why, yes. Henry Darnley, the nineteen-year-old son of the Earl of Lennox. He, too, was a great-grandson of Henry VII, and a dashing young courtier to boot. "Fair-haired, beardless, frolicsome and impatient for his rights, he was"—to quote Mary's own words— "the handsomest and best-proportioned long man" she had ever seen. She married Darnley, and thus acquired one temporary plaything and two lifelong enemies—Queen Elizabeth and James Stuart.

Queen Bess, the cousin of Queen Mary, was her opposite in many ways. Mary Stuart was an impulsive adventuress, a romantic dreamer, a passionate daredevil of a gambler, "a woman's body," as the Pope once remarked, "with the soul of a man." Elizabeth Tudor, on the other hand, was a sagacious politician, a practical realist, a calculating hunter of her prey, a man's body with the soul of a tigress.

But in one respect they were both alike. Each of them lived for a single purpose—to get the other out of the way. Yet in their frequent correspondence they purred to each other with feline protestations of friendship. "My dearest sister." "My beloved cousin." "How happy it makes me to see *you* happy."

It was in such vein that Elizabeth congratulated Mary upon her marriage to Lord Darnley. Secretly, however, she commissioned James Stuart to stir up a rebellion in Scotland and to bring about Mary's overthrow—and if possible, her death.

James Stuart, the Earl of Moray, was Queen Mary's (illegitimate) half-brother. Consumed with an ambition for the Scottish throne, he was furious when his sister removed this throne further than ever from his clutch through her marriage with Darnley. He was therefore only too glad to accept Elizabeth's commission and to put himself—secretly, of course—at the head of the insurrection against his sister. If and when he got Mary out of the way, thought James Stuart, it would then be a good idea to plan a similar exit for Elizabeth. And so these three "supreme personages" kept spinning their merry plot—a pretty triangle of royal rascality.

In the spinning of this triple web of mutual hatred, Queen Mary was at a disadvantage. For her throne had always been insecure—an island of Catholicism in a sea of Protestant agitation. Her arrival in Scotland had met with the rudest of receptions. Only a handful of fishermen and peasants had come to welcome their sovereign as she stepped ashore at Leith. One of her first experiences in Edinburgh was a hurricane of abuse from John Knox, the fire-and-brimstone leader of the Reformed Kirk in Scotland. According to Knox, there were but two ways of life —his own way, and the Devil's way. He regarded himself as the sole interpreter of God's will on earth. And woe unto those who refused to subscribe to his interpretation! Had Mary been willing to forsake "the Congregation of Satan"—John Knox's name for the Catholic Church—she might have spared herself many a heartache. But, in spite of her frivolity, the queen possessed the courage of her Catholic convictions. She refused to budge an inch.

A firm adherence to the faith and a giddy flaunting of the conventions—such was the paradoxical behavior of the heavenly-minded and earthly-hearted Mary of Scotland. She supplied her enemies with plenty of ammunition to strike against her. She played with her courtiers as a little girl plays with her dolls. At first it was the French poet, Chastelard, who was caught hiding in her bedchamber. And then it was her Italian secretary, Rizzio. Both of them paid for their rashness with their lives. Mary, on each of these occasions, protested her innocence; but nobody—and least of all Elizabeth and Moray—believed her. The web was beginning to tighten around her.

But Mary, reckless of her reputation, went on with her peccadillos. And from trivial peccadillos it was but a short step to a serious crime. Mary had grown tired of her husband. She was disappointed in him. No asset he in her struggle for the English throne. She had expected him to be a fighter, and he had turned out to be a fop. But in Scotland there *was* a man who could fight. And love. And take risks. James Hepburn, the Earl of Bothwell. A tough and burly and brilliant soldier of a man—an adventurer whose sword was as sharp as his tongue. What a royal companion *he* would make!

But to this companionship there were two drawbacks—Mary's husband and Bothwell's wife. As for Bothwell's wife, the earl was ready to divorce her. And as for Mary's husband, the earl was equally ready to murder him. And murder him he did— with Mary's consent and even, it would seem, with Mary's coöperation.

The killing of Darnley was an ugly job. The king, aware of the queen's growing repugnance toward him, had taken himself off to a castle in Glasgow. Here he stayed with his father, the Earl of Lennox, and with a protective garrison of retainers. How to reach him in this stronghold and to lure him away to his rendezvous with death? Mary and Bothwell put their heads together and hit upon a practical plan. Darnley was convalescing from a severe attack of smallpox. And Mary, with a sudden show of compunction toward her "poor, neglected, beloved husband," came to visit him and smoothed his brow and whispered honeyed words into his ear. "Why stay here in this gloomy fortress, with its damp walls and pestilential air? Let me take you to a quiet house in Edinburgh, where I can see you frequently and nurse you back to health."

Darnley submitted to her blandishments and allowed himself, ill as he was, to be taken to that "quiet house" in Edinburgh. This house, "a solitar place separat from all companie," was situated in an alley appropriately named *Thieves' Row.* Here the stricken young fellow, his face still pitted with the pockmarks but his eyes "the merriest that ever you saw," looked forward to a second honeymoon with the woman whom he still loved desperately. He begged her to cut up his meat for him, he clung to her and in his eagerness failed to notice the shudder of aversion as her lips touched his. The Judas kiss. He implored her to stay the night with him. But Mary excused herself—an important matter of state, she said, required her presence at the palace.

It is late in the evening—Sunday, February 9, 1667. The queen has just attended a wedding reception—the marriage of

[*58*]

two of her faithful servants. Bothwell, too, has been present at the reception. And now the festivities are over. The queen is asleep.

A violent knocking at the gate. What presumptuous fellow is *that?* The queen mustn't be disturbed. She's so tired from her dancing.

But the knocking persists. "The news is urgent!"

The queen is awakened, and she receives the news. Her husband the king, Henry Darnley, has just been blown up in an explosion at the quiet house. "Malefactors unknown."

III

MARY OF SCOTLAND was approaching the summit of her ambition. She had a husband (Bothwell) who shared her daring, and a son (by Henry Darnley) who would inherit her throne. Just one more step, the removal of Elizabeth, and all her dreams would be fulfilled.

It would be an easy matter, she thought, to get rid of Elizabeth. Bothwell was the ablest soldier in the British Isles, and his army of cut-throats feared neither beast nor man nor devil. A hasty charge of complicity in the murder of Darnley had been drawn up against Bothwell. But the defiant "prisoner" had come to the trial with a cavalcade of four thousand armed men, and the terrified judges promptly exonerated him from "any art and part of the slaughter of the King." And then, brandishing his naked sword, he rode through the streets and challenged anyone in the city, or in the world, to declare him guilty. "With such a man at their head," said Mary, "our soldiers will sweep everything before them."

But when the crisis came, these soldiers displayed more bluster than blows. They shouted at the enemy and threatened to disembowel them—and then, at the very first encounter, "melted away like the morning mist." Bothwell embraced his queen hurriedly—she had come to witness the battle in person—and then mounted his horse and galloped away into exile. A price having been set on his head, he set sail for Norway in a cockleshell of a boat, barely escaped shipwreck, made his way precariously to Denmark, seduced a Danish girl, finally fell into the hands of the Copenhagen authorities and after ten years of solitary confinement died raving mad.

Such was the end of Mary's last champion. The queen was left alone with her conscience—the hunted prey of her two mortal enemies, Moray and Elizabeth.

Her brother Moray made short work of her imperial dream. He compelled her—with Elizabeth's consent—to abdicate her throne in favor of her little son James. Moray appointed himself regent of the young king and waited for his opportunity to climb into the throne himself. But *his* dream, too, came to an untimely end. After several years of scheming and bathing in the blood of his peers, he received the final wages of his sin—a violent death.

And now there were left only the two protagonists in the tragi-comedy of imperial greed. Elizabeth and Mary. The Queen of England took her good time with her Scottish cousin. A long and diverting cat-and-mouse game. It was so pleasant to sip her revenge in small draughts and smack her lips and smile at the torture of her victim. Elizabeth was the malicious daughter of a malicious father, King Henry VIII, the man who had murdered several of his wives. Humanity, to Elizabeth, consisted of a billion ciphers with herself as the one integral number at the head. She would have her full measure of fun with this cipher, Mary Stuart, before she rubbed it out.

First of all, therefore, she presented Mary with her royal ring, a "symbol of friendship from a fortunate queen"—note the dig—"to a sister queen in distress." And then she took steps to perpetuate the distressful state of her "sister." She bribed the Scottish lairds—always through a third party, so that her right

[60]

hand might not know what her left hand was doing—to imprison Mary in Lochleven Castle. And finally, when Mary had managed to escape from Lochleven, Elizabeth invited her to England. "Won't you come into my parlor?" said the spider to the fly. Her ring, declared Elizabeth, would always serve Mary as a safe conduct in England. Here, she promised, Mary Stuart would find "a good neighbour, a dear sister, a faithful friend."

She arrived in England after many hardships. "I have suffered injuries, calumnies, captivity, hunger, cold, heat, flying— without knowing whither—fourscore and twelve miles across the country, without once pausing to alight, and then lay on the hard ground, having only sour milk to drink, and oatmeal to eat, without bread, passing three nights with the owls." It was on May 16, 1568, that the exiled queen disembarked on English soil. And the English queen received her, not as her guest but as her prisoner. She refused to see Mary in person but would keep her, she said, safely tucked away from all harm. And she sugared the bitter pill of Mary's captivity with her usual protestations of love. "I promise on the word of a queen," she wrote, "that no persuasion . . . or advice of others shall ever induce me to move you to anything dangerous to you or your honour."

For nineteen years Elizabeth kept Mary in "honourable custody," sending her from one castle prison to another, allowing her to "lord it" over her custodians, fetching for her the best physicians when she was ill, encouraging her to go hawking or hunting when she was well—her horse was always surrounded by a cavalcade of jailers euphemistically called a "guard of honour"—granting her, in short, all sorts of *liberties* save one— *liberty.*

At last Elizabeth grew tired of her game with Mary and decided to put her away. The incident that brought matters to a head was in itself trivial. The Countess of Shrewsbury, malicious gossip and wife of Mary's latest jailer, had brought to Elizabeth a report of the Scottish queen's "amorous relationships" with her husband, the Earl of Shrewsbury. Whereupon Mary indignantly denied the accusation and sent Elizabeth a letter in which she opened the floodgates of her wrath not only against the countess but against the queen herself. "This vile Shrewsbury woman has been slandering you as well as me." And then Mary went on with a brutal catalogue of Elizabeth's faults. She intended this letter, she said, as a friendly warning. Actually she meant it as a venomous sting. Did Elizabeth know—she asked—that the Countess of Shrewsbury depicted her as vain and vulgar and cruel beyond measure? On one occasion, it was reported, she had slashed the hand of an attendant because the latter had displayed a bit of awkwardness in the service of her dinner.

But worse than that. The Countess asserted furthermore—wrote Mary—that Elizabeth had a running sore on her leg (a broad hint that she had inherited a venereal disease from her father); that she had lost her youth but not her lust; that she was running continually after illicit pleasures—pleasures, however, which she was unable to consummate owing to her premature frigidity; that finally—and this was the deepest cut of all—"you are not like other women." Elizabeth had thought that this physical peculiarity of hers, a peculiarity that shut her off from the normal pursuits of a healthy woman, was known to herself alone. And here was her most hated enemy throwing it up to her face.

After this outburst of animosity, there was no further playing with her victim. There must be a speedy end to the game. And at this point Elizabeth hit upon a plan that was worthy of Machiavelli. She concocted a conspiracy against herself and intrigued Mary—indirectly, as usual—to become the leader of this conspiracy.

When word reached Mary that a plan was afoot to kill Elizabeth so that she herself might be elevated to the English throne, she stepped eagerly into the trap and accepted the dagger pressed into her hand for her own destruction. A clever way had been discovered—so Mary thought—for reaching her in her castle-prison. Once every week a barrel of beer was brought into the castle for the attendants. And Mary's "retainers"—in reality they were Elizabeth's spies—had replaced the bung of the barrel with a hollow cork in which a weekly letter could be concealed. In this way Mary kept up a regular correspondence—with Elizabeth herself, though she was unaware of the fact—designed to bring about Elizabeth's destruction.

The Scottish queen was now worked up to a frenzy of enthusiasm. Her lifelong ambition was to be fulfilled at last! In her letters she outlined the entire conspiracy. As soon as she escaped from her prison, she would return to Scotland, rally her forces, invade England with the help of a contingent sent by the Spanish king, and reward the king with the crown of Scotland and with the right of succession (after herself) to the crown of England.

Elizabeth was delighted with the "progress" of this conspiracy. There was but one further bit of evidence necessary to incriminate the Scottish queen to the hilt. A written statement that Mary sanctioned the murder of Elizabeth. And finally, after much teasing and urging and dangling of rosy hopes, they got their incriminating statement. Mary agreed in writing to the "tragical execution" of Elizabeth, the "pretender" to the British throne.

When Mary realized that the game was up, she asked for but one thing—an impressive death. The vainglory of the purple blood even in the shadow of the grave.

The death was impressive enough. Not only for Mary, but for Elizabeth as well. Mary had requested to exit dramatically, dressed in her finest robes. And Elizabeth was only too glad to accede to this request. It was no small thing to win a victory over such a woman!

QUEEN CHRISTINA

Important Dates in Life of Queen Christina

1626—Born at Stockholm.
1632—Lost her father, Gustavus Adolphus.
1644—Crowned Queen of Sweden.
1650—Appointed her cousin, Charles Gustavus, as successor to the throne.
1654—Voluntarily descended from the throne. Adopted Catholic religion at Innsbruck.
1657—Ordered assassination of Monaldeschi, her major-domo.
1660—Returned to Sweden in vain effort to regain throne. Tried to become Queen of Poland.
1667—Finally settled in Rome.
1689—Died in Rome.

Queen Christina

Christina of Sweden

1626—1689

THE FIRST TWO CHILDREN of King Gustavus Adolphus had
been girls, and both of them had died in their infancy. The
third child, the astrologers predicted, would be a boy. There
wasn't the slightest doubt of it. They could read it distinctly in
the stars.

The astrologers proved to be only half right. When Christina
was born, her body was so dark and hairy and her voice so
tough that everybody thought she was a boy. She turned out,
however, to be merely a tomboy.

Throughout her life, Christina possessed a preponderance of
masculine traits. She could ride and fight and swear like a
trooper, tell an off-color story without a blush, and slouch in a
most unfeminine posture with her legs flung over the arm of
a chair. She preferred short skirts—or still better, trousers—to
long dresses. "Women's clothes and women's ways were alike
insupportable to me." She had the endurance of a man, getting
along frequently with only four or five hours' sleep, working
with equal energy in excessive heat or excessive cold, and walking even the sturdier of her male companions into a state of

exhaustion. "The gentlemen and the ladies in attendance on me were made desperate by the way in which I tired them out." She appeared to them like a pellet of quicksilver—forever rolling restlessly on to new adventures. "I gave them no rest either by day or by night." Disdaining to address her by her feminine title, her attendants referred to her as *Prince* Christina.

Prince Christina, in short, displayed a masculine temperament in every way save one. She had a whirlwind habit of changing her mind. The daughter of Gustavus Adolphus was a woman after all.

II

SHE WAS BORN in the midst of the Thirty Years' War—in its origin a *German* war. All her life she was to hate war and to despise the Germans. In her childhood she heard horrible stories of the depredations of the soldiers and of the sufferings of the civilians—"of starving dogs eating men and of starving men eating dogs." An inquisitive child, she asked again and again, "What are they fighting about?" And the invariable answer was, "God knows!"

Though she admired courage, she hated brutality—especially *senseless* brutality. It made no sense to her when her father left her one day never to return. She was only four at the time. She had plucked at his beard to make him listen to her farewell speech. Her nurses had taught her this speech. "When he noticed that, he took me in his arms and kissed me, unable to restrain his tears . . . He had a premonition that he was shortly to die on the battlefield."

Christina adored her father; but she cared little for her mother—a sentimental little woman, long on sighs, short on sense. She was only too glad when, at the age of six, she was taken away from her mother to be educated under the influence of the Grand Chancellor, Oxenstiern.

[*68*]

And her education was a man's education, administered by men. She never did feel comfortable in the presence of women. Couldn't understand their queer ways. And their queer studies, such as embroidery and coquetry and court etiquette. She wanted none of this primping and pruning and simpering under the fatuous admiration of the effeminate carpet-knights. Give her a horse and a saddle—and she preferred to sit astride like a boy rather than sideways like a girl. Give her a man's food and a man's books. Essays on philosophy, treatises on politics, disquisitions on theology, dissertations on art. And linguistics. A prince must learn to discourse with many people in many languages.

She was a brilliant, though not very submissive, student. Almost a genius, yet compelled to be a queen. She hated the splendor of the golden ball and chain that kept her confined within the prison of a royal routine. A king, like a criminal, must live as a person apart—removed from the pursuits and the pleasures of ordinary men and women. No place for him in the footrace of daily competition, with the zestful hope for victory and the zestful fear of defeat. Fettered by the prerogatives of his royal position, the king in his palace possesses much the same honor, and much the same opportunity for developing his individual inclinations, as a pampered baby in its crib.

Christina, as we shall see, was courageous enough to kick her way out of her gilded crib. But before she did so, she led her nurses a merry chase.

First of all, she insisted upon putting an end to the Thirty Years' War. This step of hers was "a scandal and a revolution." Rulers, she was told, were meant to *make* wars, not to *stop* them. But she paid no attention to her scandalized advisers and signed the Peace of Westphalia. She was only twenty-two at the time.

And then—scandal heaped upon scandal!—she refused to marry and, like a good queen, to supply her kingdom with an heir. "My ambition and my pride . . . made me incapable of submitting my will to that of another, but inspired me with scorn for everybody"—especially for those "noble nincompoops" whom Oxenstiern had selected to sire her offspring.

Her next unqueenly act was the appointment of Salvius, a talented but low-born commoner, to the Senate. And when Oxenstiern expressed his amazement at her nonchalant adulteration of the good blood with the bad, she remarked with a smile that personal merit was more important than birth. "There are peasants who deserve to be kings and kings who deserve to be peasants."

Was there, perhaps, something of the peasant in this strange little tadpole of a queen? Who could tell? The meanderings of the royal bloodstream, as the courtiers knew only too well, were often dark and devious. No accounting for some of its irregular tributaries. Come to think of it, Christina did not look the part of a queen. A stunted and stocky little thing, built close to the ground. Rarely combed her hair but just tied it carelessly with a ribbon. Coarse and suntanned and heavy features, like those of a woman working in the fields. Long nose, hanging underlip, manly voice. Appeared like a kitchen wench who had accidentally strayed into the parlor. "Her convictions smelt of the gutter."

And the company she kept! Not the gentlefolk of noble blood, who—as befitted the gentry—spent their days hunting and their nights flirting and playing cards, but a rabble of base-born foreigners, who wasted their own time and the queen's time in the "worthless pursuits" of scribbling music and painting pictures and writing books. That scholar Salvatius, for example—the man who conversed in ancient Latin instead of using modern Swedish. Or that Professor Boecler, the lecturer who once had dared to remark, "I would say more if the Swedes could only get it through their wooden heads." Served him right when the Swedish students broke his own head in revenge. Or that scientist Stiernhielm, the man who tried to introduce a magical burning glass called a *microscope*. With that funny contraption of his, he had singed a peasant's beard and magnified a flea in the presence of a clergyman. The peasant and the clergyman had him arrested as a sorcerer and an atheist. Or that philosopher Descartes, the Frenchman who tried to teach Christina the mysteries of heaven when she ought to be devoting her time to the diversions of the earth. It was a good thing, though, that she insisted upon taking her lesson at five in the morning. The early hour and the Swedish climate gave him a case of pneumonia and he died.

One worthless intruder the less, thought the courtiers. But the queen still was too strongly addicted to her scholars and her books. What did Christina want with books anyhow? It was her business not to think but to rule.

Yet Christina persisted in her thinking and one day, to the amazement of the courtiers, she decided to give up her ruling. "I am going to abdicate my throne—and to change my religion." A two-forked thunderbolt. The Swedish nation was stupefied. The ways of their queen were past understanding. "This woman is reversing the very process of nature." Most people would forfeit their life to win a throne. Christina forfeited her throne to win a life. From now on—she was only twenty-eight at the time —she would cease to be a personage and become a person.

III

IN HER *Autobiography* Christina writes that she gave up her crown in order to find peace. To judge from her subsequent actions, it would seem more likely that she gave up her crown in order to get applause. She was sick of playing princess to the Swedes. She wanted to play madcap to the world. She wanted to take a leading part in a drama of her own composition. A few days after the abdication she wrote: "I know that the play in which I acted was not prepared according to the ordinary rules of the stage." This, in a few blunt words, expresses the primary purpose of Christina's life—to dazzle by breaking the rules. Her exits and her entrances in the playing of her part must be unlike those of any other woman. Her abdication was more sensational than the winning of a war—"Who ever heard of such a thing!" wrote one scholar to another—and Christina took care to keep up the sensation. Refusing to depart with the modesty expected after such a noble abnegation, she rode out of Sweden in a triumphant procession. She rifled the palace of the gold and silver plate, the furniture, the tapestries, the crown jewels. It was reported that her successor to the throne, Charles Gustavus, "found nothing in the palace save two carpets and an old bed." Though she had renounced the royal name, she retained her royal retinue. As she galloped from place to place, she kept Europe agog with a continuous bombardment of surprises. On one day the people would be told that she had cut her hair, adopted a man's uniform with a gun in her hands, and enlisted to fight in Flanders under the orders of Condé. On another day she would disappear altogether—she had a novelist's instinct for suspense—only to appear again suddenly in a dizzy escapade. Once, while the fleet was waiting for her at a prearranged port, she deliberately set sail from another port. Always she did the unexpected. Her arrival in a city "made one think of a traveling circus." Crowds gathered everywhere to cheer this "greatest curiosity of Christendom." Feasted and flattered on every hand, she sometimes presided with the dignity of a queen, at other times with the drollery of a clown.

Always anxious to surprise, to dazzle, to shock. At Hamburg she accepted the hospitality of a Jewish banker; and when the clergy denounced her from the pulpit, she retorted that Jesus was Himself a Jew and had, throughout His life, enjoyed the hospitality of Jews.

And thus she went on with her startling play, advancing the scene from Hamburg to Brussels, to Antwerp, to Innsbruck—meeting everywhere with cheering throngs, saluting soldiers, clanging bells and blazing bonfires. It was at Innsbruck that she formally adopted the Catholic faith—a final climax to the pageant of her ostentatious humility. She took her religion, like everything else, with a flourish. Her conversion was motivated, to some extent at least, by a sincere desire to seek for the truth. The human heart is a complicated instrument of many strings; and the psychologist is yet to be found who can interpret all the various motifs of all the various strings in the determination of any single human act. Yet there seems to be little doubt that a hunger for unusual sensations played an important part in her acceptance of a new religion. "One must ever begin anew," was the frequently repeated motto of her life. She had found it easy to cast off the garment of her Lutheran faith because she had always worn this garment rather loosely. As a child, and even as a grown woman, she had read her Vergil during the Sunday sermons. "No sermons for me! I have the profoundest contempt for all the preachers." And now that she had put on the garment of the Catholic faith, she found it no more cramping to the freedom of her movements. When the Jesuits of Louvain proposed to place her name on a panel of saints, she replied, "No, thank you, I would much prefer to find my name on a panel of philosophers." And when the ceremony of conversion was completed at Innsbruck, she is said to have asked for the performance of a comic opera as a dessert. "Gentlemen," she declared, "it is most proper that you should entertain me with a comedy after I have entertained you with a farce."

IV

DELIGHTED to find herself now the center of a whirlwind of discord—stormy execration on the part of the Lutherans, stormy adoration on the part of the Catholics—she made her way blusteringly to Rome and rather disconcerted the Pope by appearing for the sacrament at St. Peter's dressed in her riding breeches and a jaunty hat. The Holy Father was deeply disappointed in his new convert. He had expected to find a crowned saint. Instead, he found an uncrowned sinner. The Cardinals, too, were disturbed over this swaggering sinner in their midst. They tried to turn her heart, and she succeeded in turning their heads. Especially the head of Cardinal Colonna. This poor prelate took to powdering his hair and serenading her at night like a troubadour with a guitar. When the Pope heard of this nonsense on the part of his formerly sensible Cardinal, he ordered him out of Rome. As for Christina, His Holiness sent her a rosary with his compliments and advised her to tell her beads for the salvation of her soul. Whereupon Christina told him, with a smile of insolent sweetness, that she had found in Catholicism other and greater satisfactions than the telling of beads. And then, when the pontiff tried to upbraid her for her levity, she fell contritely on her knees and asked for his blessing.

Yet contrition, even in the presence of the Pope, was hardly one of her common characteristics. She had the vainglory of an actress not quite sure of her talents. Again and again she talks of her greatness, as if trying to convince herself against her own better judgment. "In many ways," she writes, speaking of her childhood, "I was precocious." Again, reporting a mission of Russian ambassadors to Sweden—"Everybody expected me to be frightened at the long beards and the outlandish costumes of the Russians . . . But I only laughed and said, 'Why should I be afraid of them? Tell me what I have to do, and leave the rest to me.' And I kept my word. I received my visitors, seated on the throne, in the customary manner, with a demeanor so self-possessed and majestic that, instead of being frightened, as other children are, on similar occasions, I made the ambassadors feel what all men feel when they are brought into contact with the great." Still again—speaking now of her merits as a grown woman—"My talents and my virtues . . . raise me above the rest of mankind." Her *Autobiography* is full of such passages of self-glorification. *Plaudite, cives!* Applaud, ye citizens! Exalt me for the brilliance of my intellect—"O Lord, what knowledge

Thou hast implanted in me!"—for the dexterity of my horseman-
ship, the adroitness of my diplomacy, the ardor of my passion, the
sincerity of my devotion, the audacity of my courage, the strength
of my will. Behold in me, Christina of Sweden, the Eighth
Wonder of the World!

For a time the world looked on and wondered and applauded.
And then it grew sick of her play-acting. She was more melo-
dramatic than dramatic. She had quarreled with so many people
in Rome that finally they were glad to get rid of her. And she,
on her part, was glad to get rid of the people. She had outstayed
her glory. On one occasion she had invited forty guests to dinner,
and not a single one of them had turned up. Her funds were
running low. She would go back to Sweden—her former subjects
still adored her—and raise the money for the further production
of her superdrama.

The Pope presented her with 10,000 crowns as a "good riddance" token, and Christina set sail for Sweden (July 19, 1656).

But on her way home the "vagabond queen" stopped in France
for a very interesting—yet not very savory—interlude in her
world-dazzling drama. After a stormy cavalcade through the
various French cities—"she rode astride a big white horse, pistols
at the holster, wig uncurled, complexion wild like a gypsy's, hands
ungloved and not too clean"—she astonished the world with a
new escapade, this time no less than a murder. The scene of this
latest royal hunger for sensation was the palace of Louis XIV
at Fontainebleau; and the victim was Count Monaldeschi,
Christina's Italian master of the horse. He had written a number
of letters in which the queen was insulted. The busybody queen—
"everybody's affairs are *my* affairs"—had intercepted these letters
and confronted Monaldeschi with them. Monaldeschi, confessing
his "crime," implored her forgiveness. But Christina was unfor-
giving. Calling into the room the prior of Fontainebleau, she
said quietly: "Father, I leave this man in your hands. Prepare
him for death." And then she summoned the "executioners"—

[75]

three amateur swordsmen who made a ghastly botch of the business. It took them several hours to put their terrified quarry to death.

The murder in itself was brutal. But the fact that it was committed in an atmosphere of hospitality, a palace in which both Christina and Monaldeschi were staying as guests, added the insult of bad manners to the injury of barbarous morals.

Christina had once again created a sensation. This time it was a tornado of resentment that swept her out of France. But the queen took it nonchalantly. "We Nordics are of a rough nature and not much given to tremors . . . As to my conduct toward Monaldeschi, I find it easier to strangle people than to fear them." She had been eager to try every emotion, including that of killing. And, being an ex-queen, she felt that what she did was none of the world's business. The gods and Christina had an ethical standard of their own. "To us, all things are allowed."

V

CHRISTINA, restless as ever, was seeking for a new sensation. She had already experienced the excitement of *renouncing* a crown; she now wanted to experience the excitement of *pursuing* a crown. She tried to become the king of Naples; and failing in this, she offered herself as the king of Poland. "I will prove," she declared, "to be the greatest warrior that Poland has ever known" —she who had once been "the greatest pacifist that the world has ever known." When the Polish nobles objected to her candidacy on the ground that she had murdered Monaldeschi in cold blood, she retorted—"Oh, no, not in cold blood; I took good care to have the sacraments administered to him before the end." But the Polish nobles were "deaf to her wisdom and blind to her virtues." They rejected her candidacy.

And then, still eager to astonish—"from me the world must always expect the unexpected"—she began to organize an army for the Last Crusade against the Turks. This army, like many of her other grandiose schemes, melted away in the mists of her imagination. It never came to reality. Merely another plotted, and discarded, episode in the fantastic life-drama of her own devising. "The Queen," sarcastically wrote Cardinal Azzolini, her major-domo, "is very apt to take things up and drop them again before they are half finished."

VI

AND NOW came the bitterest of her experiences—oblivion within her own lifetime. Thirty years of sputtering and crackling and fussing without a single upflare to the heavens in a rocket of showering splendor. Christina had run out of ideas. "She still loved to astound the world, and the world refused to be astounded." The play was but half over, and her audience had walked out on her. She tried a pathetic love episode—a desperate effort to warm herself at the heart of Cardinal Azzolini. But young men only laugh at old women. "Christina is now very fat and heavy, with a double chin, short rough hair, and a sash tied around her too ample waistline." She wrote letter after letter to Azzolini, imploring him to look graciously upon her. "Nothing will prevent me from loving you until the hour of death. But since the obligations of piety prevent you from being my lover, I will excuse you from being my servant, and I will remain content to live and die your slave."

And Azzolini took her at her word. The Divine Stage Manager had taken pity upon the failure of Christina's drama. He was about to ring down the curtain. Azzolini, in his capacity as her major-domo, presented her with a document for her signature. "This document will be advantageous for Her Majesty's household." Christina, too feeble to read now, signed the paper. It was a will that made Azzolini her heir. The estate was worth several million crowns.

Just one solitary spectator to applaud her final exit.

Yet rumor had it—fantastic, no doubt, but her whole life was fantastic—that there was one other presence at her bedside when she died. The ghost of Monaldeschi, the man she had murdered in the heyday of her fame.

MADAME DE MAINTENON

Important Dates in Life of Madame de Maintenon

1635—Born in prison at Niort.
1645—Educated in a convent.
1654—Married the crippled poet, Scarron.
1669—Became governess of King Louis XIV's illegitimate children.
1675—Received, from Louis XIV, money to buy an estate, and the title of Marquise de Maintenon.
1685—Became the secret wife of Louis XIV.
1686—Founded the school for orphan girls of the nobility at St. Cyr.
1719—Died in the convent at St. Cyr.

Madame de Maintenon

Madame de Maintenon
1635–1719

Iᴛ ᴄᴏᴜʟᴅ ʜᴀᴠᴇ ʜᴀᴘᴘᴇɴᴇᴅ only in France—the France of Louis XIV where fortunes were made and souls were flayed at a nod of the royal brow. The France of that period wore the periwigged head of the nobility on the suffering shoulders of the peasant. The masses were compelled to grovel upon the earth. But for the fortunate few, it was only a short journey from the earth to the sun. Along the skies of the King's fancy a handful of women reached the windiest heights of favor—and settled on a cloud-throne all a-flutter, like peacocks that had suddenly been given the power to fly. "If I told the whole truth about my life," said Madame de Maintenon, "you would not believe it."

II

Sᴏᴍᴇ ᴡᴏᴍᴇɴ begin life in easy circumstances and end in prison. Françoise d'Aubigné began life in prison and ended in easy circumstances. Her life was the reverse of the moralist's object lesson. She was born in a cell—through no fault of her own, and spent her last thirty years in a palace—through very little virtue

[*81*]

of her own. The sins of her father became the charms of the daughter.

His sins—and her charms—were many. Her grandfather, Théodore Agrippa d'Aubigné, companion to Henry IV, was a combination of baron, admiral, diplomat and historian. Her father was a universal encyclopedia of the vices. He committed murder, he betrayed his father's politics to the King and seized all his lands, he coined counterfeit money and was sentenced to a prison term at Bordeaux. And, to cap the climax of his versatility, he composed poetry and won the hand of his jailer's daughter. Drugged by the bouquet of his verses, Jeanne married the brilliant scoundrel and moved into jail with him for her honeymoon. As he was transferred from one prison to another, she followed him to serve out her sentence of love. And it was in the prison of Niort, adjoining the palace of Justice, that her third child, Françoise, was born.

Relatives took the infant from the gray walls and nursed her on her grandfather's estate. Françoise spent all her early years at the Chateau de Mursay. On a step of the impressive staircase in the hallway she learned to read an inscription—*It is hard to rise*. And as her eye wandered to the topmost step and her infant legs struggled hard to carry her to the landing, she never forgot.

When her father Constantine was released from jail, he sailed with his wife and his children for the West Indies. He settled on the Island of Martinique in a subordinate post. Here Françoise and her brothers were brought up under the care of a mother whose sufferings had made her somewhat "cracked." She allowed them to read nothing but Plutarch and "to discuss nothing but what they read there." Fine thing for a dainty little demoiselle to live on a masculine diet of Caesar and Themistocles and Alexander!

Within a few years Constantine took his family back to France, to live "on the charity of some Protestant landowners who revered his father's memory." And shortly thereafter he died.

[*82*]

Not a tear was shed at his passing. Cardinal Richelieu had once remarked politely to Madame d'Aubigné, "The greatest kindness I can do you is to keep such a man in prison." Now he was beyond reprieve. His little daughter Françoise, the descendant of an impoverished and tainted nobility, was taken out of the reach of her unsympathetic mother and abandoned in a convent like an unclaimed parcel of baggage at the railroad station. But it wasn't long before the bundle unloosed itself from its wrappings and displayed the splendor of its wares. The shy little demoiselle had developed into a marvel of beauty. Quiet as a mouse she sat at her needle work, yet every eye strayed from the center of the company to the little jewel at the fringe. At fourteen they called her "la belle Indienne." For where else but in the solution of the West Indian winds and in the conjunction of the equatorial stars and suns could such a complexion, figure and majesty have been formed?

III

PARIS was a bazaar of the odd sizes and shapes of human nature. And Paul Scarron was the feature attraction. A gay young scimitar of wit that flashed and wounded; the son of a leader of Parliament. As clever at playing the lute as playing the ladies, he tossed verses into the air like crystal balls, and pulverized ambitions and hearts under his heel. But his dissipations had ended in disease, robbed him of the use of his limbs and left him only his cynicism. He sat upon a "box with wheels" and presided zestfully over the tragedy of his life like Mephistopheles over a condemned soul. He turned his bitterness into comedies, his disappointments into verses, his midnight agonies into epigrams of laughter. The blazing beacon of his personality, though it was grounded in mud, attracted the wittiest company in the kingdom —the generals Condé and Turenne, the writers Molière and La Fontaine, the "luster of the salon" Madame Scudery, the actress Ninon de l'Enclos. And the aunt of Françoise d'Aubigné joined this delirious circle and brought her pale and timorous niece along with her. Perhaps there was a method to her madness.

Paul Scarron turned his eyes—the only healthy part of him—upon Françoise, and a thrill ran through his twisted little body. And the young girl's shrewd and observant aunt made a mental note of this. A match between a young girl with no dowry and a paralytic with influence in the highest places would not be such a tragedy after all. Beggars couldn't be choosers. And Scarron knew kings.

One day the lover ventured to speak his heart to Françoise. Theirs was an era of hard bargains. "In a situation like yours, my dear Françoise, I see only two alternatives—to accept a husband or to return to the convent . . . If you do not wish to become a nun, and if, in spite of my face, figure and helplessness, you will consent to marry me, I will do everything possible to make you happy. And I guarantee in advance that if you weep in my house it will be only on the day of my death."

And so it was agreed. The Noblesse d'épée joined hands with the Noblesse de robe. The young girl married the man "whose body might be taken for a gibbet on which the devil had hanged a soul." As the notary drew up the marriage contract, he asked Paul Scarron what dowry he would bestow upon his wife. "Immortality," answered the King of the Jesters.

For six patient years Françoise nursed him and suffered with him and shared the crazy excesses of his glory and his pain. Paul Scarron became the idol of Paris. The audiences at his plays were so great that "people were crushed to death at the door of the theatre." Suddenly in the midst of his wildest jokes, while his guests were shaking with laughter, he would shriek in a paroxysm of pain. "I am the quintessence of all human misery!" Yet he was a reckless spendthrift of his meager health. And of his abundant wealth. Money flowed through his desperate fingers like sand. The Hôtel de Troyes, where he lived with his wife, became known as the *Hôtel de l'Extravagance*. And Françoise lived up to her side of the bargain in this extravagant deal. Six years she fed him opium and sat by him in the midnight stillness when there was no need to wear the mask of laughter. It was a fair bargain. Let the gods add up the balance sheet. "You have brought to my bedside a pair of large eyes, a beautiful figure, a fine pair of hands and an income of four pounds. And I have brought to you knowledge of Latin, Italian, Spanish, an education, a position in life. I have given you a background which, for your advancement, is worth all the moneybags of the realm."

Six years of nursing; and when the final hour approached for Paul Scarron, he rejoiced. "At last I am going to be *well!*"

He was buried in a pauper's grave. He left behind a mountain of debts and a beautiful wife whom he had prepared for a splendid sacrifice. She had ministered to the lonely heart of a cripple. In a few years she would minister to the lonely heart of a king. Destiny had flung her last great irony at Paul Scarron.

IV

MEN TRIED THEIR CHARMS; but she refused to remarry. "La belle tête brune" was not easily turned. There was too much wisdom in that little head. A lover sought a rendezvous with her. She pretended to consent. And when the eager fellow arrived at the tryst he found not Madame Scarron, but his wife and his baby whom Madame Scarron had sent out to meet him. It was a lovers' rendezvous after all. The family was reunited.

Françoise retired to a convent as a "boarder of distinction" and spent her time reading philosophy. But she was religious as well as wise. "A short time ago I did not exist. A few years more and I shall cease to exist. Has a being of such limitations the right to measure God?"

Though Paul Scarron's widow lived in an age of adventure, she was not an adventuress. Was it not maddening for a lady with the face of Venus to have a heart of ice? A pulchritudinous

Puritan. God had formed her in fire and given her a chill wind for breath.

She knew the world; she was discreet. However, she had exciting friends at the court of Louis XIV. She had been invited to suppers in elaborate houses and had met the most fascinating woman in all France—Madame de Montespan, the mistress of the King. When this lady's husband, the Marquis de Montespan, finally discovered the business, he behaved in a remarkable manner. He went into mourning, draped his carriage and all his livery in black and sent out cards inviting his friends to the funeral of his wife. For she was dead to *him*. But all this belonged to the future. For the present, the liaison was known only to a select few, and the husband was not one of them.

Madame was about to have a child by the King. The situation called for the most exquisite delicacy. The King's illegitimate offspring could not be brought up in the palace for all the world to see. A house in the suburbs was needed. And a governess who would perform the duties of a mother. Madame de Montespan's eyes met Madame Scarron's at the table with a question. And then one day in March Madame Scarron came to the apartment where Madame de Montespan was being confined, walked softly through a side door with a baby girl hidden under her scarf, and entered a waiting carriage.

"Thenceforth," the chronicles tell us, "she led a double life." Five times she came softly to the side door of Madame de Montespan's house and stole away with her bundle. She lived splendidly, if ambiguously, during these interesting years. "I am not a sinner," she reasoned with herself. "I undertook this charge out of respect for the King, my benefactor, and because my Confessor considered it a good work. At the beginning I believed that I should never get to the year's end without disgust. Little by little I silenced my emotions and my regrets." The woman who bears the children is immoral. The woman who brings them up under the protection of the King is only—discreet.

[86]

It was a "thoroughly well appointed house" in which she brought up the King's natural children. Her word was law for the "two nurses, a waiting-maid, a physician, a courier, two footmen, a coachman, a postilion, and two cooks." She was provided with "an excellent coach in which she took the children to St. Germain every week, to be seen by their parents." Madame Scarron dined with the royal family and sat in the royal coach and sailed in the royal yacht. And even the King's legitimate wife, the Queen Marie-Thérèse, when at last she learned of her husband's "children of passion," could not help admiring their education. "Ah, Madame Scarron," she said, "you ought to have educated *my* children, too."

One day the King himself came unexpectedly to the house of his governess in the suburbs. And as he stood silently at the door of the nursery, he witnessed a tableau of devotion. Madame Scarron was sitting by the bed of his son, the Duc de Main, who was suffering from a fever. With one hand she stroked his head and with the other she rocked the cradle of his daughter, Mademoiselle Nantes. And on her lap lay his other son, the Count de Vexin.

So faithful a scene deserved a fitting reward. The King presented his governess with the estate of Maintenon—a splendid country house of Gothic construction, built for the pleasure of a feudal lord in the time of Philip Augustus, and redecorated and enlarged in the fifteenth century. And he bestowed upon her the title of Marquise de Maintenon.

Before long, the King had come to feel more than gratitude for the governess. He had "fallen under the spell of Madame's complexion." So, too, had every nobleman in France. "Her beauty is performing such miracles, there must be something supernatural about it." The story passed around the court that the West Indian governess had acquired the powers of a witch from a potion a Negress had given her in Martinique. It was an enchantment which made her irresistible. It wouldn't be long now, they whispered, before "la belle Indienne" would steal her way into the royal bed.

But Madame lowered her eyes. People underestimated her character. The King soon came to realize that he had to deal with a woman who was not only piquant but pious. Hitherto he had thought that only ugly women were devout. And no woman had ever been able to resist him. It began to look as if *he* would not be able to resist *her*. He would have to accept her not as his mistress but as his wife.

And why not? She dug into the records and discovered seventeen degrees of "pedigree" on her father's side—a long line dating from Geffroi d'Aubigné of Anjou, founder of one of the noblest families in France. To be sure, a few of the cynics whispered that she had made a mistake somewhere in her research; that the d'Aubignés of Anjou were in no wise related to the d'Aubignés of Niort Jail; and that she could go back no farther than her grandfather Théodore. But she shrugged off these attacks. God would know His own.

God, she felt convinced, had chosen her for a holy crusade. She had brought up the King's children. Why not bring up the King's morals? She implored him to leave Madame de Montespan. The King's mistress was an artist after a fashion; but the King's governess was one of the supreme artists of the realm. "Sire," she said, "Madame de Montespan is dear to you. But yours is a selfish love, which wounds her husband and your Queen . . . What would you do to your Captain of the Guard, if you were told that he had taken away another man's wife?"

Parbleu, but this Madame-Governess grows younger with every word! Although close to fifty, she looks thirty. She has been appointed Lady-in-Waiting to the Dauphiness, the wife of the Crown Prince. And she has completely eclipsed the Dauphiness. Whom next shall she eclipse?

Whom indeed? After all, the Queen still lives, Madame de Montespan remains in the King's favor, and Madame de Maintenon is only Lady-in-Waiting. How long can a lady wait and still remain a lady?

And then, suddenly, the death of Queen Marie-Thérèse—the most neglected plaything in the King's palace. Louis Quatorze, guided at last by the waxing of his scruples and the waning of his appetites, dismisses Madame de Montespan. And on January 12, 1648, in the Chapel at Versailles, the Sun King—secretly—makes Madame de Maintenon his wife. Françoise d'Aubigné is now a full-fledged Bourbon.

V

AND who were these Bourbons to whom Madame de Maintenon had now become legally united? Monsieur, the King's brother, had a passion for necklaces "with which he loved to decorate his person." The Duc de Bourbon, the King's son-in-law, "is as thin as a lathe with legs like a crane," wrote one of his contemporaries. "His body is bent and short; his eyes are so red that it is impossible to distinguish the good from the bad one which has been accidentally struck out." Another of the Bourbons, the Comte de Soisson, "is as yellow as saffron. His mouth is very small and full of decayed teeth; his feet are turned inward, which makes him look like a parrot." And as for the King's own son, the heir to the throne—"ah, by the grace of God, he does not seem to be very promising" either in fact or in figure. He guzzles and he gorges himself until he appears to incorporate all France in his flesh. He is "drowned in his own fat . . . He is unable to speak on any subject but cooking and hunting; he is obstinate and excessively mean." As a child he was furious with the weather when it rained against his wishes. He broke the clocks that struck the hours for his lessons. And now "his pride is such that he seems to look down from the heights of heaven on ordinary men as mere atoms to whom he bears not the slightest resemblance."

But, in this last respect, he was but the child of his father.

Louis XIV, too, believed himself to be the unique earthly image of the unique sun in the heavens. "As soon as the conversation turned on anything but himself, the King yawned and went to bed." It was a relief for Madame de Maintenon to leave the "splendors" of this court and to go into the country where she could mingle with some honest peasants. "They do not talk as well as we do, but we do not act as well as they do."

Finally, as a retreat from the vainglorious activities of the court, Madame de Maintenon decided to build a school for girls—the daughters of military officers who had lost their lives in the King's wars—an institution in which the girls were to be educated in moral and religious principles, and supplied with a husband at the age of twenty. "This is such a worthy design!" The King, who could refuse his wife nothing, invested over a million livres to build the school at St. Cyr. When the building was completed, he had a pavilion for himself erected in the main yard and he ordered the girls to pray for him when his armies suffered a defeat and to sing for him when they gained a victory. But the students must live behind their high walls in utter ignorance of the world until twenty. "I like the ladies of St. Cyr to hate the world and to love the State," announced the conceited King.

At this school Madame de Maintenon's genius for training children was put into good effect. St. Cyr became the "academy of fashion" in France. The little students, nourished on ribbons and courtesies and sweet conversation, became the actresses in a pageant finer even than that of the palace at Versailles. The courtly writer Racine, with a pen that flowed in a cascade of classic verse, was asked to write a play for the girls at St. Cyr. And he composed a supreme drama on a biblical theme—the story of Esther.

The performance was a success. "M. le Prince was moved to tears and the King applauded frequently and talked of nothing else at supper." Poor, silly, grown-up children! And as for the younger children at St. Cyr, their glory was short-lived. Under pressure from the Church—"play acting is no fit occupation for young ladies"—Madame de Maintenon transformed the academy for girls into a community for nuns. The teachers took the vows of St. Augustine, and the girls gave up their plays for their prayers.

*This was the somber epilogue of what commenced to be
The fashionable acting of a pleasant fantasy.*

VI

A FAITHFUL CONSORT must follow her husband to glory even through the fires of hell. On several of the King's military campaigns Madame de Maintenon accompanied the army in a carriage—and feasted while the soldiers fought. "The battle gained in Italy," writes Madame during the war with the Duke of Marlborough, "determines me to put on my fine dress; if Barcelona is captured I shall wear green; and rose color if the Arch-Duke is taken prisoner."

All this is charming. But not a word about the nameless soldiers who win the King's battles. And what happens when the King's armies begin to lose? *Then* the nameless soldiers suddenly find a name for themselves. *Fools!* "We might have known that King Louis is not the favorite of God. War after war since he came to the throne. Uncomplainingly we have died to win him his victories. But now he no longer wins." Even Madame de Maintenon with all her piety suddenly loses faith. Perhaps God is not a Frenchman after all!

But she is reassured. The King finally makes peace with Marlborough, loses a little territory and pride, but keeps his throne. And life goes on at Versailles in splendid fashion as before.

Yet one day, as Madame drives through the city of Paris in her carriage, the starving people crowd about her with a strange, menacing, almost vocal look in their eyes. Will they speak after

all these centuries of silence? For an uneasy moment she feels
that her life is no longer safe. They cry out her name in a chant.
This is the woman whose extravagant luxuries have left them
without bread. This is the woman at whose orders the greatest
engineers of the realm have tried to turn a river from its course in
order that it might feed more fountains for Versailles—and a
thousand men were crushed in the attempt!

And yet this day no one will harm Madame. She protests her
innocence. Several years later another woman, far less fortunate,
was also to protest her innocence—only to be carted to the guillo-
tine. But Marie Antoinette, unfortunate queen, wore a flashing
necklace when she rode past the starving mobs of Paris. Madame
de Maintenon, paragon of subtle piety, wears a modest black
dress.

VII

"There is not a kitchen maid who doesn't suppose herself equal
to the task of statesmanship," said a cynical Frenchman. But
Madame de Maintenon amazed even the French. At fifty she
married a royal voluptuary of forty-six and kept his heart for
thirty years when the most beautiful young women of his realm
had kept it for scarcely thirty nights. At sixty, "suffering in all her
joints," she danced the masquerade and rode to the hunt. At
seventy she lost her sight and her hearing and her teeth, yet she
went "frolicking piously" in the king's gondolas. As the violins
played at Versailles, she kept murmuring between her naps, "I
am a living skeleton." At eighty she accompanied the king in
his coach-and-six which he drove madly as if to chase away his
own seventy-six years. And through all this busy life she wrote
some of the wittiest epigrams in the history of French literature.
Now at last she wanted to be left alone, resting at her Chateau
de Maintenon and watching the nectarines ripen on the wall.
What a mockery of the grand passion for a decaying frame to act
a pageant, to suit the whims of a king!

But she remained at Versailles, she told herself, because she conceived of a "sacred mission"—to turn the dying king to God. If Louis could learn to love religion only through his love of a woman devoted to religion, so let it be. "Woman is the eternal saviour of man."

She was like a phantom dragged about "from bed to bed, from niche to niche." And she read him the Bible in his hours of torture. There is no more pitiable child, no creature more needy of salvation, than the man who is master of every one but himself. As he lay on the verge of death he whispered to her, "What will become of you? You have nothing!"

She made the sign of the cross and answered, "I *am* nothing. Think only of God."

She retired to St. Cyr. The role she had played was finished. She had begun it in the black garments of widowhood; she ended it in the black garments of widowhood. Thirty years ago the curtain had risen when she had buried a poet. Now it fell as she buried a king. She merely laughed a little when the grave diggers rested.

And when Czar Peter, on a trip through France, saw her on her deathbed, he asked solicitously: "What are you dying of, Madame?"

"Of laughter," she replied.

CHARLOTTE BRONTË

Important Dates in Life of Charlotte Brontë

1816—Born at Thornton, Yorkshire.

1830—Entered Miss Wooler's school at Roe Head.

1842–44—Studied in Belgium and fell in love with her professor.

1846—Published a book of poems anonymously by herself and her sisters Emily and Anne.

1847—Published *Jane Eyre*.

1849—Completed the writing of *Shirley*.

1852–53—Wrote *Villette*.

1854—Married Arthur Bell Nicholls.

1855—Died in pregnancy.

Charlotte Brontë

Charlotte Brontë

1816–1855

HAWORTH lay at the top of a slope so high it seemed to go to heaven. Twisted away in a fold of fog and rain, behind the little church, stretched the parsonage like a shaggy silent dog. No laughter came from it. The very tombstones in the cemetery which was its garden seemed like whirligigs of mirth compared to the parson and his family within the house. In the rooms guarded by the cemetery in the front and by the moors in the rear, were born six persons no less strange than you may suppose. Six Irish children—five girls and a boy. The oldest was eight when their mother died. The youngest was less than two. They lived a life according to the Calvinist precepts of their clerical father. They ate no meat, for that was a luxury. They played no games. They were indoctrinated with the sadness and the responsibility of life. "They were taught to discuss death and the hereafter when they should have been sucking their thumbs." They saw no one outside the members of their family. How could they know of a world beyond? Before the windows of the children's nursery the somber silence of the cemetery, the wild silence of the moors, Death and the Devil were waging an incessant epic struggle for the possession of their bodies and their souls.

And their stern Gaelic father in his mourning clothes, with yards of white silk handkerchiefs wrapped around his neck as a protection against the cold, was he not the God of the awful struggle between the elements?

The children learned their lessons from Aunt Branwell, their father's sister. Once a week the Reverend Mr. Brontë called them into his study for an oral examination. Like little old people they stood obediently before him. "Anne, what does a child like yourself lack most?"

"Age and experience, Papa," replied Anne, a blue-eyed little scholar of four.

Emily was next on the carpet. "Tell me what I must do with your brother Branwell when he is naughty?"

And the five-year-old Emily replied, "Reason with him, and when he won't listen to reason, whip him."

Excellent children, conscientious little Puritans after his own heart! He turned to Charlotte, homely little eight-year-old elfin with a large, crooked mouth, and with eyes like the eyes of a child out of Mother Goose. "What is the best book in the world?"

"The Bible—and nature, Papa."

Next came Maria. "Tell me, child, what is the best way of employing one's time? Think carefully before you answer. Look into your heart, child."

And the ten-year-old replied, "I believe the best way of employing one's time is by laying it out in preparation for eternity."

And now Branwell, the boy upon whom Mr. Brontë had placed all his hopes. A rogue, a tiger of a child. Seven years. "What is the best way to know the difference between the intellects of men and women?"

Branwell puckered up his face. "By considering the difference between them as to their bodies, Sir."

This reply rather stumped Mr. Brontë. But Branwell was a genius.

And now the interview is over, the sun is high and the six sad little Christians go scrambling with their dog over the heathen moor. By a strange alchemy during these few precious hours, the loneliness of the children, who seem to have been neglected by other children, penetrates the loneliness of the moors that seem to have been neglected by God—two isolated groups of motherless souls become one.

II

PARSON BRONTË sent his girls to Cowan Bridge school near Bradford. But the poor food and the bleak life broke the fragile bodies of Maria and Elizabeth, the two oldest children, and spilled their lives.

Back at Haworth, Charlotte was now the oldest child. She taught and organized and protected the other children and read the morning paper to her father while he took his coffee. She led a mass assault of the children upon Tabby, the servant, for ghost stories, and she made believe that she was on a lonely island with the Duke of Wellington, her favorite hero. At Haworth it was necessary to populate the air for company, for very little real company ventured inside. And thus, the most fascinating souls in history were these children's for the imagining. They crowded their notebooks with the exploits of fabulous races—images of themselves reflected in the thousand-and-one mirrors of their fancy. They created a whole world in the likeness of one another.

But Papa decided that Charlotte must undergo a more conventional education. And he sent his daughter of fourteen to Roe's Head School. As she stood in Miss Wooler's parlor on the first day of the term, shrinking and blinking in the light, the other girls were half-amused, half-terrified, half-moved to tears. "She looked so puny . . . as to pass for a child of ten . . . Her hands and feet were tiny beyond belief. Her extreme near-sightedness gave her the look of a mole brought suddenly into broad daylight." Her hair was frizzled, her green woolen dress had been worn by her Aunt Branwell a generation ago, her movements were like a frightened little animal's.

Miss Wooler examined her and found that she was deficient in the most elementary mathematics and geography and grammar. But when she put a pen into her hand, the amazing child glued her nose to the paper and covered page after page of an improvised story. "Please, ma'am, I have written twenty-two volumes of stories at home," she murmured.

And when Miss Wooler shook out the little lady's curls, she found them truly magnificent. She prescribed a diet of animal food—meat and soup and gravy—for the first time in the life of that little body. Charlotte grew plump and almost beautiful. Poor little wet mouse taken out of the rain. And in the dormitory at night, how she kept the girls awake with stories of the moors! She launched out into terrible, fantastic, hair-raising improvisations. Her eyes grew brilliant, and her face changed to fire. "One night," writes a schoolmate, "Charlotte caused a panic of terror by telling of the wanderings of a sleepwalker. She brought together all the horrors her imagination could create, from surging seas . . . towering castle walls, high precipices . . . She brought out, in almost cloud-height, her somnambulist to walk on shaking turrets. She told it all in a voice that conveyed more than words can express. A shivering cry of terror seized one of her audience, a recently recovered invalid . . . After a pause, a subdued cry of pain came from Charlotte herself. And tremblingly she called out for someone to go for help. She was in terrible tears and distress . . . For weeks we could not prevail upon her to continue her tales."

Her imagination was supreme. She related little incidents about her two dead sisters and suffered as she spoke. When surprise was expressed that she could have known about them when they were so young and she was even younger, she replied, "I began to analyze characters when I was five years old." And she produced notes she had taken on two guests who had stayed at Haworth during her early childhood.

An active mind in an inactive body. "In our play hours she sat or stood still with a book. Some of us once urged her to be on our side in a game of ball . . . We soon found she could not see the ball, so we put her out." Her sight could never tally with the ball thrown by other folk. She was too weak-sighted—and too strong-sighted—for the games of her schoolmates. The lights and shadows of Haworth had trained her to a different perspective.

III

THE QUIET DAYS AND NIGHTS at Haworth merged into quiet years. Charlotte was now a teacher at Miss Wooler's school. But she didn't like to teach. She sent some of her poetry to Robert Southey and asked him whether he could encourage her in a literary career. And the acid old Puritan replied, "Literature cannot be the business of a woman's life and ought not to be." She sent part of a novel to Wordsworth; and the elderly poet, who had long since changed from a man into an institution, declared that he was unable to determine whether the author was a "notary's clerk or a demented seamstress." That was sufficient. She accepted a job as governess with a middle class London family. But she found herself dreadfully unhappy. "One of the pleasantest afternoons I have spent here," she wrote with her accustomed sarcasm, "was when Mr. Sidgwick walked out with his children and his Newfoundland dog, and I had orders to follow a little behind."

As for the "dear little children," they reveled in their filth, "spilled their milk on the table, plunged their fingers into each other's mugs, wiped their mouths and hands on their mother's skirt . . . bellowed like bulls, and spat, either into each other's faces or into the workbag of their governess!" Why should children obey a little woman who looked like an elf in a midsummer night's dream?

She left her job in confusion. Her failure had only aggravated the sense of her own inferiority. What was she to do? Marriage, she felt, was out of the question for a girl "with no beauty and no fortune." She had noticed, she commented wryly, "that after a stranger has once looked at my face, he is careful not to let his eyes wander to that part of the room again."

Charlotte was not doing at all well. Neither were the other members of the family. The Brontës seemed to be not of the clay of this world. Poor Anne, who could not bear to look strangers in the face, was suffering miserably in her employment as a governess. Emily was unwilling to seek employment away from home, for she clung to the moors like a lover. Branwell, the chief hope of his father, had made a few unsuccessful attempts to sell his stories and was now wasting his time in the taverns where he found an audience who appreciated him—chiefly because "he could write two letters simultaneously with his two hands" and tell witty Irish jokes. Whenever a traveler stopped at the inn at Haworth, the landlord would tell him of this "brilliant young fellow at the Parsonage near by, who will certainly come down and have a glass or two to pass the hour." Poor Branwell was playing a role of Shakespearean tragedy for the Yorkshire farmers!

Something had to be done to rehabilitate the family. And Charlotte felt the responsibility of her years upon her. It was up to her to extricate the Brontës from the swamp.

And the opportunity presented itself. She received a letter from a school chum who was attending a *pensionnat* in Brussels, and an idea struck her. She would take Emily to school with her in Belgium. A year on the continent acquiring the savoir-faire, and then back to Haworth to open a fashionable school for girls.

So the prim little old maid of twenty-six set sail for the Land of the Cathedrals.

IV

SHE ENROLLED at the *pensionnat* of Monsieur and Madame Héger. And she was instantly attracted to Professor Héger. He was a married man with five children—"and the most repulsive male in the world . . . German in origin, short-legged, with a domed cranium, thick dark hair clipped close, eye-glasses set astride his nose, behind which his eyes burn like coals . . . a little black being, with a face that varies in expression. Sometimes he borrows the lineaments of an insane tomcat, sometimes those of a delirious hyena." Her exact opposite in age, inclination, temperament. He was keen, vivacious, would fly into a passion at nothing, lose all control of himself, and sob tears of rage in the midst of his lectures. But he was the first keen intellect she had met in a man.

He had singled her out as his favorite pupil. She went through the most sacred first impressions by his side. He gave her special lessons and he made a "strong masculine mind" out of what had been the mind of a precocious child. He revealed to her a world of philosophy and science and art, and he opened up for her a new dimension of human experience.

At the end of her term, Charlotte came back to Haworth. But Professor Héger wrote a letter to her father telling how much he desired his exceptional student to return. And Charlotte, "drawn by an irresistible impulse," went back to Brussels. For what was Haworth to her now?

Inexpressible delight! He asked her to teach him English lessons. Now she would be alone with the man who had become all-in-all to her!

Madame Héger coolly observed the symptoms. This shy little Englishwoman spoke to no one, smiled at no one, but her husband. When they were together, "her face would light up and acquire a beauty of which she was unconscious." She would become transformed—almost—into a desirable woman. Madame played her game skillfully as befitted her years. With exquisite tact, she rearranged the Professor's schedule so that his leisure hours would not coincide with his pupil's. She hinted that Charlotte would no longer be welcome to use the family living room as her own.

Did she really fear Charlotte? That artless girl had written, "Love, as I understand it, is nothing that is not right, noble, faithful." Charlotte wanted no caresses. She wanted to be with him, "to catch his glance, to listen for an hour to the sound of his voice," to gather in her drawer the cigars he had left half-smoked behind him. That was all she asked. And even *that* was denied her.

For two years longer she stayed in Brussels. He did not see her passion. He did not feel. He talked to her of passion as if it were an abstract idea. And she went almost dead with the excess of her emotion.

Two years she stayed in a midnight without friends. And then, as she wandered distractedly through the neighborhood of the Rue d'Isabelle, she came upon a friend. It was the Church of Sainte Gudule. She looked for a moment through the door into the light of the candles. And then she did what her father and her sisters would never understand. She walked through the entrance into the bosom of this Catholic friend and knelt by the grate of the confessional, ready to pour out the whole story of her love.

But how could she begin? The formula was unfamiliar and alien. Could she say, "Father, I am a Protestant and I seek the blessings of confession"? Slowly the church bells tolled. And the great stone bosom of the church seemed to breathe out her incense with the gentleness of a mother. Like a little child Charlotte confessed her secret. And then she packed her luggage and came back to Haworth.

She took up her pen and wrote to him—fervid, impetuous, eager letters, the lava of a smoldering heart. "Sir, the poor do not need very much to sustain them in life. They ask only the crumbs that fall from the rich man's table. I also have need only of a little affection from those I love. I would not know what to do with a whole and complete devotion: I am so unused to the thought . . . And yet I am conscious that there are cold reasonable people who would say if they read it, 'she raves.' My revenge is to wish that these people might for one day know the tortures that I have for eight months experienced; we should see then if they, too, would not also rave. One suffers in silence as long as one has the strength; but when that strength gives out, one speaks without measuring words."

There was no reply. He was "correct." He did not care. He did not see. He did not feel. Again she took up her pen. "I have sought to forget you. I have done everything; I have tried to keep occupied . . . Why cannot I feel for you just the same degree of friendship that you feel for me, neither more nor less? I should then be so free! I could then be silent for years! . . . Sir, I have a favor to ask. Talk about your children . . . Speak what you please, my master, if only you speak . . . For me it means life . . . To forbid me to write, to refuse to reply, would be to snatch from me my sole happiness in this world, to deprive me of my last privilege." And at last a reply. "Your letter," she writes, "served to nourish me for six months. I must have another now, and you will send it to me, not out of friendship, for you cannot feel much of that, but because you have a compassionate heart and would not condemn anyone to prolonged suffering in order to spare a few boring moments . . ."

And then she took her pen again to keep from going mad. But this time no letter came as the rain beat down. She turned her suffering into a novel for the ages.

V

JANE EYRE swept England by storm. "Writers are wrong, morally wrong in making their heroines beautiful as a matter of course,"

Charlotte had told her sisters. "I will prove that they are wrong. I will show you a heroine as plain and small as myself."

Within a fortnight of the publication of the book, concert halls and tea rooms buzzed with pleasure and horror at the sensation. Who was this author who called himself "Currer Bell"—obviously a pseudonym—who had dared to write this unconventional love story of a homely governess in love with a man married to a lunatic wife? Was it the work of a scoundrel? Few guessed that it was the work of a woman.

Thackeray, who was reveling in an "equally unconventional" best seller he had just written, recognized a kindred genius. With the grin of a satyr he sent an inscribed copy of *Vanity Fair* to the author of *Jane Eyre*. Did he realize that the author of this book was a clergyman's daughter?

Charlotte Brontë returned the compliment by dedicating the second edition of her book to Thackeray. And the English public, aware now of her identity, decided that she must be Thackeray's mistress, for "two such souls dripped in brimfire" could not live long apart in this world.

But neither Thackeray nor any one else could guess the true proportions of the melodrama that was the life of Charlotte Brontë.

While "Currer Bell" tasted glory in the bookstalls, Charlotte Brontë tasted grief at home. Branwell, who had cast not the least grotesque of the shadows at Haworth, was dead at thirty-one. He had gone to London to paint, and he had succumbed to the dissipations of his fellow artists. He had taken a position as instructor to a rich man's children and had been dismissed when it was discovered that he was planning to elope with their mother. He had worked for a time as ticket agent on the railroad. But when the inspector checked his ledgers he found, in place of the account of the money taken in, nothing but sketches of the head and the bust of Venus and snatches of poetry. And then, when Branwell had reached the very bottom of the world's esteem, he translated the *Odes* of Horace into the finest English poetry, took a final drink and passed on. And his eyes looked as if his heart had burst with the mighty question, "What is the meaning of all this?"

A few weeks later, dark-eyed Emily followed him across the stream of darkness. Shy, reserved as a peony in the parlor, her lips silent but her heart a cathedral on fire, she had written a book called *Wuthering Heights* with as little fuss as she made when she churned the butter. In all her life she had never lingered over any task that lay before her, and she did not linger now. She followed the voices calling from the moors to the sources of the wind; and Keeper, her dog, barked in vain for her to come home again.

A month later Anne, "the little one," coughed as Emily had coughed. The fatal consumption! Charlotte carried her off to the seashore, hoping desperately that the salt air might save her. But Anne knew better. She held Charlotte's hand and whispered, "Take courage." The distant ships "shone like burnished gold on the sea" the afternoon she died. Charlotte stood in the light of the setting sun. Nodding and dreamless she heard the words that Emily had flung against the night:

> *Though earth and moon were gone*
> *And suns and universes ceased to be,*
> *And Thou were left alone,*
> *Every existence would exist in Thee.*

VI

ONE EVENING the footman at Mrs. Harriet Martineau's announced a "Miss Brogden" to the company. And in walked "the tiniest lady the guests had ever seen except at a fair." The lady had given her name in such a low voice that the footman had got it wrong. It was "Miss Brontë," the guest of honor herself. Miss Brontë thrust at her hostess a cold tiny hand, "like the claw of a little bird," and sat down to blink in a corner. She had dared to emerge from Haworth one Saturday for a timid visit to her publishers, Smith and Elder, on Paternoster Row. And it had taken all their powers of persuasion to convince her to go through the busy schedule of a celebrity—visits to the National Gallery, dinners in the country, lectures, splendid rooms in London, "morning and evening a fire in her bedroom and wax candles." The cognoscenti were frantic to make a lioness out of this ewe. But Miss Brontë "seemed possessed with the most unfeminine lack of desire to please." She simply refused to roar. A galaxy of distinguished guests gathered at Mr. Thackeray's house to listen to Miss Brontë's "brilliant conversation." For several hours no one spoke. Finally one lady turned desperately to the silent little authoress on the sofa. "Do you like London, Miss Brontë?" Miss Brontë pursed her lips and paused dramatically for a moment of deep concentration while all breathing stopped. "Yes— and no," she replied. Whereupon Mr. Thackeray stood up, excused himself from his guests and went off to his club to get drunk.

She wished "she could hide under the furniture." The presence of people gave her physical pain. At the opera, at public readings, "the very cream" of society parted in two rows and gaped as she walked by—and she trembled on her escort's arm. Finally, when her publishers allowed her to select her own amusements and to visit the sort of people she really wanted to see, she went to two prisons, the Hospital for Foundlings and the Bethlehem Lunatic Asylum.

She made one last surrender, however, to the society of Regent Park. She sat for a portrait by Richmond—who failed to catch the haunting sadness in her eyes. And then she returned to Haworth.

Two more books came from her pen—sequels to *Jane Eyre*— and she wrote these books "painfully, as if paid with her flesh." She took up the threads of her autobiography from the days when she had served as governess in London. She wrote *Shirley,* a book commemorating her sister Emily and the curates who sat and joked in the parlor when life was to be had for the asking. One of these curates had been a very bashful suitor. He had sent valentines to all the sisters, for he had no intention of "embarrassing" the one that he really loved. And now he was dead and his secret with him underground. And nothing belonged to the present but memories; everything was of the past.

Then she turned her memory upon the trip to Belgium and the *pensionnat* of Professor Héger. And as she wrote *Villette,* the air was so still "you could catch the ticking of the clock in the kitchen, or the buzzing of a fly in the parlor, all over the house."

Quiet—and restless. When the people who had come up the windy path to visit her at Haworth went to bed at night, they heard her pace the floor until they fell asleep.

How old was this woman? they asked in London. Nearing forty. And those who saw her declared she looked nearer sixty. Too old by far for romance.

Yet there were rumors that a clergyman who lived near by had made her a declaration of love. The rumors were based upon fact. A neighboring curate had indeed offered her a second chance at life. He was an obscure and uninspired child of God. She was a sad and gifted lady of fame. It was a match! She laid out her wedding dress and slept with the dreams of a young bride till the churchbells tolled. "After a hard and long struggle, after many cares and much sorrow, she is tasting happiness at last." It was on a Christmas afternoon that she stood beside him, dressed in her white muslin and "looking like a snowdrop." Once more there was a woman who loved a man at Haworth since the day when a hard-pressed mother of eight children lay dying in an upper room. For thirty years nothing of a pleasant nature had happened here until this wedding day.

Months pass. And then the news comes from Yorkshire to London. Charlotte is going to have a child. Paint the walls bright and put up the curtains that laugh and dance with color. There are going to be new eyes at Haworth to look upon the great play of life with its topsy-turvy fortunes, its ups and downs, its gladness and its madness . . .

She is ill and tired and takes to her bed. The doctor reassures her. This is to be expected in her condition. No cause for alarm. She looks out of the window. "Storms of rain are sweeping the garden. The moors are hidden in thick fog." She feels a morbid strength in her weakness. Side by side with the stirrings of life there is the growth of death in her body. Both spread and grow and suck her food and wrestle like the ancient furies to overmaster her. Slowly she loses all desire for the child, loses all curiosity, all joy in its coming. "I am too tired to care much, now . . . but perhaps . . . later on!" . . . She lifts her head to her husband. "I am not going to die. He will not separate us. We have been so happy!"

But when the winds of March went out, they carried her along with them. Across the Dark River, to her second chance at life.

GEORGE ELIOT

Important Dates in Life of George Eliot

1819—Born in Warwickshire, England.

1844—Commenced her intellectual life by translating Strauss' *Life of Jesus.*

1851—Became assistant editor of the *Westminster Review.*

1854—Began living with George Henry Lewes as his wife.

1857—Wrote *Scenes from Clerical Life* for *Blackwood's Magazine* and commenced her career as a writer of fiction.

1878—Death of George Henry Lewes.

1879—Marriage to John W. Cross.

1880—Died.

The following are her major works:

1859—*Adam Bede;* 1860—*The Mill on the Floss;* 1861—*Silas Marner;* 1862–3—*Romola;* 1866—*Felix Holt;* 1868—*The Spanish Gypsy* (drama); 1872—*Middle-March;* 1876—*Daniel Deronda.*

George Eliot

George Eliot

1819–1880

WHEN people first looked into her face they were left with an extraordinary impression. "Her eyes were gray-green. They looked as if they were newly washed." The upper part of her face was heavier and more masculine than most men's; the lower half was more sensitive than most women's. When she was lost in a mood of sadness, she looked as "homely as a horse." But when she smiled, she was divinity itself.

Her smiles, however, were few. "She lacked some aroma of hope, some felicity of virtue." She wore a look like that of Proserpina spending six months as a frightened guest in the world of sunshine. Everybody felt the effect of her loneliness, "a loneliness of one dwelling sadly, sublimely apart."

Mary Anne Evans was born on St. Cecilia's Day, at the edge of the Forest of Arden. Her father was a midland farmer, an "honest old Tory" who pronounced the word "government" in a manner that stunned his children into religious awe. He evaluated estates for the country nobility, sold anything for a commission, and knew that the Duke of Wellington would "set things right" by chastising all radicals as he had chastised Napoleon. Solid as a coffin he was, and as faithful as Scripture. There was nothing about him, or about his wife, that suggested the slightest deviation from the ordinary. But here was their child, Mary Anne, who walked on wind. She had a temper and an imagination, a code of justice and of retribution all her own. A cow was not a cow to her. Nor was a doll a doll. When she was angry at humanity—for some thing Papa did—she drove nails into the head of her doll. And then, like a very goddess, she repented and applied poultices. At five she was "a quaint thing with strongly marked features and great seriousness of expression, whom the older girls petted and called 'Little Mama.' " At eight she found religion as an active force. Before she was twelve she taught a Sunday school class of Nuneaton farm boys and girls. At thirteen she decided that orthodoxy in religion was not necessary to nobility in character. She read Wordsworth. And the older people were startled, in the midst of the average placidity of the Evans farm, to see two shining eyes that stood out like stars in a barren field of night. They called her *Clematis,* which in the language of the flowers means *moral beauty.*

Yet the moral little scholar had the savage in her. She roamed the fields and didn't mind if the brambles drew blood from her feet. She wrestled with her brother until her hair was caked in mud. She loved to fall and to go to sleep in untidy places, and to squeeze a blackberry as if it were alive. And when she went to church in her Sunday clothes, she felt as out of place as a piccaninny in a palace.

But at last the inevitable years washed away her awkwardness. She grew tall, even graceful—and self conscious. And she discarded nearly all of her childhood "playthings." But she retained the books of Goldsmith, and Scott, the essays of Lamb, the fable of Bunyan. Her interests now were deliberately cultivated, not nature-bestowed. She read Pascal's *Meditations* and listened to the Bach masses and the Handel oratorios. For a while she stopped going to church. She became the mistress of many tongues and unconventions. At a time when other women put on airs and cosmetics to catch a man, she put on spectacles to catch the muse of learning; and she carried her pedantry like an aroma that kept away all men of a romantic turn. She was still a gipsy —no longer a gipsy child, to be sure, but a gipsy philosopher. She would never "stay put" and settle down to warm herself by the fireside morality of her generation. She would travel along an itinerary of morals and mishaps and revelations all her own. She would shock the fathers and the husbands of England. Whoever heard of a respectable woman in Victorian England learning life by trial and error? A wife and a mother should endure many *trials,* to be sure, said the men. But there must be no *errors*—and certainly no *learning.*

But Mary Anne Evans at twenty-one was more than an Englishman.

II

SHE came up to London and was appointed assistant editor of the *Westminster Review.* She overwhelmed the sophisticates with her sophistication. She became interested in the new science of phrenology—the reading of a person's character by the shape and bumps of his head—and had herself shaved clean to the scalp in order that the phrenological society might experiment with a plaster cast of her own skull. For weeks she wore a hat in ballrooms and theaters until her hair grew back, and she consoled herself in her private hours by translating the *Life of Jesus* from the ponderous German of David Strauss. When this work was finished, she spent her evenings translating the *Ethics* of Spinoza from the Latin, after her fifteen-hour-a-day chore as a reviewer on the *Westminster Review.* There was no more formidable man-eating shark among the literary critics than this little lady. Her comments on the modern novels were terrifying and to the point. She exchanged wares of gossip with Carlyle and Huxley and Mill and Tyndall and other leading merchandisers of thought. She sat in restaurants with illustrious émigrés, political refugees from the continent, aspiring writers. She discussed the science of socialism with Louis Blanc, and the art of insurrection with Mazzini.

And at this point in her life she met the archangel of the art of theorizing, Herbert Spencer, then known as the author of *Social Statistics*. All his life was to be paved and sustained and fortified with statistics. Now he took Mary Anne Evans to "so many" operas, "such and such" a number of theater openings, "so and so many" walks by the Thames. And friends began to whisper anxiously that the two mental navigators had discovered among their equipment a stowaway emotion that might take over and steer the ship. After such an honorable and analytical courtship, Herbert Spencer was expected to declare himself. He admitted publicly—and to himself—that he had never before met a woman whose powers and weaknesses at every point were so like his own. And Mary Anne found in the daring architect of theories and figures the embodiment of an ideal husband. But the proposal did not come. Herbert Spencer had added up the final column of his statistics and had found that the sum read —bachelorhood.

Soon the couple were no longer seen together. Mary Anne retired discreetly to her front office and allowed her bitter afterfeelings to spend themselves in work. Life had caught up with her at last and had wrenched her loose from her superior attitude toward life; had reminded her that she was a woman and that she could be hurt. At thirty she had considered herself ancient, too ancient to be touched by time; now she was considerably over thirty. Yet in her sudden old age she felt young again, too young to be *mended* by time. Once this Minerva of wisdom—it was before she had discovered that she wore the heel of Achilles— had said prettily and truly, "To the old, sorrow is sorrow; to the young, it is despair." Then she had *said* it; now she *knew* it, knew every fathom of the agonizing gradation from sorrow to despair.

She spoke of herself no longer in terms of learning. "I feel in my sad moments as if a great procession has swept by, and the last notes of its music have died away, leaving me alone with fields and sky."

But as time went on, she remarked with a sarcastic dignity— "The weather and I are better, having cried ourselves out and used up all our clouds, and I even contemplate living six months longer."

III

IN LONDON lived a scholar out of the Arabian nights—George Henry Lewes—critic, philosopher and actor extraordinary. He was so ugly that children ran away from him. People joked that the chimpanzee in the London Zoo had died from jealous anxiety that George Henry Lewes would usurp his place. And Mr. Lewes was as learned as he was ugly. Every day he "breakfasted off a chapter of Kant and dined on a poem by Goethe."

Mary Anne Evans met him socially. She marveled at the ironical trick that nature had played upon this man by giving him a body too repellent and a mind too large for the world. The story of his life was no less amazing than his appearance. As a youth he showed a talent for writing—and was placed in an attorney's office to write deeds. His salary was paid in "compliments." He kept the books of a Russian merchant, was attracted to medicine and then to philosophy, and spent his evenings at a Spinoza club. He rushed to Germany and entered the field of science; but "incapable of doing anything long," he turned actor, became a member of a company of players organized by Charles Dickens, and scored a great success as Shylock. Then he left the stage, wrote plays, taught a dozen languages, published a novel on the French Revolution and a history of philosophy, married the beautiful daughter of a member of Parliament, and started a magazine with a partner who concluded the bargain by running away with his wife. Thereafter he wrote critical reviews, amazed society with his brilliant and audacious utterances, and went home to his lodgings night after night the loneliest and bitterest man in England—until one evening he met the loneliest and bitterest *woman* in England, the editor of the *Westminster Review*.

Then a most shocking—and entirely logical—thing happened. Mary Anne Evans ran off with George Henry Lewes. Owing to the law and to his scattered finances, Lewes had been unable to obtain a divorce from his former wife. No matter—Mary Anne Evans was a law unto herself. When the news broke that the homeliest woman in London had joined "unholy hands" with the homeliest man in England, the couple was already beyond the range of insular criticism. They had fled to the continent, to commence their life together in foreign surroundings.

Their honeymoon was a perfect blending of minds. They came to Weimar where Lewes, at work on a Life of Goethe, caught glimpses of the spirit of the master. They heard Liszt as he conducted *Ernani*. They spoke to the red-headed Berlioz over the table in a Brussels hotel and saw something of the fantastic symphony in his eyes. They shouted with laughter at two crabs fighting by the seashore. They found a little girl sleeping in the fields and put a penny into her hand. But when they returned to settle down in England, they found nowhere a smile for them. Mary Anne's father and sisters and brother refused all communication with her. Boldly she signed her name "Mrs. George Henry Lewes" in the hotel registry. But all England shrank from her touch.

Lewes had taken upon himself the support of his former wife who was now destitute. And he sent his boys to an expensive boarding school. The couple found it hard to keep up financially, since they were "neither philanthropists nor swindlers." Furiously they worked to feed seven mouths with the meager earnings of their articles and reviews. For lack of space they worked in one room during the day. But at night the room opened up its walls as if by magic into a universe as they read the *Iliad* together in the original Greek.

She called him "Little Pater," and he called her "Madonna" or simply "Polly." They were left severely to themselves. For days they saw no one, received no visits. "To know the high initiation of love, a woman must often tread where it is hard to tread, and feel the chill air, and walk through darkness."

It was a life of "joyous desolation." Lewes, watching his "Madonna" carefully, realized that she must somehow free herself from this existence in one room, that she must soften the keen edges of her suffering, or sorrow would kill the better stuff in her. He had read some sketches of fiction she had written at random. "You must write a story, Polly. I'm convinced that you have it in you to become a great novelist."

The idea was tempting. But what could she write about? And then one day the words of Sir Philip Sidney flashed into her mind and set it on fire. "Look into your heart and write!"

IV

"SEPTEMBER 1856 made a new era in my life," she wrote in her Journal. For on that day she began a series of *Scenes from Clerical Life*—short stories about the country folk she had known as a little girl. These stories were promptly accepted for publication in *Blackwood's Magazine*. Whereupon she set to work on a full-length novel. She had come to fiction from philosophy with a relish at the change of scene. Hers would be a literature of the "little people"—the derelicts and the outcasts whom nobody cared about. "Paint us an angel, if you can . . . but do not . . . banish from the region of art those old women scraping their work-worn hands, those heavy clowns taking holiday in a dingy pothouse, those rounded backs and stupid weather-beaten faces that have bent over the spade and done the rough work of the world . . . These commonplace people—many of them

—bear a conscience, and have felt the sublime prompting to do the painful right; they have their unspoken sorrows and their sacred joys; their hearts have perhaps gone out to their first born, and they have mourned over the irreclaimable dead . . . Is there not a pathos in their very insignificance?" She placed the name *Mary Anne*, critic of the *Westminster Review*, into the files for pedants, and she took for her new public the pen name *George Eliot*—George, in honor of her husband George Henry; Eliot, because it was "a good mouth-filling word."

She wrote the story of Adam Bede, the carpenter, and of his love for Dinah Morris, the Methodist preacher. The book scored a huge success. All England was alive with inquiries about this *George Eliot*. What manner of man was he? Various rumors were bandied about. One county judge claimed that he had discovered the identity of the author. It was none other than a Mr. Liggins who lived in Nuneaton—"the son of a baker, a man of no mark at all in his town, so that it is possible you have not heard of him . . . They say he gets no profit out of *Adam Bede*, and gives it freely to Blackwood."

Immediately a host of admirers came down into the country to see this shy, retiring, and marvelous "author." They found him washing his laundry at a pump. "He has no servant and does everything for himself." And he inspired them "with a reverence that would have made an impertinent question impossible." Sums of money were raised by subscription all over England to put poor Mr. Liggins—a little the worse for drink— on his feet. Distinguished guests came flocking in growing numbers to this shrine by the pump. And all the while this poor Mr. Liggins, who had suddenly leaped into fame "for doing nothing at all," humbly bowed in reverence before his new-found devotees. Other disturbing reports reached the real George Eliot, until finally she stepped forward and revealed herself as the author of *Adam Bede*.

Then she wrote her second novel, *The Mill on the Floss*. She composed this book with as much misgiving as if she were not famous. She had never been afraid of obscurity, only of artistic failure. And then, when she had scored another success with this autobiographical study of brother and sister love, she turned from the House of Tulliver to the story of Silas Marner, the Weaver of Raveloe—a bitter, stooped, cynical outcast from society, who builds up a treasure of gold and comes home one night to find his hoardings gone and a little child on his doorstep. "Of such is the Kingdom of Heaven."

But George Eliot's restlessness would not long permit her to remain and nurse a child in Yorkshire. She wished to embrace within the grasp of her imagination the experiences of all human minds at all periods. She traveled to Italy, plunged into a study of the Renaissance and "relived" the fifteenth century of re-awakened philosophy and music and poetry and art. And then she wrote an historical novel about the life and times of Savonarola, the martyr of Florence. Another literary sensation and financial success.

But the work "ploughed into her and left her an old woman." She "took a vacation" by writing a dramatic poem on the Spanish gipsies during the Crusades; and then, "refreshed and relaxed," she returned to England to create the portrait of a radical workman, Felix Holt. One book more on the provincial life in the Midlands, and then her restlessness carried her off again to the Continent. She went to Holland and visited a Hebrew synagogue in order to study the habits of the Jewish people. "Not a woman was present, but of devout men not a few . . . The chanting and the swaying about of the bodies—almost a wriggling—are strange to the sense; but I fairly cried at witnessing this faint symbolism of a religion of sublime, far off memories." Then she wrote the story of Daniel Deronda, and of his ardent dream for a homeland in Palestine.

She finished the book, and traveled on.

This woman living with a married man was on trial. Perhaps

she felt a little like a goddess who had stumbled on to earth—
and forgotten her way back to heaven. She had broken a rule of
these queer little earth-people. And now she was on trial before
them. She could not sneer and rage to win herself an acquittal.
She must invoke their sympathy in the name of heaven. But first
she must tell a convincing story of human love and of human
pity. "The tale of the Divine Pity was never yet believed from
lips that were not felt to be moved by human pity." That is why
Hetty Sorrel, little Eppie, Maggie Tulliver were born.

V

BEFORE she was forty, George Eliot was queen only of George
Henry Lewes. Before she was sixty, she was queen of the most
brilliant salon in London. She had found her friends again. She
was rich and famous and dyspeptic—altogether a hostess of fascinating and somewhat unpredictable moods. She had taken a
house in Regent Park and she named it "the Priory." George
Henry had accepted the editorship of the *Fortnightly Review,* and
he used his name to lure Browning and Huxley and Tyndall over
the threshold of its covers.

On Sunday afternoons at "the Priory" Herbert Spencer handed
his portfolio to his assistants and posed for charades; Emerson
from America rubbed shoulders with the Russian novelist, Tur-
genieff; and Richard Wagner talked about his new opera, *Tann-
häuser.* And all were agreed that George Eliot was "the most
popular fellow in London." The gracious hostess spoke a few
moments to each of her guests in an "indescribably charming
voice."

But she was not a great conversationalist. It was her husband
who possessed the knack for keeping the small talk on the go.
He scurried from one group to another like a whimsical gnome
and from time to time, when a quip had told, he stood in a
corner with a smile of triumph at the success of his little mischief.

He was happy beyond words. His big generous heart was beating for the life of another—his Polly. She was the shrewd genius; he was the happy warrior enlisted in the shrewdness and the genius of her cause. It was not for him to taste the cup of fame. But at least he could hold it to the lips of the goddess he adored. He had cut a great figure upon his little stage until he found a better player for the part. And then he made for the wings with the graciousness of an artist who cared solely for the best performance. If necessary, he would "hold up the stage in his hands" for her play to go on.

Yet in spite of his whole-hearted devotion, he managed in his spare hours to deliver a series of lectures on *Life from the Simple Cell to Man,* to complete a book on Aristotle, to study insanity, to visit asylums, to observe the effects of chloral and to do research work on protozoa.

But at last his health began to give way. As his wife grew richer, he grew gradually more deaf. From Regent Park they moved to a more spacious house in Surrey. They were served by flunkeys and rode in carriages. But Lewes was perfectly content with looking through his microscope and planning a new philosophy for a few pounds. An admirer of his wife's genius sent him a cane. And as his strength declined, he kept it by his bed and used it for every step he took. But no one had sent him a cane for *his* genius. No matter. He couldn't figure out the crazy patch of life. Here the climate was "Scotland wedded to Warwickshire." For a time it cleared his head and gave him a feeling of false security. He walked, played, told better jokes than ever. He sang songs a little off key to Polly's accompaniment on the piano. And then one day he died in his sleep. He had not realized that he was going to die or he would most certainly have made his bravest joke and sung a jaunty song about it.

VI

GEORGE ELIOT corrected his last manuscript and sent it off to the publishers. Then she established in his name a scholarship for physiological research. "Our dead are never dead to us until we have forgotten them." And gradually her spirits revived, her love for life reasserted itself and by God's mercy she began to live again. She accepted the tributes that were bestowed upon her. And these tributes came to her in a continual stream of adoration from every part of the world. One Swiss gentleman in his old age wrote that he had learned the English language for the single purpose of "reading her novels in their mother tongue." Another admirer begged that his ashes might be placed as near as possible to her grave. But the greatest commendation came from a young English banker, John Cross. He married her.

There was a difference of twenty years between Mary Anne Evans and John Cross. He was forty-one and she was sixty-one. But that did not matter. So long as a woman employs the magic of her pen to create youth and beauty in her writings, she is young and beautiful. So long as she *writes* about the spring, she *is* the spring.

"Our thoughts are often worse than we are, just as they are often better than we are,"—but they are never as old as we are. She went with her husband on a grand tour of the continent just as if forty years had not passed since her first view of the cathedrals and the Rhine. They gathered roses in the garden of Jean Jacques Rousseau, and they read Dante's *Divine Comedy* together. The summer heat in Milan proved too much for him, not for her. She seemed strong and serene. She nursed him as he lay abed. Together they read Goethe's *Faust* and her lips quivered slightly as the old philosopher, who had bought his days of youth again for the price of his soul, implored the passing hour never to leave him. "Linger awhile; thou art so fair!" Linger awhile

. . . Do not hurry. If only she, too, like Faust, could sell her soul to the devil for one more lifetime!

Ah, but it was a silly thing to wish for twice as many home-comings from a summer on the continent to a chill fall in England and to learn that another beloved has passed away. The great author in his foolishness gave Faust a second life; but the Great Author in His wisdom gave Goethe only one life—gave to all created things one life, and a hope . . .

Oh may I join the choir invisible
Of those immortal dead who live again
In minds made better by their presence . . .

Time was no dawdler. Seven months after she had taken the marriage vows she caught a draft in a concert hall in England.

They could not place this gipsy queen of letters in Westminster Abbey by the side of kings. For she had loved a man outside the code of civilized morals. So they buried her instead by the side of the man she loved, in ground unblessed by any other kind of religion save this love—a gipsy poet in a gipsy spot where nature wore her hair unkempt for her banished children.

ELIZABETH BARRETT BROWNING

Important Dates in Life of Elizabeth Barrett Browning

1806—Born at Coxhoe Hall, Durham.

1819—Saw publication of her first book of poetry, *The Battle of Marathon.*

1826—Published her second book, *An Essay on Mind and Other Poems.*

1833-46—Wrote and published several other volumes of poetry.

1845—Received first letter from Robert Browning.

1846—Married him.

1847—Settled, with Robert Browning, in Florence. Published *Sonnets from the Portuguese.*

1849—Gave birth to only child, Robert Wiedemann Barrett.

1851—Visited England.

1857—Published *Aurora Leigh.*

1861—Died, June 30, in Florence.

Elizabeth Barrett Browning

Elizabeth Barrett Browning

1806–1861

H ER FATHER, brought up as a slave-owner, treated his twelve children like slaves. In his vocabulary there were two words that stood out above all the others—*Command, Obey.* His was the mission to command; his children's, the duty to obey.

He was kind to these helpless little serfs of his own flesh and blood, just as he was kind to his dogs. But he exacted the last possible drop of their undeviating devotion, without a bite or a bark. He built for them and for his wife—without ever consulting any of them—a mansion of oriental magnificence; and then he placed every one of them away in a gilded cell and locked the door.

Many a morning, Elizabeth tells us, she longed

> *To slip downstairs through all the sleepy house*
> *. . . . . and escape,*
> *As a soul from the body out of doors,*
> *Glide through the shrubberies, drop into the lane,*
> *And wander on the hills an hour or two,*
> *Then back again before the house should stir.*

But the slave must never wander away from the watchful eyes of the master. The physical adventures of other children were not for Elizabeth. She had to content herself with her *mental* adventures. And here Mr. Barrett interposed no obstacles. Indeed, he encouraged the full play of her imagination. Proud of her poetical skill—she began to "versify" almost in her cradle —he allowed her to roam at will in his library. "You must make sure, however, to read only the books on *this* side, not on *that* side." For on *that* side of the library were the *forbidden* books, such as Gibbon's *History,* Fielding's *Tom Jones,* and the like. On *this* side were the *permitted* books—*Plato, Shakespeare, Homer, Milton,* the *Holy Writ.* On this side, too, through an oversight on the part of Mr. Barrett, were Tom Paine's *Age of Reason,* Voltaire's *Philosophical Dictionary,* Goethe's *Werther,* Hume's *Essays*—"books which I was never suspected of looking towards . . . but which did just as well as the *forbidden* works."

A sturdy soul in a stunted body. An elfin child wandering in a world of fairy dust. "Books and dreams were what I lived in." Especially the dream-books of Homer. The siege of Troy. The wanderings of Ulysses. The tragedy of Hector. In her garden she had cut out of the turf a gigantic figure of Hector, planting it with blue eyes, crimson cheeks and a breastplate of gold.

She was not a sculptor, however, but a poet. At eight she delighted her family with a "little clasped notebook" of odes and lyrics. At nine she presented them with an epic. At ten she composed a French tragedy which her brothers and her sisters acted in the nursery. At thirteen she completed an epic in four cantos on the Battle of Marathon. Her father was so proud of this poem that he had fifty copies of it printed. And Elizabeth was so proud of her father's pride that she dedicated her poem to him. "To the father whose never-failing kindness, whose unwearied affection I can never repay, I offer these pages as a small testimony of . . . gratitude." Elizabeth, like all the other

Barrett children, adored with a slavish adoration her father's reign of benevolent tyranny.

The benevolent tyrant hired a tutor for his two oldest children —Elizabeth and Edward. The education must be purely classical; arithmetic was one of Mr. Barrett's taboos. To the end of her days Elizabeth "envied" the people who could multiply "three times six without doing it on their fingers."

A poor mathematician and a passionate pagan. Under the influence of her tutor—a blind scholar by the name of H. S. Boyd—she became so enamored of the ancient Olympian divinities that she offered secret sacrifices to them.

Her father, unaware of her pagan tendencies, encouraged her in her Greek studies. Pious Christian that he was, he would have been terribly shocked to hear his daughter's nightly prayer: "O God, if there be a God, save my soul if I have a soul."

The rumblings of civil war on Wimpole Street. One of the Barrett chattels was getting out of hand.

II

ELIZABETH was twenty-six when she made her first move along the road to open rebellion. She selected for translation the most revolutionary of ancient Greek poems—the *Prometheus* of Aeschylus. The titan Prometheus had dared to question the authority of Zeus, father and ruler of the gods. In choosing this subject, Elizabeth implied that she too would like to question the authority of Zeus—father and ruler of the Barretts.

But it was a mild form of rebellion on Elizabeth's part. Her translation of *Prometheus* was a hint rather than a declaration of her attitude toward the despotism of her father. Furthermore, it was a *subconscious* rather than a *conscious* hint. She herself was not yet aware of the fact that her father was in the wrong. She chafed under the weight of her chains, but she still felt vaguely that those chains might be a good thing for her. Because her father had said so. Surely her father was no *heartless* tyrant. He could be so gentle at times. And so thoughtful. So full of taste and pleasantry and good humor. That is, when you didn't cross his will. He had a way of bringing stacks of books to Elizabeth—reading matter that seemed to *him* good for *her*. And pictures—a Rembrandt, a Titian, an Andrea del Sarto. Anything that would please her—provided it pleased him first. She was an invalid now—a congestion of the lungs in her adolescent years had sapped her strength for life. She stayed all the time in her room, rarely opened the windows, hardly ever drew aside the curtains to let in the sun. And her father was so good to her. He read to her and pampered her and brought the drugs to her when she asked for them. Not that he was in favor of her drugs. "You'd be better off if you took less medicine and more meat." But since she insisted on medicine, very well. "Let her have her whims."

Yet there was one whim that she must *not* have—companionship other than his own. Mr. Barrett was insanely jealous of his children's love. No one but himself must share it. He never invited anybody to dinner, never allowed his children to invite anybody. Let no one contaminate the Barretts with the poison of an un-Barrettlike conversation. As for the conversations in the books that he allowed his children to read, he always passed them beforehand through the censorship of his dictatorial approval.

In his censorship of Elizabeth's associates, Mr. Barrett made one exception. He allowed her the company of her spaniel, Flush. Next to Elizabeth and her father, Flush was the most interesting character of Wimpole Street. This cantankerous puppy was the *little* tyrant, just as Mr. Barrett was the *big* tyrant, of the family. Lazy and wine-colored and overplump, he was as fastidious about his food as a pampered lady. He would come to his meals only after persistent coaxing; and then, if the food were not prepared exactly to his taste, he would turn away disdainfully. His chicken and his mutton must be roasted, not boiled. If his coffee came with muffins, he drank it; if without muffins, he sniffed it away. His macaroons must be soaked in sugar and cream; otherwise they were taboo. As a general rule he disliked salt; but his cream cheese must be liberally salted, and under his very nose, before he would deign to touch it. His meat must be cut into small pieces and fed to him on a fork, or else he would have none of it.

Yet in spite of his squeamishness, he was Elizabeth's constant amusement. And her constant anxiety. He had a way of allowing himself to be kidnaped by the dog catchers—"I do believe he does it on purpose"—who insisted every time upon a ransom of ten guineas (about fifty dollars). Elizabeth was only too happy to pay the price and to restore her little tyrant to his mastery of the Barrett household.

And this mastery, like Mr. Barrett's, included a selfish demand upon Elizabeth's exclusive affection. He snapped whenever anybody came into the house. Nobody must wean her away from him—not even that handsome young man who dropped in occasionally when Mr. Barrett was away. Flush didn't like the idea at all, and he showed his dislike in his growling. If only he could speak to Mr. Barrett and warn him!

But for a time Mr. Barrett was blissfully unaware of the fact that his daughter was receiving the visits of a young poet. And he was equally unaware of the fact that this young poet had corresponded with his daughter for several months even before his first visit. This was one of the two secrets that Elizabeth kept from her father. Forbidden books and forbidden love. He had told her to stay out of *that* side of the library and *that* side of life. But on *this* side, too, there managed to slip in occasionally a prohibited book and a prohibited personality. The *Age of Reason* and Robert Browning. Logic and love had found their way into the invalid prison of Elizabeth Barrett. And the jailer slept through it all.

But Elizabeth trembled at the thought of what would happen when the jailer awoke from his sleep.

III

FOR THE LONGEST TIME Elizabeth had tried to discourage the letters and the visits of Robert Browning. Not that she was displeased with them. On the contrary, they brought her the keenest happiness she had experienced thus far. But she was terrified at the reaction of her father. His one commandment—*thou shalt not!*—must be at all times obeyed. And now more than ever there was need for obedience. She had crossed him once, and with tragic results. She had insisted, against his will, upon going on a vacation to the seashore and taking her brother Edward along with her. Edward was her favorite among all the Barretts. She affectionately called him *Bro*—abbreviation for brother; and he, in turn, addressed her as *Ba*—the first syllable of baby. The devoted companionship of *Bro* and *Ba* was the outstanding topic of their family conversation. But when Elizabeth suggested an excursion with Edward to the seashore at Torquay, Mr. Barrett was furious. "A vacation for a *woman* is crazy enough. But a vacation for a *man*—who ever heard of such a thing?" Elizabeth, however, had kept on imploring for Edward, and finally Mr. Barrett had yielded. "Very well, Elizabeth, but the responsibility is yours."

"I'll take it, father!"

And so Edward had come along with her to Torquay. And one day he went sailing in the harbor with another young man, a sudden squall, and the two dead bodies were washed ashore . . .

From that day on, Elizabeth had a mortal dread of taking the responsibility against her father's consent. It was therefore with a mingled feeling of joy and anguish that she received a letter from Mr. Robert Browning. She had just published a volume of her poems; and this truly great young poet—how infinitely greater than herself! she realized—had written such glowing words to her. "I love your verses with all my heart," the letter began. She caught her breath, and went on: "I do, as I say, love these verses with all my heart, dear Miss Barrett—and I love you, too."

She read the last words again . . . "and I love you, too." Gallant words from a gallant young god. But meaningless, no doubt. They had never met. Apparently Mr. Browning didn't know that she was an invalid, that she was a self-convicted murderess, that she had driven her brother to his death through her "unpardonable" opposition to her father's will. Mr. Browning must never come to see her, must never be disillusioned about her. They must remain forever apart—for Mr. Browning's sake, and for her father's sake. Mr. Browning was too good for her, too strong and too young—seven years younger than herself, to be precise. She was almost forty now, a "next door neighbor to the grave." Why saddle this vigorous demigod of a poet to a decrepit old friendship like hers?

Besides, what would her father think of such a friendship, assuming even that it were possible? He had already shown his attitude toward the male friends of his daughters in the case of her sister Henrietta. A young officer had dared to come in to see her. Mr. Barrett, meeting this young man unexpectedly in his house one day, threw him bodily out of doors. Mr. Barrett was obsessed by a monomania against any sort of "conviviality" on the part of his children. For conviviality might lead—horrible thought—to marriage; and the marriage of his children, he was firmly convinced, was at the very bottom of the scale of the world's worst crimes.

His aversion to marriage was one of the strangest idiosyncrasies of this strange man. His own married life had been far from unhappy. But now that his wife was dead, he regarded himself wedded to his children; and woe unto any of them if they dared to "commit bigamy" by wedding another.

And so Elizabeth, as Browning kept courting her in his letters, stood hesitantly poised between *yes* and *no*.

"Yes," I answered you last night;
"No," this morning, sir, I say;
Colors seen by candle-light
Will not look the same by day.

What seemed possible in the candle-light of romance, appeared incredible under the glare of her father's anger. Again and again in his letters Browning implored her to let him pay her a visit. But always she came back with a vague suggestion that this visit must be put off to another year, another month, another day. "Some time in the Spring we shall meet." And when he wrote to her that *his* Spring began early in February, she replied that *hers* began late in May. And finally, when his persistence won him a definite tryst, she still hesitated and reproached herself for her "unseemly" impetuosity. "Headlong I was at first, and headlong I continue—precipitately rushing forward through all manner of nettles and briars instead of keeping to the path."

It was on May 20, 1845, that Browning was at last permitted to come to Wimpole Street. The time for the visit, she had written him, must be "after two and before six." It was always at six that Mr. Barrett returned from his business in the city. He must not, under any circumstances, find this strange young man in his house.

Browning arrived at three o'clock. His first greeting met a snap and a snarl on the part of Elizabeth's spaniel. But Elizabeth quieted the dog. "Down, Flush! Keep still!"

The dog lay down and looked on with a hostile eye while the two poets conversed on this and on that and on every other topic save the one that lay nearest their hearts. And little by little the spaniel became accustomed to the presence of the intruder. An impetuous, energetic, voluble and lovable young fellow. His visits were like a tonic to his invalid mistress. Under the sunlight of his encouragement she actually got out of bed and walked down the steps to the library. And one day—miracle of miracles!—she took a little stroll with him down the street, with Flush tagging at their heels. The dog was actually beginning to like this young fellow. The tyranny of Flush, after all, was not so inexorable as the tyranny of Mr. Barrett.

It was a lucky thing that Mr. Barrett was unaware of Browning's visits to his daughter. Once or twice, indeed, Browning offered to meet him. "I am sure, when I speak to him, that I can sweep away his objections to our friendship." But Elizabeth knew her father. "You might," she said, "as well think to sweep off a third of the stars of Heaven with the motion of your eyelashes!"

Compelled thus to keep their secret from her father, they drifted rapidly from sympathy to friendship and from friendship to love. What they dared not say aloud in each other's presence, they wrote to each other immediately after his return from his visits. "If only I could tell you," he confessed in one of his letters, "*tell* you!—what would be supreme happiness to me in the event—however distant—" And she replied: "If only I were different in some respects and free in others . . . I would accept the great gift of your happiness . . . not, I *do* accept it, observe! . . . I *would* accept it."

For she still hesitated. "If only I were different . . . and free . . . " Sounder in body, stronger in will. She was far too gone in sickness, she believed, ever to enjoy the happiness of married life.

> *We have met late—it is too late to meet,*
> *O friend, not more than friend!*
> *Death's forecome shroud is tangled round my feet,*
> *And if I step or stir, I touch the end.*

[*137*]

And even if she were physically strong enough to accept his love, she did not feel mentally free enough to do so. She had disobeyed her father once and had lost him a son. She dared not disobey him again and lose him a daughter.

But Browning kept impetuously on with his courting; and finally Elizabeth, "saying she would ne'er consent, consented." Their marriage, however, must be secret, she insisted. Were she to tell her father of her intention, "he would wish to see me dead at his foot—and he will say so, and mean it, and persist in the meaning."

And this is precisely how he reacted when his daughter took matters into her own hands and set sail for Italy as Mrs. Elizabeth Barrett Browning. "My daughter is now in her grave," he remarked drily. "Let us forget the dead."

IV

A NEW HAPPINESS FOR ELIZABETH. And an old sorrow. The shadow of her father's tyranny loomed over her wherever she went. Before her marriage it was his constant nagging that had depressed her—and now it was his constant silence. Again and again she wrote to him, begging his forgiveness. But never a word in reply.

Yet her happiness enabled her at times to forget her sorrow. Browning never left her for a moment. She was well enough to walk now, yet her poet-husband insisted upon carrying her upstairs for the sheer pleasure of the burden. They had settled at Pisa for a time, a playtime of reckless abandon for the three of them—Elizabeth and Robert and Flush. A trio of spoiled vagabonds. Thoroughly reconciled to Browning, the dog had adopted the holiday mood of his master and his mistress. He went off adventuring into the streets of Pisa, fraternizing with the Italian dogs, and coming home full of caprices and fleas. And then Elizabeth and Robert would sit on the floor with a basin of water and scrub him and comb him and overwhelm him with an avalanche of petting and scolding and laughter. A long-drawn-out interlude of carefree relaxation. No household duties and no financial worries—they had an income of about £400 a year, more than sufficient for their vagabond program. Meals sent in from a near-by restaurant—eggs and coffee for breakfast, thrushes and chianti for dinner, coffee and milk-rolls for supper, and a snack of grapes and roast chestnuts at nine in the evening. And for Flush, his roasted mutton, his salted cream cheese, and his sugared macaroons. And thus they lived—"the prophet Elijah or the lilies of the field took as little thought for their dining."

Such was the atmosphere out of which came the minted gold of their poetry. One morning she slipped into his pocket a little parcel of forty-four love sonnets. "Please don't read them until I am out of this room."

He looked through the poems. Intimate revelations of a dying invalid recalled to life. The conquest of Death through Love.

"Guess now who holds thee?"—"Death," I said. But, there
The silver answer rang . . . "Not Death, but Love."

The story of Elizabeth's renascence. The renunciation of Paradise for happiness here below.

I yield the grave for thy sake, and exchange
My near sweet view of Heaven, for earth with thee!

He read the sonnets again. The personal outpourings of an overfull heart. Written for his eyes alone. And yet, there was a universal quality about them. They represented the triumph of love for every lover. Here was a treasure not for himself but for the world. He had no right to keep it hidden away.

At first she wouldn't hear of their publication. "These poems must remain our own secret. Like our letters."

"But, my dearest, they're the finest sonnets since Shakespeare!"

"Nonsense. You overestimate them as you overestimate me."

He pleaded with her, pointed out the excellencies of her poems, urged upon her the duty of sharing them with her fellows. "You have no more right to hoard your genius than to hoard your money." At last he prevailed upon her. "Heaven intends our gifts to be spent." Very well, she would lavish the coin of her heart upon the lovers of the world.

But it must come to the world as an impersonal philosophy rather than as a personal emotion. After all, you can't dissect your heart for the contemplation of your friends. Let the poems be disguised as translations from a foreign tongue. "*Sonnets from the Bosnian.* How would that do?" No one knew Bosnian, and so no one would guess her secret. But he suggested a better title: *Sonnets from the Portuguese.* "The public will then think that the poems were written by Caterina to Camoens, and not by Elizabeth to Robert."

And *Sonnets from the Portuguese* was the title under which these love poems were published. "One of the most exquisite translations in the history of literature!" exclaimed the critics. And the critics were right. This sonnet sequence is indeed one of the most exquisite translations of the divine fire into human words. For it represents the one permanent consistency in the impermanent diversity of things—"Love that endures from Life that disappears."

V

FROM PISA they went to Florence; and from Florence to the mountains of Vallombrosa, where they found fir trees that breathed of Heaven and biscuits that tasted like sawdust. Here, though the bread "stuck in the throat like Macbeth's amen," they would have remained for several months to feast upon the mountain scenery. But the Abbot of Vallombrosa drove them out after five days. The friars in this "monastery of the shadows" feared that they might be contaminated by the presence of Elizabeth and her maid. These friars abhorred three things—dogs, pigs and women. "And the women are the most obnoxious animals of them all . . . Better to clean out a pigsty with our bare hands, without spade or shovel, than to touch the little finger of a woman."

Elizabeth took both the insult and the injury in the gayest of spirits. "We were driven out of Eden," she wrote, "—for did not Milton take his description of Paradise from Vallombrosa?" They went back to Florence. "And what Florence is, the tongue of man or poet may easily fail to describe. The most beautiful of cities, with the golden Arno shot through the breast of her like an arrow . . ."

Here, in the cool rooms of the Palazzo Guidi, they reached the apex of their happiness. A son was born to them—just three days after Elizabeth's forty-third birthday. A lusty lollipop of a bantling, full of chins and dimples. "Too strong by far," smiled Elizabeth, "to seem like a child of mine."

And from her new-born babe Elizabeth acquired a new-born strength. No more languishing on the couch and waiting passively to be waited on. On the contrary, it was she now who was the impatient member of the family. "Let's be up and about!" Excursions to Bagni di Lucca, to Spezzia, to the marble cliffs of Carrara. Climbs over the precipitous mountain trails on the back of a donkey. Journeys to Venice, Milan, Geneva, Paris. And, finally, a trip to London in an effort to conciliate her father.

Repeatedly she had written to her father, but always without result. She told him about her son Wiedemann—they called him *Penini* from his attempts to pronounce his name—how he would race with Flush to pick up articles rolled by his parents across the floor. "This little rascal of ours is always up to mischief, upsetting the water-jugs till he is drenched (which charms him), pulling the broom to pieces, and having serious designs upon cutting up his frocks with a pair of scissors. He laughs like an imp when he can succeed in doing anything wrong." But there were times—she wrote to her father—when the child would "sit quietly on his mother's knee, listening while his father played the piano, putting up his little mouth for a kiss every two minutes."

And in answer to all these letters—silence. When Elizabeth came to London, her father refused to see her. He ordered his servants to "tell her, if ever she comes to this house, that I am not in."

This final rebuff from her father, whom she still adored with a blind adoration, was a severe blow to Elizabeth. Her health began once more to fail. Her lungs could not stand the harshness of the London fogs. Back to Paris, and then to Italy and to the consolation of her pen. In spite of her waning strength—or rather, because of it, for she felt that her time was short—she undertook the most ambitious of all her works. *Aurora Leigh,* a novel in verse. It was largely a fictitious transcript of her own life. The plot was fantastic, the situations were unreal and the characters overdrawn. But the poetry of *Aurora Leigh,* like the poetry of the *Sonnets from the Portuguese,* revealed—to quote Robert Browning—"an entirely angel nature, as divine a heart as God ever made."

And many of the critics agreed with Browning. Barry Cornwall acclaimed it "a hundred times over, the finest poem ever written by a woman." Walter Savage Landor said he had no idea "that anyone in this age was capable of so much poetry . . . I am half drunk with it." John Ruskin was even more extravagant in his praise. "I think *Aurora Leigh* the greatest poem in the English language, unsurpassed by anything but Shakespeare— *not* surpassed by Shakespeare's *Sonnets,* and therefore the greatest *poem* in the language."

Elizabeth read these reviews, and felt duly flattered, and shook her head with a smile. The blindness of the critics! Here they were acclaiming the lamplight flicker of her own verse while they remained unaware of the sunlight splendor of her husband's poetry. The stupidity, the unfairness, the pontifical finality with which the *judges* of the world handed out their prizes to the *contestants* of the world.

Well, she would be happy not in the glamor of her own littleness but in the obscurity of her husband's greatness. "Some day," she said, "they will praise *him,* who is worth twenty of *me.*"

But she didn't live to see that day. Her strength was rapidly flowing out. A quiet, contented drifting, marred by a single grief—her father's inexorable silence. And then, an end to the silence. A letter from her father, and a package. Tremblingly she opened the letter. It was a note addressed to Browning— short and straight to the point. "In the accompanying package you will find the letters sent to me by your wife. All these letters, you will note, have remained unopened. The seals upon them are still intact."

VI

HER FATHER DIED shortly after the return of the letters. The news of his death brought a collapse from which Elizabeth never recovered.

Browning was sitting at her bedside. They had been married over fourteen years now. It seemed to them like fourteen days —a brief fortnight of a honeymoon. But their honeymoon was not yet over. Many more days of poetry and devotion. It was so pleasant lying here within the protective shelter of his eyes. She stretched out her arms to him, and he held her close. She dozed off; and when she awoke, she found herself still lying in his arms. She smiled. "You're so good to me, Robert." And then, as she trailed off into sleep again, "If you could hold me like this . . . forever . . ."

"Yes?"

For reply, she placed her head on his cheek.

Once more she closed her eyes. And when he next spoke to her, there was no answer.

FLORENCE NIGHTINGALE

Important Dates in Life of Florence Nightingale

1820—Born at Florence, Italy; named after that city.

1844—Began to visit hospitals.

1849–50—Made trip to Egypt.

1853—Studied nursing organization in Paris. Established a "Hospital for Invalid Gentlewomen" in London.

1854—Organized group of trained nurses to serve in Crimean War.

1856—Returned home at the end of the war.

1857—Founded the "Nightingale Home" for the training of nurses.

1858—Published book on the health problems of the British Army.

1862–90—Assisted in the establishment of several schools for nurses.

1907—Received the Order of Merit (at the age of 87).

1910—Died in London.

Florence Nightingale

Florence Nightingale

1820–1910

"Forward, the Light Brigade!
Charge for the guns," he said:
Into the valley of Death
    Rode the six hundred.

        * * *

Theirs not to reason why,
Theirs but to do and die:
Into the valley of Death
    Rode the six hundred.

        * * *

When can their glory fade?
O the wild charge they made!
    All the world wonder'd.
Honor the charge they made!
Honor the Light Brigade,
    Noble six hundred!

THIS IS Tennyson's romantic picture of the battle of Balaclava, in the Crimean War. But here is Florence Nightingale's realistic picture of the scene that *followed* the battle:

"At the hospital (in Scutari) there are no clean shirts . . . The men have only rags saturated with blood . . . The hospital has been transformed from a barrack . . . and underneath its imposing mass are sewers loaded with filth, through which the wind blows fetid air up the pipes into the wards where the sick men are lying. Wounds and sickness, overcrowding and want of proper ventilation contribute to the foulness of the atmosphere . . . The wards are infested with rats, mice and vermin. Flooring is defective; furniture and even the commonest utensils for cleanliness, decency and comfort are lacking . . . The vermin might, if they had but unity of purpose, carry off the four miles of bedding on their backs and march with them into the War Office in London."

Tennyson speaks of the heroism of the men in the field. Florence Nightingale speaks of the stupidity of the men in the War Office. "The iron beds from England have arrived at Scutari, but the legs for the beds were put into another ship and sent on to Balaclava. The sick and the wounded at Scutari lie on mattresses on the stone floors." In another letter—"The officials in London have sent us plenty of rations, but they have forgotten to send us kettles to cook them in." And when finally the kettles arrived—"The meat was ordered to be cut into uniform pieces of the same size . . . Sometimes a patient got a lump entirely gristle, the next might be entirely fat or entirely bone; the fortunes of war."

The trouble with the (non-combatant) officials, said Miss Nightingale, was that they regarded the soldiers as military machines. "Suppose you break them and throw them into the dump heap; what then? We've got plenty of others to take their place."

Even the soldiers had come to look upon themselves as mere machines unworthy of the consideration of their superiors. "In going round the hospital with me," writes Miss Nightingale, "the Duke of Cambridge recognized a sergeant of the guard who had had at least one third of his body shot away, and said (the

Duke) to him with a great oath, calling him by his Christian name and surname, 'Aren't you dead yet?' The man said to me afterward, with tears in his eyes: 'So feelin' of 'Is Royal 'Ighness, wasn't it, m'm? Bless 'is 'eart, 'e wondered why I ain't dead yet.' "

Into this cauldron of incompetence and pitilessness and suffering stepped Florence Nightingale with her heroic band of thirty-eight nurses, and created order out of chaos. Within a few months after her arrival at Scutari, the death rate in the hospital had been reduced from forty per cent to less than three per cent.

II

WHEN Florence first announced to her parents that she wanted to become a nurse, they looked upon her with open-mouthed astonishment. What? The daughter of one of the richest families in England to enter into one of the lowest of professions? Why, nursing was not even a profession in those days. "Most of the nursing"—we are quoting a contemporary physician—"is done by drunken prostitutes who, when brought into the police court, are given the option of going to prison or to hospital service . . . They are often found in sleep under the beds of their dead patients whose liquor they have stolen."

When, therefore, she announced her decision to her parents, "it was as if I had wanted to be a kitchen maid." It was not for *such* a career that they had raised their daughter. Mr. William Shore Nightingale, the master of Embley Park in Hampshire, had meant Florence to be a lady, like her elegant mother. Why, this girl was the prettiest and the most accomplished of all the Nightingale children. They had given her an education fit for a princess—higher mathematics, music, art, science, literature. Italian, German and French—and she spoke these languages as fluently as she spoke English. And the ancient languages, too,—"a capital young lady," once remarked the geographer,

Sir Henry de la Beche, to the archaeologist, Warrenton Smythe, "a capital young lady, indeed, if only she hadn't floored me with her Latin and Greek."

A brilliant young lady, and as charming as she was brilliant. Had traveled all over Europe, and had gone up the Nile. Could converse with all sorts of people on all sorts of subjects. Had even attended the receptions of the Queen. And all the eligible young men of England were at her feet. What in the world did she want?

"I want to get away from the boredom of it all." She had an independent way about her. And a temper. And a biting tongue in that pretty little mouth of hers. "Piling up miscellaneous instruction," she said, "is the most disgusting of all pursuits." And almost as disgusting was the piling up of miscellaneous acquaintances among the smart set. Watching Lord Melbourne snore after dinner in the royal presence. Applauding Prince Albert for his "imaginary" skill at billiards. "Dowagering out with Papa" to "pay her respects" to people for whom she hadn't the slightest respect. Complimenting Lady So-and-so on her "oh, so becoming" diamond brooch—which, in reality, became her like a "raspberry tart on a pumpkin."

Florence Nightingale wanted to get away from all this painted and powdered artificiality. She wanted to come to grips with life. To know real people in their real moments. Their moments of suffering. Her father frequently made her read aloud to him. A Victorian book of good manners entitled *Passages in the Life of a Daughter at Home*. She preferred to read by herself, and a book of a quite different tenor. *The Annual Report of the Fliedner Institute*.

This Institute was a German training school for nurses. Flo Nightingale had been born with a passion to nurse the wounded and the sick. Even as a child she had frequently left her games to mend her dolls and to bandage the wounds of the cottagers' animal pets in Embley. At the age of six, she tells us, she was already conscious of a "call" to a mission of mercy. As she grew older, she became more and more conscious of the star that she was bidden to follow. One afternoon—she was about eighteen at the time—Florence was walking with a friend on the lawn in front of the drawing room at Embley. "Do you know what I always think when I look at that row of windows?" she said. "I think how I should turn it into a hospital and just how I should place the beds." For a time, during her twenties, she thought of marrying and settling down. She even had a love affair or two. But she put out of her mind the thought of a married life. This sort of thing was not for her. In marriage, she noted, she might find satisfaction for her "intellectual nature" and her "passional nature," but not for her "moral nature." And it was her moral nature that won out. In 1850 she wrote in her diary: "I am thirty now—the age at which Christ began His mission . . . No more childish things, no more vain things, no more love, no more marriage."

She was ready now to follow in His footsteps and to enter upon her own mission.

"Father, mother, I am going to be a nurse."

"Why, you're insane!"

"Maybe I am. All I can say is, thank God for my insanity."

III

FLORENCE NIGHTINGALE had stolen many an hour from her social activities to study anatomy and to visit the county hospital. Once, on a trip to Germany, she spent two weeks at the Fliedner Nursing School. At first Herr Fliedner was afraid of her "frail aristocratic hands." But he didn't know her sturdy democratic heart. "You won't want to scrub that corridor floor," he said. "Just try me," she replied. And when he tried her, he knew that she was made for nursing.

Before long she proved to the English skeptics, too, that she was made for nursing. Appointed manager of the Harley Street Sanitarium—an "Establishment for Gentlewomen during Illness"—she showed that she could not only scrub floors but bind wounds and, what was even more important, revive hopes. And, figuratively speaking, slap faces. How she did love to slap the faces of the bigots! "Clarkey, dear," she writes to one of her friends. "My committee refused me to take in Catholic patients, whereupon I wished them good morning, unless I might take in Catholics as well as Jews and their rabbis. So now it is settled and in print that we are to take in all denominations whatever . . . provided *I* make myself responsible for their visitors, receive the obnoxious animals at the door . . . and bring them downstairs again in a noose, and out into the street. Amen . . . From bigotry and all deceits, Good Lord deliver us!"

It was a herculean job that she undertook as the first female manager of a hospital. Chaperoning the "obnoxious animals" who came to visit the non-Protestant patients; supervising the untrained and ill-disciplined nurses; spraining her back as she lifted a patient to the operating table; catching a hot stovepipe in her arms to keep it from falling upon a sick child; holding down a blind woman who was threatened with insanity when an operation to restore her vision had failed; and defending herself against the petty jealousies and the continual bickerings of her male—and therefore her "superior"—colleagues.

Yet, with all her inexperience, she stood the ordeal and came out triumphant. "She seems as completely led by God as Joan of Arc," said the novelist, Mrs. Gaskell.

Led by God into a definite road. Reports were reaching England about the terrible conditions in the Crimean hospitals. "The old pensioners sent out to nurse the sick and wounded are not of the slightest use; the soldiers have to attend upon each other." "No sufficient preparations have been made for the care of the wounded . . . No bandages, no dressers, no nurses." The public began to clamor for a remedy to this evil state of affairs. And

finally the clamor became crystallized into a single name—
Florence Nightingale. "Why will not Florence Nightingale give
herself to this work?" wrote Cardinal Manning to the London
Times.

And Florence Nightingale heard the cry, and answered it. She
sent a letter to Sir Sidney Herbert, an intimate friend of hers
who was then serving as the British Secretary at War. "A small
private expedition of nurses has been organized for Scutari, and
I have been asked to command it . . . We shall feed and lodge
ourselves there, and are to be no expense whatever to the
country . . ." And then, realizing the stodgy skepticism of Victorian officialdom, she added a postscript: "Would you or some
one else reassure the War Office about my qualifications? Please
tell them that 'this is not a lady but a real hospital nurse.' "

Reluctantly the War Office consented to let the lady play the
nurse. The whole thing would be a failure—no doubt of it! But
let the madcap have her way.

And so, on October 21, 1854, Florence Nightingale set sail for
the Crimea. The excitement of the trip, the tossing of the boat—
there was a hurricane in the Mediterranean—and the management of the thirty-eight none-too-obedient nurses whom she had
taken along with her—all these proved too much for her strength.
She was ill when she arrived in Scutari. The soldiers carried her
stretcher in relays, fighting for the honor, from the pier to the
chaplain's house.

But she rapidly recovered from her illness. Who had time to be
sick when there were so many wounded to be cared for? And
so many mistakes to be corrected? And so much stubbornness to
be overcome? The officials in charge of the hospital insisted that
"everything is just as it ought to be." And they wanted no woman
"to interfere with the efficiency of our organization."

Their "efficiency" had resulted in a welter of misery and dis-
organization and filth. It was the fault of no one man, but of an
entire stumbling system which tried to advance toward the future

with eyes turned toward the past. Of the Scutari hospital, as of Dante's Inferno, it was said: "All hope abandon ye who enter here."

But there was one who entered and who did not abandon hope. Florence Nightingale created sanity out of confusion through the simple process of cutting red tape. Shortly after her arrival, a consignment of 27,000 shirts was landed at Scutari and only waited to be unpacked. But the official "Purveyor" refused to allow the unpacking "without the permission of the Board." For three weeks the sick and the wounded "lay shivering in their nakedness" while Miss Nightingale kept vainly begging to have them clothed. Finally the Board got around to the matter "in the regular routine of business" and issued the necessary permission. On the very next occasion when a consignment of shirts arrived at the hospital, Miss Nightingale took matters into her own hands. She ordered the nurses to open the bundles and to distribute the shirts, while the "Purveyor" stood by wringing his hands and muttering that the world was going to "the women and the dogs."

But the women, under the leadership of Florence Nightingale, had their way. They scrubbed the floors and the walls of the hospital, they reorganized the wards and the kitchens and the laundries, they rearranged the distribution of the food so that nobody was obliged to go hungry, and they added to the menu a number of strengthening "appetizers," such as soups and wines and jellies—"preposterous luxuries!" growled Dr. Hall, the officer in charge. And they were able to do all this because they spent none of the government's money upon their "innovations," but depended upon Florence Nightingale's own funds, supplemented by generous contributions from a number of forward-looking men and women. "What a needless waste of money upon useless rubbish!" wailed Lord Stratford de Redcliffe, the British ambassador to Turkey. "I do wish they would spend this money upon a *worthy* object, the building of an Anglican Church in Constantinople!"

When one of the wounded soldiers heard of this, he said, "This 'ospital is our church, and Miss Nightingale is our ministerin' angel." The grateful patients at Scutari came to regard her as "the lady with the lamp." Her mere presence restored to life many a man whom the surgeons had given up as beyond hope. The soldiers idolized her. They kissed her shadow as she passed through the wards. These battle-scarred men, who knew the meaning of fatigue, were amazed at the indefatigable energy of this angel of mercy. There were days when she would spend eight hours on her knees, dressing wounds and smoothing blankets over aching limbs. Sometimes she would assist the relays of surgeons at their operations for twenty hours at a stretch. How she found time for all her work was a mystery. For, in addition to her nursing, she attended to all the administrative and to many of the menial duties of the hospital. "I am really cook, housekeeper and scavenger, washerwoman, general dealer, storekeeper." And writer of letters extraordinary. Hundreds and hundreds of them. Letters with a *sting* to them, to awaken her sleeping countrymen out of their complacent dreams. "When I write civilly I have a civil answer—*and nothing is done*. When I write furiously I have a rude answer—*and something is done*."

Throughout her stay at Scutari, it was a continual struggle between an iron will and a granite wall of opposition. And the granite gave way. Amazed at her treatment of the soldiers as if they were human beings, the conservative officials kept grumbling, "You'll only spoil the brutes." And Miss Nightingale replied, "That's precisely what I want to do. I want to spoil them as brutes and transform them into men."

IV

SHE RETURNED HOME an invalid for life. But her work, far from being over, was only just begun. Scutari was not the only hospital. The entire world was a sick room that needed nursing.

But again that intolerable opposition of the complacent and the blind. People praised her, and came in throngs to catch a glimpse of her, and did nothing to help her in her work. The government had offered her a man-of-war to bring her home to England. But she had refused it, preferring to slip into her country quietly and unannounced. "I don't want adulation, I want understanding."

And understanding was the last thing she was able to get. She tried to open a training school for nurses—a place where it would be possible "for a woman to be a person." And she was anxious to bring about a drastic reform in all the military hospitals and barracks of England. She interviewed every important personage in the government; she even secured an audience and a "God bless you" from Queen Victoria. But always, when the road seemed open, some obstinate official would get in the way.

One of the most obstinate of them all was Lord Panmure, Sir Sidney Herbert's successor as Secretary at War. Lord Panmure—because of his immovable stubbornness Miss Nightingale called him "the Bison"—had nothing personally against her. He merely disliked what he called "her busybodiness." The Crimean War was over, the country was at peace, and he, Lord Panmure, might be pleasantly engaged in his grouse shooting but for Miss Nightingale's silly notions about schools for nurses and military hospitals and sanitary reforms. What troublesome piffle! He would put a stop to all this—not by refusing his help, but by offering it and then giving as little of it as was humanly possible.

And so he began his campaign of benevolent negligence. And behind him stood a whole battalion of reactionaries—dear, devoted friends of Miss Nightingale's, every one of them. "You are so tired, and ill. Why don't you rest for a while, and then we can discuss the whole matter."

She replied to the Bison and his "lords of the out-of-date" in one of her trenchant letters: "I am lying without my head, without my claws, and you all peck at me." And then, to convince the

public when she had failed to convince the *peers,* she wrote a long
and provocative book on the subject—*Notes on Nursing*—and
personally attended to its publicity until it was translated into
several languages and reached into hundreds of thousands of
homes.

The public listened and came to her assistance with petitions
and contributions. And finally even the Bison allowed himself
reluctantly to be led by her steady hand. The training school for
nurses was opened, the military hospital was built, and the sanitary reforms were instituted.

But the Bison, even in his captivity, tried to make one last show
of his masculine prerogative. What would a woman know about
the building of hospitals? It was he, Lord Panmure, who would
order the plans for the building. The plans were duly drawn up
and the construction was already underway before Miss Nightingale had an opportunity to visit the project. And then to her
consternation she saw that the new hospital was designed to
reproduce all the worst faults of the outdated hospitals of the
past. She urged the Bison to stop the work, but without avail. *He*
knew what was best. "Look at the spot I have selected, and the
front view!"

There was but one thing to do—make an appeal to Lord Palmerston, the Prime Minister. Point out to him, with appropriate
charts, the evils of the old and the advantages of the new. And
so, armed with her documents and her wrath, she visited the
Prime Minister, spent several hours in his office, and left him
convinced that she was in the right. "It seems to me," he wrote to
Lord Panmure, "that (in the new hospital) all consideration of
what would best tend to the comfort and recovery of the patients
has been sacrificed to the vanity of the architect, whose sole
object has been to make a building which should cut a dash when
looked at from the Southampton River . . . Pray, therefore,
stop all further progress in the work until the matter can be duly
considered."

The work was stopped; and after the matter had been duly considered, the hospital was rebuilt in accordance with the plans of Florence Nightingale.

V

FOR THE MOST PART NOW she was unable to be on her feet. But she went on with her work. An extraordinary invalid. She lay in the upper room of a little house she had bought on South Street, received the visits of statesmen and generals and artists and poets and peers, and manipulated with her capable pale hands the strings of a hundred reforms. On very rare occasions she wentiout for a drive in the Park. And then the eager crowds pressed around her carriage. "Let me touch your shawl, Miss Nightingale."—"Let me stroke your arm."—"Let me just glance at those radiant eyes." The people adored her. For she had opened the windows of their old stuffy world to let in the air of a new physical strength. And religious faith. One of the most interesting of the manifold activities of her old age was the writing of a three-volume interpretation of the old Christian truths in the light of modern needs. *Femina sum.* "I am a woman, and therefore I am interested in everything that appertains to the children of the human family." She was eighty-two now, but not ready as yet to lay down her work. When her nurse tucked her in at night, she got out of bed to tuck in her nurse. And throughout the day, thinking and planning and dictating letters for the building of better hospitals, better churches, a better world.

And now she was ninety, and no longer able to work. "The black camel that kneels at every house" was slowly approaching her door. One by one her mortal faculties left her—"the excess baggage for the immortal journey of the soul." First it was her hands that died, and then her eyes, and then her mind. Fitful, fragmentary visions of the past kept flying over the broken screen of her memory. One night she woke with a start. "Am I the one who stood on that Crimean height?"

Yet before the end, one final flash of light. "Do you know where you are?" a friend asked her one day.

"Yes," she replied. "I am watching at the altar of murdered men." Then, with that old-time determination in her voice, "And as long as I live, I shall be fighting their cause!"

SUSAN B. ANTHONY

Important Dates in Life of Susan B. Anthony

1820—Born at Adams, Mass.

1852—Organized first woman's state temperance society in America.

1854—Began her lifelong career of agitation for woman's rights.

1856—Assumed active part in American Anti-Slavery Society.

1868—Started a weekly woman's rights paper, *The Revolution*.

1869—Became Vice-President of the National Woman Suffrage Association.

1872—Arrested for casting a vote in the presidential election.

1884–87—Collaborated on a 4-volume *History of Woman Suffrage*.

1899—Her last public appearance as a delegate to the International Council of Women (London, England).

1900—Public celebration of her eightieth birthday.

1906—Died at Rochester, N. Y.

Susan B. Anthony

Susan B. Anthony

1820–1906

SHE WAS NOT LIKE OTHER CHILDREN. "The girls of the nineteenth century," said her teacher, Miss Deborah Moulson, "must behave precisely as the girls have behaved in all the other centuries . . . The sanctity of tradition must be always upheld." But Susan believed neither in precision nor in tradition. She had a mind of her own—an unheard-of crime in Miss Moulson's Select Seminary for Females. The curriculum at the Seminary was based upon the time-honored triangle of Morality, Love of Virtue, and—above all—Humility. Susan couldn't be humble. She tried her best, but in vain. Children, insisted Deborah, must rarely be seen and never heard. But Susan liked to be heard as well as seen. One day she laughed in class out of turn. "Traitor," snapped Deborah, "remember the fate of Judas Iscariot!" All letters written by the students to their parents, declared Deborah, must first be submitted to her censorial scrutiny. Susan prepared a letter containing some "private" information and tried to send it off to her father uncensored. Deborah intercepted the letter. The memory of the scene that followed brought tears to Susan's eyes years afterwards.

But the climax of her "unregenerate conduct" came on the day of the spring housecleaning at the Seminary. In her eagerness to sweep a cobweb off the ceiling, Susan jumped upon Deborah's desk—and broke it! This was a misdemeanor that demanded nothing less than a public scolding before the entire school. Miss Moulson assembled the school and, after the solemn reading of a chapter from the Scriptures, consigned Susan to those regions where "the worm dieth not and the fire is not quenched." Miss Deborah's homilies, wrote Susan in her diary, "made me indeed feel like a worm . . . But there were times when I preferred to be a worm rather than a girl. For then I could do my wriggling without the eternal scrutiny of my fellow worms."

II

HER ATTENDANCE at Miss Moulson's Seminary gave Susan two things: a stiff literary style—"whenever I take my pen in hand I seem to be mounted on stilts"—and a wholesome disrespect for the "conventions of the ant-hill." She came by her rebellion from her father who, though himself a Quaker, had defied the rules of his order by marrying a Baptist. And his young bride, Lucy Read, was not an orthodox Baptist at that. She was fond of pretty compliments and pretty clothes, she sang at her spinning wheel—a frivolous indiscretion in the second decade of the nineteenth century—and she danced until four o'clock in the morning just a few days before her marriage—an *unpardonable sin* in the second decade of the nineteenth century. She developed, however, into a sensible wife and sensitive mother. And her eight children—of whom Susan was the second—inherited their mother's sensitiveness as well as their father's rebellion.

Susan's early years were spent in an atmosphere of "comfortable hardship." Her father was the owner of a small cotton mill. The older children had their hands full in helping their mother to take care not only of the younger children, but of the mill hands who boarded in their house. During one summer, with a nursing baby in her arms, Mrs. Anthony was obliged to board eleven "guests." No time now for the mother to sing at her spinning wheel. Or for the children to play. Too many hours to spend in washing, ironing, weaving, sewing, cooking, baking. On one of the pages of her diary, Susan makes the following casual entry—"Made twenty-one loaves of bread today." Recreation was not meant for the womenfolk of the world. Theirs was the business "to attend to the household work, to fear the Lord and to hold their tongues."

But Susan was not the one to hold her tongue. Her father having lost his mill in the panic of 1838, she was obliged to help out the family budget with the two dollars a week she earned as a school teacher. Her contract, however, was not renewed after the first term. Her acts and her speech were too free. Warned again and again that she must not jeopardize her position through her association with the "niggers" of the community, she finally answered the warnings with this rifle-shot of defiance: "Since school today I have had the unspeakable satisfaction of visiting four colored people and drinking tea with them."

Though she felt pity for the black sheep of the human family, she had nothing but contempt for the white bullies. She was now teaching in another school, a whirlpool of ruffianism from which the male teacher had just been dismissed for his failure as a disciplinarian. The farm louts who attended that school had enrolled there not for study but for sport—the hoodlum sport of teacher-baiting. They soon found, to their sorrow, that Miss Anthony was a teacher not to be baited. Cutting a heavy stick from a birch tree, she trounced the leader of the rowdies into so abject a state of submission that from that day on the entire school treated her with the proper respect. "By gosh, this woman's got the nerve of a man!"

And the *brains* of a man. Appointed as the principal of the girls' department in the Canajoharie (New York) Academy, she made a profound impression upon the citizens of that village. "This woman," said one of the trustees of the school, "is the smartest man that ever came to Canajoharie."

Several of the local "magnates" proposed marriage to her. These men, however, were attracted not so much by her wisdom as by her vigor. "A fine figure of a woman," said one of them— the owner of a sixty-cow dairy. "She'll do a good job milking those sixty cows." Susan politely but emphatically refused this man as well as her other suitors. "No, thank you, I don't want to be any man's legalized servant."

She preferred to stick to her independence. Her shoulders were sturdy enough and her heart stout enough to sustain the burden of her livelihood. But what of those millions of women who were neither strong enough nor courageous enough to stand up against the injustices of a man-made world? One day in the summer of 1848, she read about a convention of women that had been held in Seneca Falls, New York, for the purpose of discussing their "social, civil and religious rights." The idea intrigued her. She began to study the social, civil and religious status of women in the United States—and was appalled at the revelation. The legal code of America, like that of every other country in the world, had relegated the women to a position of undignified inferiority. In accordance with this code, every woman was a perpetual minor. She could never grow up to legal maturity. If she married, she became the property of her husband. And if she remained a spinster, she was obliged to assign her property to a male guardian. No married woman was allowed to sue for breach of contract, to retain the wages that she earned for her work, or to receive damages for injury done to her person or character. In every case the husband was the beneficiary. He was not only the arbiter of her fate and fortune but the owner of her children. He could give or will away the children without the mother's consent; and even though he were proved to be a degenerate or a drunkard, he became the children's sole custodian in the event of divorce. A

[*166*]

man was allowed to beat his wife, his children and his dog; and a woman was not allowed to divorce her husband even on the ground of cruelty. Every American woman, in short, was a slave.

When the women attempted to break the chains of their slavery, they were met everywhere with a howl of derision. The delegates to the Seneca Falls Convention were characterized as "atheists, hermaphrodites, hyenas in petticoats." A few courageous voices, however, had dared to approve of the women's Declaration of Independence. One of the approving voices was that of Susan's father, Daniel Anthony. In his own cotton mills he had regarded his workers like human beings. But in *most* of the cotton mills, he learned from the speeches of the convention, the workers were treated merely like so many mechanical hands. Especially the women. For a working day of fourteen hours they received thirty-one cents. The same situation held true in all the other trades open to women. For sewing a coat, a woman received forty cents; for a pair of trousers, twelve cents. But—most deplorable of all—these working women, if married, had no claim to their own wages, but were compelled by law to turn every cent over to their husbands. And many of these husbands, it was pointed out, wasted their women's earnings on drink or on other women.

The Anthonys discussed these matters around the dinner table. Daniel Anthony told Susan about another woman's rights convention, held at Rochester, which he had personally attended. He related an amusing anecdote about that convention. One of the speakers, Mrs. Elizabeth Cady Stanton, had been taken to task by a married clergyman. "The Apostle Paul," the clergyman scolded her, "recommends silence to women. Why don't you mind him?" Whereupon Mrs. Stanton retorted, "The Apostle Paul also recommends celibacy to clergymen. Why don't *you* mind him?"

Susan laughed when she heard this story. "Mrs. Stanton," she said, "is a woman after my own heart. I should like to meet her."

III

IT WAS some years before Susan Anthony met Elizabeth Cady Stanton. For at the time of the Seneca Falls Convention, Miss Anthony was interested in reforming the men rather than in liberating the women. An ardent rebel like her father, she had allied herself not only with the Abolitionists but also—and especially—with the Prohibitionists. Equally pernicious with the curse of slavery, it seemed to her, was the curse of drink. For drinking, in those days, was a serious matter. The pioneers were men of leathery throats and fireproof stomachs. Everybody drank, and almost everybody drank to excess. At a banquet given in honor of Daniel Webster, at which there were twelve hundred invited guests, the champagne consumed amounted to exactly twenty-four hundred bottles—two bottles to every guest. And this was merely the appetizer for the stronger drinks.

The excessive taste for alcohol was a reaction against the Puritanism of the age. The conscience of America forbade the people to play; and the people, out of revenge, decided to drown their conscience in a deluge of whisky. Almost the entire male population, from the workingman in the factory to the judge on the bench, went about their business in a perpetual fog of intoxication.

Such was the state of affairs when Miss Anthony joined the Temperance movement. At that period she hadn't the slightest interest in votes for women. Or in votes for men, either. For she had been brought up in a Quaker community, and the Quakers were philosophical anarchists who did not believe in voting. But the Anthonys did believe in speaking their minds. Especially Susan. One day, when she was attending a Temperance Convention in Albany (1852), she stood up and tried to make a speech. Whereupon the chairman promptly silenced her. Women, he declared bluntly, must listen and learn but they must never talk. Furious over the ungallantry of the dominant sex, she stalked out of the room. If the men refused to give the women equal courtesy, the women would begin to demand equal rights. On that day Militant Feminism was born.

As soon as she joined the Feminist movement, Susan became one of its leaders. For everybody recognized her dynamic personality and her extraordinary intellect. Yet she knew her own limitations. She was a great organizer, but she was not a great writer or speaker. And so she supplemented her own talents with those of the two other leading Feminists of the day—Elizabeth Cady Stanton and Ernestine Rose. These "three musketeers" organized themselves into what may be called the first "female triumvirate" in history. Susan Anthony, who was the most practical member of the triumvirate, supplied the plans for the campaign. Elizabeth Stanton, who had a feeling for poetical phrases, put the plans into winged words. And Ernestine Rose, whose eloquent tongue had distinguished her as "the Queen of the Platform," delivered the speeches. These three women were socially and economically so far apart that only in America could an intimate alliance have been possible between them. Susan Anthony was the daughter of a poor Quaker. Elizabeth Stanton was the wife of a wealthy attorney. Ernestine Rose was a Jewish immigrant.

Together the three went traveling over the country, organizing meetings, encouraging the women and upbraiding the men. It was a long and uphill fight, at first without the benefit of publicity from the press. "Who would be interested in reading about these crazy female ranters?" But little by little the editors became scurrilously interested. They tried to drown out the movement in a deluge of Rabelaisian innuendo. "What do the leaders of the woman's rights organization want?" asked the elder Mr. Bennett in the New York *Herald* (September 12, 1852). "They want to fill all the posts which men are ambitious to occupy, to be lawyers, doctors, captains of vessels and generals in the field. How funny it would sound in the newspapers that Lucy Stone, pleading a cause, took suddenly ill in the pains of parturition . . . Or that the Reverend Antoinette Brown was arrested in the pulpit in the middle of her sermon from the same cause . . . Or that Dr. Harriot K. Hunt, while attending a gentleman patient for a fistula in ano, found it necessary to send for a doctor, there and then, to be delivered of twins."

And then, when they saw that the Feminist movement was gaining adherents, the editors descended from derision to denunciation. The Feminist triumvirate had advocated, among other things, divorce for drunkenness and birth control for drunkards' wives. "Such heresies," wrote the Syracuse *Star,* "would make demons of the pit shudder to hear." Even those who sympathized with the principles of Feminism were aghast at the spectacle of a woman speaking in public. "That was a magnificent address," said a prominent journalist after one of Ernestine Rose's speeches. "But . . . I would rather see my wife or my daughter in her coffin than hear her speaking . . . before a public assembly."

Allied with the journalists in their denunciation of the Feminist movement were the politicians. When Susan Anthony presented a petition for woman's rights to the New York Legislature, the anti-Feminist lobbyists began to quote Scripture for their purpose. "Are we, sir," cried Assemblyman Burnett, "to give the least countenance to claims so preposterous, disgraceful and criminal as are embodied in this petition? . . . Are we to put the stamp of truth upon the libel here set forth that men and women . . . are to be equal? We *know* that God created man as the representative of the race; that after His creation the Creator took from His side the material for woman's creation . . . and that they thus became one flesh and one being, the man being the head." And if the women persisted in demanding their rights, continued Mr. Burnett, "there would be no way of preserving men's honor except by locking their wives behind bolts and bars."

But the women refused, mentally as well as physically, to be locked behind bolts and bars. Little by little the flower of American womanhood—Lucy Stone Blackwell, Lucretia Mott, Isabella Beecher (the sister of Harriet Beecher Stowe), Antoinette Brown, Anna Shaw and Carrie Chapman Catt—added their brains and their determination to the cause. For a time, in order to "sensationalize" the menfolk out of their "fossilized prejudices," the leaders of the movement cut their hair short and dressed themselves in bloomers. "There's no publicity like a shock." And the male population of America was shocked indeed. What? Release the women from their seven layers of underwear, their starched and quilted petticoats, their tight corsets, their long and dust-sweeping skirts? How preposterous! Why, dressed in her bloomers, a woman was almost as free as a man!

Before long, however, the women gave up their bloomers. But not their fight for freedom. They went on with their endless and tireless crusade for the "right of women to their earnings and their children." And the most tireless crusader of them all was Susan B. Anthony. They called her the Napoleon of the Feminist movement. Though she had none of the cruelty of Napoleon, she had much of his genius—his ability to organize, his power to command, his insensibility to pain and his persistency in the face of defeat. The harder the odds against her, the more eager she was for the fight. Through dint of constant practice, she had become a competent speaker. And now she went about the country, agitating and educating and organizing all by herself. Elizabeth Stanton and Ernestine Rose had fallen by the wayside. They were glad to rest from their labors. But Susan Anthony knew no rest. Her physical endurance was one of the miracles of the century. Her tall, spare frame had become a legend as it sloshed its way through the sleet and the rain, hurrying, hurrying, fighting against time and the weather, plunging through the snowdrifts and breasting the wind, always anxious to bring her message to the women of the next village or town. On one occasion, she wrote to her "good folks at home," the train on which she was traveling over the Rocky Mountains had become "stuck in a snowdrift eleven feet deep." But she managed, somehow, to keep her appointment for the next lecture. Again and again her health broke down. There were times when she stood on the platform with frost-bitten feet, or with her back almost bent double with pain. Once in the dead of winter she was obliged to take the "water cure." It was a heroic measure for Spartan souls—wet sheets, ice packs, sitz baths followed by cold showers and heart-straining gymnastics, all this self-inflicted torture repeated four times a day. And she survived the ordeal. For more than half a century she was in the forefront of the Feminist Revolution—shuttling back and forth over the country, raising hundreds of thousands of dollars for the cause, accepting a wage of only twelve dollars a week for herself. Her amazed friends began to look upon her as an immortal goddess—a poverty-stricken goddess with a rheumatic body and a flaming soul.

And through all her poverty and her hardship and her pain, she retained her saving sense of humor. Her tongue, though never deliberately cruel, could on occasion administer a vigorous thrust. "Miss Anthony," mocked Horace Greeley during one of her interviews, "you are aware, are you not, that the ballot and the bullet go together. If you get the vote, are you also prepared to fight?"

"Why, certainly, Mr. Greeley," came the instant reply. "Just as *you* fought in the Civil War—at the point of a goose-quill."

IV

MISS ANTHONY lived to see the flower, but not the fruit, of her labor. Once, for trying to vote, she had been arrested and sent to jail. But now she was no longer an object of ridicule. The women of the nation had learned to worship her, and even the men had come to look upon her as one of the makers of American history. And she had indeed made history. Largely as the result of her agitation, the women of America had crowded the progress of a thousand years into the short span of a half-century. In 1865, Vassar opened its doors to higher education for women with a curriculum equal to that of the best colleges for men. Within the next decade, no less than fourteen state universities adopted the system of indiscriminate co-education. By 1880, the number of colleges admitting both sexes had grown to a hundred and fifty-four.

Fortified by their higher education, the women had begun to enter the professions. In 1850, there were only a few women who taught school. In 1900, two-thirds of the school teachers in the United States were women. In art, in medicine, in literature, in theology and in law the women were rapidly taking their place side by side with the men. In 1879 the first woman was allowed to plead before the Supreme Court—a landmark in American history.

Most important of all was the civil emancipation of the women. By the end of the nineteenth century, nearly every state in the Union had abolished the old legal disabilities against married women. They now were given the right to own and to control their property, to sue and to be sued, to retain their earnings, to make contracts and to exercise a joint guardianship over their children. Marriage was no longer an enslavement, but an agreement—a mutual compact between equal partners.

All these radical reforms Miss Anthony lived to see as the flowering of her life's work. But the fruition of her life's work she did not live to see. Although a few isolated states had enacted a law to allow votes for women, the national amendment for woman suffrage was not passed until 1920, fourteen years after her death.

But to the last day of her life she labored to bring the final victory nearer. Her vitality remained undiminished to the end. Especially her *mental* vitality. "Miss Anthony," wrote the Chicago *Herald* in 1895, "has grown slightly thinner and more spiritual looking . . . With her transparent hands, her thin face, and her keen eyes flashing light, she looks like Pope Leo XIII. The whole physical being is as nearly submerged as possible in a great mentality."

Yet her "submerged" physical strength enabled her, as a climax to the labors of a lifetime, to take a trip to Europe and to climb Mount Vesuvius. And then, at the age of eighty-four, she attended a Feminist convention in Germany, lecturing, writing, entertaining, arguing—an inexhaustible fountain of perpetual youth. "How do you manage to keep your energy?" asked an admiring friend. "By being the leader of an unpopular cause," she replied.

Her stay in Germany was marked by an incident which served to illustrate the backward-looking mentality of the Prussian government. To while away her time during a rainy spell, she wrote a number of letters to her friends in America. All these letters were interspersed with her customary slogans—"no just government can be formed without the consent of the governed"—"taxation without representation is tyranny." The entire batch of these letters was returned to her hotel with the following official notation: "Such sentiments cannot pass through the post office in Germany."

V

SHE DIED at the age of eighty-six—and in harness. There was to be a birthday celebration in her honor at Washington. She had recently suffered a paralytic stroke, and the doctors ordered her to stay in bed. But "Aunt Susan" laughed at the doctors. "If the hammer must fall," she said, "let it fall while I'm on my feet."

And it was practically while on her feet that she received the blow. She went to the birthday dinner and, in answer to the ovation, stood up to make her final fiery speech. "What I ask is not praise, but justice." And justice, she declared, was bound to come in the end. "Failure is impossible!"

She collapsed immediately on her return home. They buried her in a blizzard—a fitting exit for a heroine who all her life had ploughed her way through the snowdrifts.

FRANCES E. WILLARD

Important Dates in Life of Frances E. Willard

1839—Born at Churchville, N.Y.

1859—Graduated from Northwestern Female College.

1871–74—Served as president of Woman's College, Evanston, Ill.

1874—Became corresponding secretary of the Woman's Christian Temperance Union.

1876—Enlisted in the cause of woman suffrage.

1879—Elected to the presidency of the W.C.T.U.

1883—Became the leader of a worldwide temperance crusade.

1890—Elected president of the National Council of women's societies in America.

1892—Visited England.

1892–98—Served as editor-in-chief of the *Union Signal*.

1898—Died.

Frances Willard

Frances E. Willard

1839–1898

THEY were having an "Indian fight" in the playroom. The two girls, Frances and Mary, had piled up a stockade of chairs and were defending themselves against a "band" of savages—two boys and a dog. The fight was going against the girls, when suddenly Frances thought of a happy idea. Running to the pantry, she came back with a piece of spare rib. "Here, doggie, have your meat and stop your fighting."

The dog "listened to reason" and went over to the girls' side of the stockade. The defenders had won the battle through a judicious bit of strategy.

This was the way of Frances Willard throughout her life. Conciliation rather than contention. "Have your meat and stop your fighting." It was her principle to win the enemy over, rather than to win over the enemy.

II

SHE SPENT HER CHILDHOOD in pioneering with her parents. At the time of her birth her father was the manager of a store in

Churchville, New York. Two years later, however, came the panic of 1837 and her father found himself out of a job. He decided to move his family to Ohio, where he hoped to enter Oberlin College—he was already over forty—and to prepare himself for the ministry. Nothing was too hard and no time was too late for the Willard clan. "The name *Willard,* you know, means *he who wills.*"

And so he packed his family into a covered wagon—Frances was huddled amongst a heap of bedding on top of her father's writing desk—and started off for a new life in the West.

At first it was great fun for Frances—this jolting over the bumps in the road and bouncing back and forth like a rubber ball between the desk and the roof of the wagon. But after a while it wasn't so funny. "Mother, Sissy's dress hurts!" And mother would remark with a smile to her husband: "Just listen to the child, Josiah. She already knows it isn't her real self but her mortal dress that suffers."

And this "mortal dress" of hers was destined to still further suffering before her family could settle down. After a few years of study at Oberlin, Josiah Willard took sick with tuberculosis. "An outdoor life," ordered the physician. "Farther West."

Another trek into the West—a journey of three weeks with rests on Sundays, and then they pitched tent on a bluff overlooking Rock River, in Wisconsin.

Here Josiah built a home and tilled the land and grew strong and prospered. And brought up his family of three children— two others "had gone back to God." It was a beautiful spot they lived in. "The bluffs rose about it on the right and left. Groves of oak and hickory were on either hand; a miniature forest of evergreens almost concealed the cottage from the view of passers-by . . . Through the thick and luxuriant growth of shrubbery were paths which strayed off aimlessly, tempting the feet of the curious down their mysterious aisles."

And the feet of Frances—they called her Frank—were curious

indeed. She was such an adventurous little redhead of a tomboy. Never cared to do the housework. Always liked to explore the "wilderness" that surrounded their Forest Home; to saddle her goat with a picnic lunch and to go off "pioneering" to the prairie —that sea of golden grain that stretched beyond the horizon.

She had come from beyond the horizon. Such a big world of interesting places and interesting people. Did they all live in homes like her own? she wondered. Homes in which the parents were strict enough, to be sure, but so gentle in their strictness. "Mind your parents and tell the truth"—this was practically the only rule they went by. Homes of laughter, frolic, singing, birthday cakes and holiday puddings. Houses filled like her own—she remembered the words often used by her mother—"with the peace of God and the love of mankind."

As she grew older, she learned from her parents that not *every* home was like her own. In some of them—too many of them— there was too little money and too much misery.

"And what is the reason for it?"

"There are many reasons," replied her father. "Greed, dishonesty, selfishness, corruption, fraud, trickery, and the curse of intoxicating drink."

Most of these expressions meant very little to Frank. But one of them she understood. Intoxicating drink. She had once seen a farm hand at Forest Home who suffered from this sickness. A *terrible* sickness. It turned a man into a pig. Her father had spoken to them about it. Had asked them to "sign the pledge." All three of the children—Oliver, Frank and Mary—had written their names on a blank page in the family Bible, right under the pledge. A funny little jingle, but it made good sense:

> *To quench our thirst we'll always bring*
> *Cold water from the well or spring.*
> *So here we pledge perpetual hate*
> *To all that can intoxicate.*

But for the present, Frank was interested in other matters. The work on the farm. Feeding the poultry, herding the sheep, harnessing the mare. And taking care of her "living dolls"—turkeys, goats, calves, colts, peafowls and her two pet rabbits, Beauty and Brighty. And reading books. *That* was the best sport of them all. Her mother had taught her to read and to write—she had been a schoolteacher before her marriage. What a world of adventure in those books! The wanderings of Aeneas, the plight of the Ancient Mariner, the ride of John Gilpin, the antics of Falstaff and of Sir Toby Belch. But no novels. "Fiction is not fit for young girls," said her father.

And then, one day, came her emancipation. It was a long time coming. She was celebrating her eighteenth birthday. Her father was working in the fields. When he came home toward evening, he found her sitting in her mother's rocker, nonchalantly reading Scott's *Ivanhoe*.

"I thought I told you not to read novels, Frances!"

"So you did, Father. But you forget what day this is."

"What do you mean, child?"

"I am eighteen today—a grown woman. And a grown woman, you know, can do as she likes."

Her father was about to take the book away, but she looked at him with laughter in her eyes. "It's a very interesting story, Father. Have you read it?"

Mr. Willard joined in her laughter. "I guess you *are* a woman, Frances. And a chip of the old block!"

III

FRANCES WILLARD took great pride in her womanhood. "Next to being an angel," she said, "the greatest bestowment of God is to make one a woman." Yet she chafed against the indignity, just as she gloried in the dignity, of her sex. "When my brother grew to manhood," she writes, "he went with his father to vote. Standing by the window, I looked out as they drove away . . . and I felt a strange ache in my heart, and tears sprang to my eyes. Turning to my sister . . . I said, 'Don't you wish we could go with them when we are old enough? Don't we love our country just as well as they do?' And her little frightened voice piped out, 'Yes, of course we ought . . . But we mustn't tell a soul—we should be called *strong-minded!*' "

That was the difference between Mary—between *Everywoman* —and Frances Willard. Others were afraid of appearing strong-minded. But Frances wasn't.

Frances wasn't afraid of anything. When, together with her sister, she entered the Northwestern Female College, she was set down by the other girls as "snooty." But her "snootiness" was merely a combination of outspoken frankness and an assumed hauteur to conceal her embarrassment over her homely face.

For her face—as one of her classmates bluntly told her—was decidedly "farmerish." And so were her clothes. But she had one outstanding ornament—a chip on the shoulder. One day a girl remarked that her red bonnet on top of her red hair was a "regular scream." Frank promptly knocked the girl down and made her "eat" her words.

Her red hair—in later years it turned to a beautiful auburn— was a source of constant humiliation to her. Accordingly she had it bobbed, whereupon her father drily remarked—"The fool and her hair are soon parted."

She was a proud, defiant and fighting young creature in her college days. And full of fun. A spirited colt of a girl. For a time her teachers found her unmanageable. One evening together with Maggie, another student tomboy like herself, she put on a pirate's rig—high-top boots, red sash, bandana kerchief, wooden bowie knife, pistols—placed upon the table a bottle of ginger ale as a substitute for whisky, crossed her legs and put between her lips a big lighted cigar.

A knock at the door; and without waiting for a summons, in

walked Miss Dickinson, one of Frank's teachers. Frank and Maggie almost collapsed in their chairs. But Miss Dickinson was equal to the occasion. "What a lucky thing!" she cried. "The mosquitoes have almost eaten me alive. Won't you please come into my room and smoke them out?"

And smoke them out they did. Choking and spluttering and protesting vigorously, the two "pirates" were compelled to burn their cigars down to the very butts. A dizzy, nauseating headache, and Frank came out of the incident a wiser if not a sadder girl.

Indeed, she was soon acclaimed as the wisest member of her class. She became the editor of the college paper, the president of the debating society, the guiding spirit of the student socials— though she preferred books to people; "in books the best self of the author meets the best self of the reader"—and the valedictorian of her class. And with all these activities she worked herself into a protracted siege of typhoid fever, so that she was unable to attend her own Commencement.

The Willard spirit was always greater than the Willard strength. The manifold interests of a developing character had almost ruined her health. And they destroyed her sister's life. Mary Willard was only nineteen when she succumbed to the family curse—tuberculosis.

Her sister's death served as the final textbook in the formal education of Frances. It deepened her social feeling toward the sisterhood of all women. Accepting a position as teacher in the Pittsburgh Female College, she inspired in her pupils so strong a devotion that the rival teachers accused her of employing hypnotic spells.

But it was merely the hypnotism of a strong personality consecrated to the task of developing other personalities to the full. Her purpose as a teacher was "not to let study interfere with education"—not to dispense facts but to build characters.

After a few years of teaching, however, she found that her own character was in need of further building. And so, in the spring of 1868, she set out on an extended tour of Europe with one of her friends, Kate Jackson. Her father had just died—the old disease had recurred after many years. It was partly to escape from the poignancy of her sorrow that she left for Europe. But, like the old Latin poet, she learned that "he who sails across the main, changes the spot but not the pain."

She looked upon Europe with eyes stimulated by curiosity, saddened by pain. She not only saw new places and people, but she saw them in a new light. At first she marveled at the palaces, the museums, the picture galleries, and she contrasted these "fine things" with the "emptiness" of her own country. But one day she spoke to a peasant in Ireland. "America," he said, "is a country where they develop *fine men*. A place where they give everybody a chance. I'd go there on my hands and knees, only for the water being in the way."

So *this* was the picture that the Europeans had of America. "A place where they give everybody a chance." Greatly exaggerated, of course. But why couldn't this Irish peasant's *ideal* of America be made *real?* Why couldn't she, Frank Willard, help to *make* it real?

A new feverish ambition had taken hold of Frances Willard. One day, as she climbed over the Simplon Pass to the Monastery of St. Bernard, she recalled a story she had read about Napoleon in McGuffey's *Third Reader*. When Napoleon arrived at this pass with thirty thousand men, he asked the guide whether it would be possible to cross it in May, while the snow lay deep upon the ground.

"It may not be *im*possible," said the guide, "but——"

"Move forward the legions!" rang Napoleon's command.

And now Frances was ready to carry her army of fellow Americans out of the valley of poverty, over the mountain passes of education and into the summit of a new hope.

"This may not be *im*possible, but——"

"Let's go ahead!"

IV

SALVATION THROUGH KNOWLEDGE. And the Eternal Feminine shall lead the way. On her return to America she accepted the presidency of the Evanston (Illinois) College for Women. Her objective in this new position was to wean the women of America away from a slavish past and to convert them to a free future.

But she was still restless. The office of a small college was no rostrum for a woman who wanted to enlighten the world. Her talents needed a bigger, more comprehensive job. And this job presented itself in the Woman's Temperance Crusade. This Crusade had just swept in a drama of triumph over the states of the Middle West. In Ohio, no less than two hundred and fifty saloons had been closed within a period of two months. *Here* was a movement for the energy of Frances Willard! One day in Chicago the street corner hoodlums had insulted a procession of women. She volunteered to march in the next procession, publicly excoriated the hoodlums—and silenced them. "That woman has magic in her voice!"

She was eager to throw herself heart and soul into the movement. But how could she find the time? She had a living to make for herself and for her mother who depended upon her. The temperance movement was poor. The people of means were keeping aloof. There were but meager funds for salaries. How, under the circumstances, could she devote herself to the cause? "This may not be *im*possible, but——"

"Let's go ahead!"

She went ahead. Resigned her office at the college, and entered the temperance ranks. She now felt completely happy for the first time in her life.

Everybody thought she was crazy. That is, everybody save one —her mother. When Frances discussed the bread-and-butter problem with her, Mrs. Willard urged her to stop worrying about it. "Trust in the Lord and do good." They would manage to be fed, somehow. "St. Courageous," Frances called her mother.

And St. Courageous looked trustingly on while her daughter marched through the streets, walked into a saloon, with "its sawdust floor, its all-too-convenient vomit-barrels," its sickening fumes, its leering men. Looked on while Frances knelt and prayed, and one by one the men dropped on their knees and joined the prayer. "It was glorious, Mother! Never in my life, save at Mary's dying bed, have I prayed as truly as in that saloon."

But what about their food and their rent? In the first abandon of her zeal, when the women elected her to the presidency of their Chicago chapter, she forgot to say anything about the matter of compensation. And the women, convinced that she had other means of support, took her at her silence and paid her nothing. Again and again she was obliged to walk across the city to her meetings because she didn't have the nickel for her carfare. Once, as she spoke to a derelict in the slums, she said: "I am a better friend than you think. I know just exactly how you feel. For, bless God, I too am hungry."

Before long, however, her co-workers realized her need and voted her just a bare, body-and-soul-preserving salary. It was all they could afford.

And now she felt fabulously rich as she kept rising higher and higher in her descent to the underworld. It was a complete transformation in her manner of life that she had undergone. From respectability to disrepute. "Instead of the sweetness of home," she writes, "I was to become a wanderer on the face of the earth; instead of libraries, I was to frequent public halls and railway carriages; instead of scholarly and cultured men, I was to see the dregs of saloon and gambling house." She had broken up her own home in order to rebuild the homes of other people.

She had adopted the hardest of human vocations. Like the prophets of old, she had become a traveling merchant of hope— a most unpromising commodity among the despised and the dispossessed. The human wreckage that she dealt with preferred the mirage of intoxicating drink to the reality of sober fact. "What have we got to look forward to if we give up the pleasures of the saloon?"

"The comforts of home."

"Just listen to her, will you? As if the likes of us ever had any comforts!"

And Frances Willard began to realize that drink was but a secondary evil. It was an escape from reality—a forgetfulness of poverty, of injustice, of distress. The root of the evil lay in the exploitation of the workers, in the degradation of their homes. It was up to the women, the *makers* of the American homes, to vote their menfolk out of the mire! Out of the sweatshops and the gutters and the saloons and into the sunlight of better wages, cleaner homes and cleaner hearts!

This, then, was the threefold mission to which Frank Willard was now dedicated: the abolition of the bar-room, votes for women, justice for men. She was still wedded to her career as a teacher—but a teacher on a wider scale, with the entire country as her classroom. Elected to the presidency of the national Woman's Christian Temperance Union, she set out on a speaking tour that took her into every American town of five thousand population or more. Her life had become a shuttle-journey between the pullman car and the lecture hall. And a journey beset with hardship and derision and contempt. Even her fellow-workers in the W.C.T.U. were aghast when she first espoused the cause of labor and of woman suffrage. It was their business, they insisted, to keep men sober, not to keep them fed. Feeding the poor was God's affair, not theirs. As to votes for women, there was quite a scene when Frances Willard first ventured to advocate it in public at the Newark Convention of the W.C.T.U. (1876).

"When I had finished speaking," writes Miss Willard, "a lady from New York, gray-haired and dignified, who was presiding, said to the audience: 'The national Woman's Christian Temperance Union is not responsible for the utterances of this evening. We have no mind to trail our skirts in the mire of politics.' "

And the hall broke into pandemonium when Frank Willard retorted: "Then raise your skirts so they won't trail!"

V

LITTLE BY LITTLE, Frank Willard got the women of the W.C.T.U. around to her way of thinking. Under the triple banner of *Prohibition, Woman's Liberation* and *Labor's Uplift,* she kept building up the national unit until it numbered a million members. And this membership consisted—again after a vigorous fight on the part of Frances Willard—not only of Protestants but of Catholics and Jews as well. It was her life's ambition, she said, to rid America of three contemptible evils: the scourge of drink, the scourge of greed, the scourge of intolerance.

And after America—the world. Her cause was the cause of the human race. Early in her public career she had adopted the slogan, "For God and Home and Native Land." She now amended it to the more inclusive slogan, "For God and Home and *Every* Land." Were it not for the intrusion of the sea, she said, the shores of Europe and of Asia "would be part and parcel of our land. We are one world of tempted humanity."

And of *suffering* humanity. Frances Willard felt herself—to use her own expression—"born to a fate." It was her fate to serve as one of the nurses in the battlefield of life—to remove the wounded soldiers from the carnage, to bind up their wounds, and to restore them to a vision of peace. She was another Florence Nightingale working in a less dramatic but more extensive conflict—the eternal conflict between need and greed. She organized the motherhood of the world in a crusade for "purer, healthier, happier homes." And, in an effort to further this crusade, she addressed a polyglot Petition, translated into fifty languages, to all the leading governments in the two hemispheres. In this universal petition she implored the various governments to prohibit the liquor and the opium traffic, to raise the living standards of their workers and to establish a code of justice upon a basis of Christian morals.

She tried, in short, to build a worldwide Kingdom of Heaven. In keeping with the liberal tendencies of the nineteenth century, she called this utopia of her dreams the *Republic of God*. The earth must become a place where all God's creatures are to be treated with equal dignity and with equal fair play. When she heard of the Turkish government's persecution of the Armenians —"they, too, are my brothers"—she organized a fund for their relief, she built homes for the homeless refugees, she sent agents to bring food and seed corn and medicine to the devastated land, and she induced our government to call upon the Turkish government for a cessation of its massacres. "The supreme duty of statesmen is the protection of the home—anywhere and everywhere upon the face of the earth."

This was the climax of her life, and it brought her beyond the summit of her strength. Her health began rapidly to decline. A trip to England, where she tried in vain to recover her strength at the estate of her British co-worker, Lady Somerset. The death of her mother—"it was a beautiful passing from life unto life." A protracted illness, whose hours she beguiled with the preparation of her autobiography—a book of 1200 pages written by an invalid in less than 12 weeks! A visit to the eastern states—"I came from that section, you know, and I wanted to say good-bye to those familiar places before the final trip." And then the return home to Evanston. It was here that she had begun her career as an educator, and it was here that she wanted to end it. "When I reach heaven, I want to register as from Evanston."

And it was at Evanston that she waited for the call to the final registration. But it was no patient waiting—not for Frances Willard. Almost to the end she kept on saying, "Let me dictate just one more letter. It's so important!"

And in the moment of her last exhaustion she whispered: "Other work, in another world."

But her work is well remembered in *this* world. For today her statue—the only woman's statue—stands in the Statuary Hall in the National Capitol.

CATHERINE BRESHKOVSKY

Important Dates in Life of Catherine Breshkovsky

1844—Born.

1869—Entered revolutionary party.

1873—Exiled to Siberia for "preaching the gospel of liberty."

1896—Released from Siberia. Organized Socialist Revolutionist Party.

1904—Visited America. On return to Russia, again sentenced to Siberia.

1917—Welcomed back to Russia by Kerensky government.

1918—Left Russia because of her opposition to the Bolsheviki. Opened school for children in Czechoslovakia.

1934—Died in Czechoslovakia.

Catherine Breshkovsky

Catherine Breshkovsky

1844–1934

IN 1904, WHEN Catherine Breshkovsky came to Boston on her first visit to America, she casually remarked that on her long railroad journey she had had nothing to eat all day. One of the reporters expressed his horror, but the little grandmother of the Russian Revolution laughed it off. "Oh, one day—what is that?" What was one foodless day to a woman who had consecrated herself to a lifetime of hunger and exile and privation and cold? Like Saint Francis, she had given up a life of luxury to be wedded to poverty. But unlike Saint Francis, she had received a fifty-year term in the ice-fields of Siberia as a wedding present.

II

EKATERINA KONSTANTINOVA BRESHKO-BRESHKOVSKAIA—such a long name for such a little lady!—was a product of the Russian nobility and the Polish aristocracy. As a child she had a quick temper and a tender heart. Once, at the age of three, she struck her mother with a stick and then spent the whole day tearfully castigating herself for her "sin." A strange child, so different from

[*195*]

the other children of the rich landowners of Tchernigov. But, then, her parents were different from the other parents. The fat Duke Baratov, for example—the man whose "god lived in his belly" and who made his fortune by selling his grain over and over again to a number of merchants, receiving a deposit from each and delivering his goods to none. And when the merchants complained, he had them arrested for questioning the honesty of the nobility. Or the Countess Shivia, who in a single season spent two hundred thousand roubles on her half-wit son, Fedia, and who flogged her peasants when they whimpered that their children didn't have enough bread. These noblemen and noblewomen were very patriotic—with the lives of their serfs. But Katya's parents looked upon their serfs as "body-and-soul-creatures" like themselves. They never flogged them or starved them or subjected them to unnecessary humiliation. "Your estate, Constantine," sneered the neighboring gentry, "is a republic."

And it was as a little republican that Katya was brought up. She shared her tidbits and her playthings with the children of the servants. And sometimes—to her mother's dismay—she would come home without her coat or her dress. "But there's no need of overdoing it, child!" her mother would remonstrate. And Katya would plead: "Don't be angry, Mother. Didn't you show us in the Bible where it says that if you have two coats you must give one of them away to the poor?"

How to befriend the poor, how to "find justice" for them, was the paramount question of her life—she tells us—from the age of eight. She had a great and, to her childish imagination, very workable dream for the emancipation of the serfs. She would go to California, dig up "heaps of gold," return with all the gold to Russia and buy a huge tract of land—"as huge as the sky"—where all the unfortunate people of the world would live in a comfortable house like her own, with plenty of food to eat and with plenty of clothes to keep them warm.

And when her parents made fun of her dream, she looked at

them with naïve incredulity at their ignorance. Didn't they know that everybody found gold in California? "Maybe," said her father with a good-natured smile. "But most of these people spend their money in a *sensible* way."

Whereupon Katya shook her head emphatically. "The only sensible way to spend your money is to make the poor happy."

III

WHEN the other girls of the nobility went out to their "silly soirées," Katya stayed home and read. "I hated the bowings and the scrapings and the stuffy ceremonials of the decayed flower of the aristocracy . . . I preferred the free society of such thinkers as Voltaire, Rousseau, and Diderot . . . I knew the French Revolution by heart." And also the German Revolution of 1848. Like most of the girls of the Russian aristocracy, she had learned French and German in her nursery; not, however, like the others merely to *prattle,* but to *think* in French and in German as well as in Russian. She became an adept in the universal language of thought. She had given up her childish idea of digging for gold in California. There was a better kind of prospecting to be done. She began to dig for ideas in Russia. She opened a school for peasants. "I found the peasant an abject, ignorant creature . . . He could think only of his mud hut and his plot of ground . . . As for the government, he knew only that in peace he must pay money; in war, lives." The so-called "liberation of the serfs" had meant complete starvation in freedom instead of semi-starvation in bondage. For the government had driven them off the land to which they had been tied in their serfdom. Abandoned cattle without a pasture. "If you take away my land, how can I feed my little ones through a Russian winter?" But the government, instead of helping the peasants, "crippled them with the knout" for their grumbling.

"I now saw how ineffectual were my attempts as a mere

teacher," wrote Catherine. "I felt that tremendous economic and political changes must be made." But what sort of changes? Her ideas had not as yet been clarified. Thus far her social outlook was that of a liberal, not of a radical. She wanted to reform, not to uproot. She met a young liberal like herself and married him. "Sensible thing," said her mother. "Now you will settle down to a respectable life, as befits your station. The running brook will become a quiet lake."

But one day she met a revolutionist, a handsome young prince who had given up his property and his titles in order to work among the poor. "For hours he discussed with me the problems that were rushing upon us. His words thrilled like fire." The name of this ardent young prince was Peter Kropotkin.

Catherine's mind was now made up. In order to teach the peasants, you must live among them, be one of them. To be understood, you must learn to understand. "If you want to know how the shoe pinches, put it on." One day she told her husband about her decision to dedicate herself to a life of hardship. "Are you ready to join me?"

Her husband was an idealist, but he was not a martyr. "No," he said, "I am not ready to go to that extent."

"Very well, then, I will go myself."

Though about to become a mother, she left the luxury of her home and set out upon the road that was bound to end in prison or in exile—perhaps even in death. "If necessary, I am ready to die for the cause."

At first she went to Kiev, where she stayed with her widowed sister, Olga, until her son was born. She supported herself by tutoring—and earned as much as a hundred and forty roubles a month. Her evenings she spent in "agitating for the New Day." And then, delivered of her child, she left it with her brother and his wife. "My heart felt torn into a thousand pieces." But she had made her choice. "I knew that I could not be a mother and

[*198*]

still be a revolutionist." And she was not alone in her decision. "Among the women in the struggle for Russian freedom there were many who chose to be fighters for justice rather than mothers of the victims of tyranny."

In order to prepare herself for her mission of rebellion, she learned the trade of dyeing and painting and then started off with two companions, Masha Kalenkina and Yakov Stepano-vitch. Masha had learned the same trade, and Yakov had fitted himself to be a cobbler. It was in the summer of 1874 that the three "flame seekers," disguised as peasants, launched upon their career as the founders of the Russian Revolution.

They had supplied themselves with false passports. Catherine's passport described her as a country woman from the province of Orlov, 40 years of age—in reality she was only 30, but she had braided and wrinkled and muffled herself up to give ten added years to her appearance. She wore enormous shoes of birch-bark, a thick canvas blouse, a skirt of heavy burlap, and a black jacket fastened with a red belt. "A nice little peasant woman," remarked a laborer as they boarded a boat on the Dnieper, "but where did you get such soft and dainty hands?"

"I was servant to a wealthy nobleman," she explained, "and he made me do only the lighter tasks."

The laborer winked with a knowing smile. "I understand."

They disembarked at the city of Tcherkass and set off on the swampy road from town to town and from village to village. For Catherine it was an Odyssey of torture. The soles of her feet were blisters, the peasant food nauseated her, and the pack pressed down upon her shoulders "like a ton of brick." And the sleeping quarters! Hovels decorated with cobwebs, carpeted with vermin and ventilated with rat holes. Once, when Catherine timidly suggested that she'd like to wash the floor of her lodging, the hostess remarked, "Get some warm manure from the field and mix it with lime. It makes a good cleanser."

Dark, dismal kennels and dark, dismal minds. "It isn't the

government that's responsible for our sufferings," the peasants kept saying, "it's the nobles."

"But what about the Czar?" asked Catherine, trying to stir within them the germ of an idea.

"The Czar, God bless him, is our little father. We are his children. He loves us."

"But he's not on your side. He's on the side of the nobles."

"Our poor little father doesn't know. The nobles don't tell him. If only somebody told him how his children suffer!"

"Then why don't you tell him?"

"They wouldn't let us speak to him. So he doesn't know. And what can he do, God bless him, if he doesn't know?"

And so on and on. It was impossible to draw them out of this petrified circle of a single idea. The little father was good but he didn't know, and the nobles knew but they weren't good. Catherine tried to awaken them by means of the printed word. She told the peasants that she would read something to them. The rumor passed around that this "something" was the "good chapter" which the Czar had inserted in the book of laws and which the nobles had torn out. "At last she will show us the Czar's truth!"

But when Catherine came to the reading, she protested that these were no "miracle papers stolen from the law book" that she had brought them. "I have other papers, written by men who really love you. These men have described the wrongs you have suffered, the outrages committed against you, and the rights you ought to demand as human beings."

And then she read to them a story called *Moses and His Four Brothers*—a revolutionary pamphlet presented in the form of a sugar-coated allegory. The peasants listened with open mouths.

"Good God, what golden words!"

"And how true they are!"

"If our little father could only read them!"

"He would then punish the nobles and take our part!"

[200]

Catherine tried to explain to them that they were wrong. "It isn't the nobles alone who are to blame for your misery. It is the nobles and the devil—and the Czar."

The peasants looked at her in amazement. And then silently, one by one, they stole out of the hut.

The following day a gendarme came to examine her passport. "So you are a peasant from Orlov?" he said after he had scrutinized the paper.

"Yes."

"And you can write?"

She nodded.

"And read"—he paused for effect and then shot out—"revolutionary trash?"

But Catherine was not to be bullied. "This is no trash I've been reading to the peasants. It's the sort of stuff will make them think."

"Well, how would *you* like a little chance to think? A nice dark place where nobody will disturb you."

They took her to the *Black Hole*—the name of the local prison. "As I went down," she writes in her diary, "two drunken wretches were stumbling up. I was pushed in, the heavy door slammed, and the bolts rattled in total blackness. I took a step forward, and lost my footing, for the floor was slippery with excrement . . . Deadly sick, I sank down on a heap of straw and rags. A moment later I was stung sharply back to consciousness, and sprang up covered with vermin. I leaned against the walls and found them dank. So I stood awake all night in the middle of the Hole." A place indeed to make one think. "And this," concludes the passage, "was the beginning of my journey to Siberia."

IV

FOR TWO YEARS they shifted her from one Russian prison to another, and then they sent her off upon her Siberian exile. "They gave me five years as a hard labor convict in the mines—the punishment ordinarily meted out to a murderer. And then, my term served, I was to be an exile in Siberia for several years longer."

They placed her in a *telega*—a covered wagon—"squeezed in between two gendarmes." For weeks at a time the wagon bumped over the roads without stopping more than ten minutes for a breathing spell. Agony of sleeplessness. Worse agony of perpetual surveillance. "The gendarmes were ordered never to take their eyes off their prisoners." On very rare occasions she was allowed, together with the other prisoners, to sleep at an *étape*—wayside jail—"reeking, crawling holes infested with scurvy, consumption and typhoid . . . The plaster on the walls was red with bedbugs killed by tormented prisoners." They slept on long benches "devoid of bedclothes." Through the walls of her cell, Catherine could hear "the endless jangling of fetters, the moaning of women, the cries of sick babies." And then, after a night of torture, the "criminals" were once more hustled into their *telegas*. The march of the million exiles—this was the number of Russians sent by the government over the White Siberian Way from 1875 to 1900. "You ask me for scenes and stories," she said to a reporter when she visited America in 1904. "But, you see, we were so busy thinking of our Dream that we had no time to watch the misery of our external existence." One incident, however, she did notice. "As we passed through Krasnoyarsk, the mother of one of the prisoners, a young student, tried to kiss him good-bye. She had come a long way for this final parting. But the gendarmes wouldn't allow her to get near him. They jerked him into the *telega* and galloped off. As I came by, I saw her white, haggard old face. Then she fell beside the road."

Arrived at the mines of Kara, Catherine discovered that the political prisoners were condemned not to hard labor but to the even harder punishment of enforced idleness. And then, after an enervating term in the purgatory of Kara, she was hounded into the inferno of Barguzin, a frozen city in the Arctic Circle of Siberia. She had been sent all the way from Kara to Barguzin —a distance of over a thousand miles—on foot. "All the prisoners were shivering with the cold; nobody spoke; and the white silence of the snowfield was broken only by the whistling of the wind." Again and again, as they continued their silent "funeral march," they came upon the "gaunt and almost naked" bodies of exiles who had died on the way. "We have no time to bury those swine," remarked one of the gendarmes laconically.

They reached Barguzin in February, with the thermometer at forty-five below zero. Another succession of shivering years of compulsory idleness. She was anxious to teach the children of her fellow-prisoners, or at least to nurse them in their illness. But this was contrary to the laws of the Russian Czar. "Exiled teachers are not allowed to heal." Nothing to do except to sit for long hours planning her escape.

And finally she managed to make her escape from Barguzin. Together with three young students she set out one night, under the guidance of an old Siberian peasant who "had made the journey" many years before. But soon their guide found that he was himself misguided. As they became entangled amidst the rocks and the chasms of the Taiga forests, the peasant scratched his head and confessed that he had lost his way. "Siberia is such a big country, and it has so many directions." Several hundred miles of zigzagging over the mountains, and then they were captured by the police.

Another term in the prison-mines of Kara, on a diet of black bread and a few ounces of putrid meat. Fifty per cent of the prisoners died of scurvy, but Catherine didn't even take sick. She was protected by her broad shoulders, her deep chest and her unconquerable Dream. This Dream, she was determined, would never leave her until Russia was free. "Mr. Kennan," she said to the American correspondent who visited her in Siberia, "we may die in exile, and our children may die in exile, and our children's children may die in exile, *but something will come of it at last.*"

V

RELEASED from Siberia in 1896, she visited her old friends of the nobility in their luxurious homes. She preferred her hardships to their luxury. "They are worried about their coffee; they are worried about their garden; they are worried about everything. I have had no baggage for thirty years, and I am not worried about anything."

After a brief stay with her friends, she went back to her revolutionary work in order, as she laughingly remarked, to relieve these friends of their worries. Once more, as in the past, she disguised herself as a peasant. Time and again the gendarmes attempted to arrest her, but she always managed to elude them. On one occasion, when she was visiting her relatives in the country, the gendarmes surrounded the house. It happened that this was the cook's day off. The gendarmes searched the house from garret to cellar while Catherine, dressed in the cook's clothes, stood nonchalantly cooking the dinner in the kitchen.

This was but one of the many roles she was obliged to assume —and to assume with histrionic perfection—in her continual hide-and-seek game with the police. She had become an expert in the art of masquerade. Once, during her American visit, a wealthy admirer presented her with a trunkful of beautiful clothes. "What in the world will I do with all these dresses?" she asked in perplexity. And then her face brightened. "I know! I will use them for my disguises when I return to Russia."

VI

HER VISIT TO AMERICA was part of an extended trip she had undertaken in an effort "to enlist the sympathy of the world in the cause of a free Russia." It was a tour of triumph. Everywhere, when she appeared on the platform, "the audiences rose *en masse,* handkerchiefs waved, hats were flung up into the air, words of affection in many languages were rained upon her from all parts of the hall, and the applause was deafening." People shouted and laughed and wept—one audience almost tore her clothes off in the universal effort to embrace her—while the silver-haired *Babushka,* the little grandmother, accepted her triumph with the same smiling tranquillity with which she had accepted her martyrdom. "Only her eyes betray the sufferings of the years."

Her friends begged her to remain in America, where she would be safe from future molestation. But she wouldn't listen to them. "I cannot stay longer; they need me in Russia. Some day I will come back—when Russia is free."

And so she returned to Russia—and to another term of exile in Siberia. This time (1912) she was sentenced for life. To a reporter who expressed his sympathy on the eve of her departure, she said: "Don't let this disturb you; I have been through it all before."

The officials thought that two or three winters of the Siberian frosts would put an end to this "stubborn little troublemaker" of sixty-eight. But they were mistaken. She seemed to grow stronger with the years. One of her fellow-exiles describes her on her second Siberian journey: "A full figure with rosy face (I paid special attention—there were no wrinkles), sparkling eyes, and gray hair hanging over a forehead so radiant it was hard to believe that she was almost seventy years old." Another exile writes about her at a later stage of the journey: "It seemed to me that since 1905 . . . she had grown younger. She was in excellent spirits . . . And this was after five days of a difficult march, all the time under a pouring rain, with the nights passed in barracks or around camp fires."

The gendarmes were astonished at her endurance. "Looks as if nothing can kill her. This woman is bewitched." They appointed two spies to watch her, and then four, and finally six.

"No telling what she may do. Old as she is, she is reckless enough to attempt another escape."

And she did attempt it—and this time almost succeeded. She was recaptured after she had traveled thousands of miles—"how she managed to cover that distance," wrote a fellow-Siberian, "we cannot understand." And it was just an hour or two before she had reached the border that the police succeeded in intercepting her. "So seemingly near to freedom and yet so far," she observed quietly. "But with Russia," she added, "it's just the opposite. So seemingly far from freedom and yet so near."

Her words about Russia were more prophetic than she was able to realize at the time. They sent her to the northernmost point in Siberia where even the sturdiest constitution would succumb to the cold. "Here," she said, "I am kept like a salted herring in a hogshead. And here I suppose I shall die without ever seeing the liberation of my people." She cared little about her own fate, but she sorrowed over the fate of Russia. "The road is so long, and the night so dark . . ."

And then, suddenly, the dawn. A message to Catherine Breshkovsky, to all the political prisoners in Siberia. "Russia is free!"

VII

SHE WENT BACK TO MOSCOW and threw herself once more into her work—this time to steel the Russians not against the cruelty of the Romanoffs but against the savagery of the Hohenzollerns. She insisted that the Russians must remain in the war (1917) against Germany. "I do not wish to see the destruction of the German people, but I do wish to see the destruction of their criminal and inhuman disrespect toward every other nation." She warned the Bolshevik government against a premature peace with the German military machine. But her warning was in vain. Lenin concluded the treaty of Brest-Litovsk. "You have overthrown one tyranny only to subject yourself to another tyranny," she said and sorrowfully betook herself once more into exile. This time it was a voluntary exile in Czechoslovakia.

Her main work was done. The little grandmother of the Russian Revolution had lived to see the fulfillment of her Dream. It was not exactly as she had dreamed it, to be sure. But she was wise enough to understand, even though she was not patient enough to accept, the difference between the final structure and the original plan. Realization must always fall short of expectation. "After all, we have only our imperfect human building-blocks to work with."

She opened a school for poor children in Prague, this young little old woman of seventy-six. And here, for the final fourteen years of her life, she tried to inspire new minds with new dreams. "A great era is coming—I feel it with all my soul—an era in which all the nations will be united into one human family."

SARAH BERNHARDT

Important Dates in Life of Sarah Bernhardt

1844—Born in Paris.

1856—Baptized as a Catholic.

1857—Entered the Conservatory for Actresses.

1862—Made her début at the Comédie Française.

1880—Visited America and scored a hit in La Dame aux Camélias (Camille).

1882—Married Jules Paul Damala.

1915—Leg amputated. Continued her acting.

1916—Played for the soldiers in the trenches.

1923—Died while making a film.

Her most famous roles include:

Hamlet; Theodora; Tosca; Phêdre; Camille; Dona Sol in Victor Hugo's Hernani.

Sarah Bernhardt

Sarah Bernhardt

1844–1923

Sᴀʀᴀʜ's ʟɪꜰᴇ was the greatest drama she played in. The morbid-minded destinies who sat in the box seats on the opening night of her life could not have found a play that began better to their liking. Sarah was born of an unwedded Jewish mother, a young milliner of Paris who sang like a half-frozen little bird in a café, and who fell a victim to the blandishments of penniless soldiers. Bereft of her father at an early age, she found herself thrust unwanted into the streets and condemned to live on her cunning and her courage. It seemed as if some angel, in the busy routine of heaven, had forgotten to call the attention of God to her. Yet somehow God had noticed her just the same. In spite of her cruel surroundings, Julie had wonderful golden-red hair, every strand curled by the divine finger, and eyes into which the divine spirit had looked before her birth and left the memory of His glance.

In the Latin Quarter strange love matches are made, but few of these matches possess the ingredients that bring forth genius. However, Julie met a wild student of the law, an amorous adventurer from the provinces. And in this haunt where every student and his mistress mingle their candles for one brief moment and then pass on each with his half-light alone, Julie and her lover set up house for a time and then went off each in a different direction—he to the provinces to practice law, she into the richer quarters of Paris to practice love. But these fly-in-the-night Bohemians left behind them a monument of genius to mark forever their indiscretion. For in October, 1844, Sarah was born.

II

JULIE VON HARD rose from a millinery shop to the salons of the greatest titles in France. She wore a pearl for every professional tear of love that she shed. Her pretty head remained unvexed either with the cares or with the duties of motherhood. She placed her baby with a nurse on a farm in Brittany and promptly forgot all about her. The nurse in time married the janitor of a tenement house in the Parisian slum and took along the child to live with her in her new home—a single stuffy, dark and ill-smelling room. She put Sarah, together with the dirty socks and underwear of her husband, into the wash tub and scrubbed them all at the same time. When the child grew older, she was assigned to the task of scrubbing all the floors in the building for an education. She played in the dirty, unsavory alleys of the neighborhood. Her first language was seasoned with the spicy obscenity of the slums. She was pale and thin and anemic. At the age of five she was dangerously close to tuberculosis. An abandoned, fatherless and motherless little waif. The nurse had written many letters to her mother, and had received not a single answer. Money for the child had ceased to come in. But one afternoon the sister of Julie, Sarah's aunt who also, like Sarah's mother, had achieved success in her love affairs, drove up to a neighboring house on "professional" business. Sarah, who had seen her aunt on several similar occasions, was playing in the gutter when the carriage arrived. As she stepped from her carriage, the magnificently gowned lady turned at the sound of a sharp little voice. "Tante Rosine! Tante Rosine!" And a little girl rushed up to her in excitement with two big tears like diamonds in her eyes.

The lady drew back uncomfortably. But the sharp little voice pursued her. "Take me away, Tante Rosine! They suffocate me, these walls—always these walls. Take me away, Tante Rosine! I want to see the sky again, and the flowers! . . ."

A crowd of people had gathered at Sarah's outcry. And Aunt Rosine, to avoid further embarrassment, hurried the child indoors and asked the nurse for an explanation. And all the while the little girl, shaken with sobs, screamed: "Take me with you— take me with you! I shall die here!"

It was the desperation of a pathetic little soul fighting for its life. But what could Aunt Rosine do about it? It was of course unthinkable for her to take this drab and sickly little child of the slums back to her apartments and her lovers. And so she tried to put her off. "I will come and take you home tomorrow."

But Sarah knew that Aunt Rosine would not come back tomorrow. Slowly she went to the window and watched as her aunt stepped into her carriage and very daintily daubed away a tear with her lace handkerchief. And then, as the carriage started off, Sarah hurled herself through the window down to the pavement below. She fell just a few feet from the carriage. The broken little body was taken home to her mother.

III

As a result of her fall, Sarah remained an invalid in her mother's house for two years. She was scarcely able to step down from her bed. Then she grew gradually stronger. Seven years old now, but as yet she could neither read nor write. Her mother decided to send her to a boarding school. It was a good way to get rid of her again.

When Sarah came before the principal of the school, she was too bashful to say a word.

"A very stupid child, you see," Aunt Rosine explained to the principal.

"I don't know where she got her stupidity," added her mother with a sigh. "I'm sure it's not from *me*."

But a teacher of the school said kindly, "She has your eyes, Madame. So intelligent!"

Thereupon her aunt and her mother kissed her fastidiously and drove away. Julie went home to have another baby.

What *could* be done with this strange little waif? Hardly had she been placed at the school when word came to Julie that Sarah got into fits of temper which left her feverish for days. Julie frowned between her kisses for her latest lover. She took Sarah from the school and deposited her in a convent. Here the child would not *dare* to carry on.

For two years all seemed well. And yet—"Do you know, Monsieur le Duc," said Julie to her lover, "the child is always in some passion or other. If it is not a passion for evil, it is a passion for good. She has become a religious fanatic ever since she was baptized into the Catholic Church. She wants to be a nun." The Duc de Morny and all the other members of Julie's circle roared with laughter. Sarah could never be a nun, really. Three times before she had reached fifteen she was suspended from the convent for her bad behavior. Once she fainted at a school ceremony and played dead until the Mother Superior was beside herself with anxiety. Then she opened her eyes. It had all been a joke. An unruly child. She spent all her leisure reading forbidden books and eating bonbons that the janitor smuggled in to her. One evening she led six other girls down from the dormitory window and over the convent wall on a ladder of twisted sheets. And the following noon they were discovered throwing rocks at the horses of the King's guard. They had learned always to expect the unexpected of her. They caught her flirting with a young dragoon who had tossed his plume over the wall. And when the nuns tried to stop her, she clambered over the wall in her nightgown and hid in the chill darkness until she almost caught her death of cold. This was the final straw. When she came out of her fever, she was told to leave the convent for good.

What is to be done with this wild madcap of fifteen? "She is thin, weedy, shock-headed, and suffers from a violent cough that shakes her body into paroxysms. She has dark rings under her eyes which show only too clearly that her anemia has not been conquered." Ah, but this anemia, this bloodless transparency, has it not a charm of its own? "Her pallid complexion gives to her face a species of extraordinary beauty which is enlivened by the extraordinary play of expression in her eyes as she talks. Her features reflect every change of mood, and her moods are many."

Many moods—and not a single plan for the future. She likes painting, has quite a talent for it. But *that* is no career for a young girl. Her father, now a successful attorney, has left her a sum of money to fall due when she is twenty-one—provided she gets married. But Sarah does not want to marry. One suitor asks for her hand, and she says no. Another proposes, and she empties a glass of champagne over him. A vicomte offers her his lands and his title, and she slaps him in the face.

A family council is held. And when a decision is reached, Sarah is summoned. "My child," observes the Duc de Morny, "we are at our wits' end. We are going to send you to the Conservatory for actresses. Maybe there's a chance for you on the stage."

Sarah's face grew livid with anger. "I don't want to be an actress!" she cried.

"Listen to her—she doesn't want to be an actress!" mocked her mother. As if it mattered what *she* wanted. "I tell you I shan't waste another penny on you after you're twenty-one!"

The Duc de Morny tried to pacify Sarah. "My child," he said not unkindly, "your mother and I will take you to a performance at the Comédie Française tonight, and you shall see for yourself what a really fine profession we have chosen for you."

Sarah, hard-eyed with suspicion, was led to a box to witness her first play. "Not so bad after all!" And then her family overwhelmed her with books on acting and with plays by Corneille and Racine and Molière—to read and to study in her preparation for the Conservatory. She had only nine weeks in which to prepare—a course which ordinarily took eighteen months. At the end of her preparatory work she was introduced to Monsieur Auber, President of the Conservatory, who advised her never to get stout, to open her o's and to roll her r's, and to aim at a life that would be serious as well as happy. And then, after much rehearsing and memorizing and scolding and prompting, the great day of the examination arrived. As she left for the Conservatory, her mother dismissed her with the parting shot: "You're too stupid to be much of an actress, but it will keep you out of mischief."

Several of the girls ahead of her have finished acting out the scene they have chosen for the judges. Sarah's name is called. She mounts the platform, deathly white, and makes a curtsy. "I shall recite the poem of the two pigeons."

"Come now, Mademoiselle," snaps one of the judges gruffly, "have you not prepared the lines of a play? One acts here; one does not recite fables."

At last she feels at home. She has been crossed. *"I shall recite the fable of the two pigeons!"* she shouts, as her eyes flash fire.

And then the judges recognize in her the true temperament of an actress.

IV

SARAH distinguished herself at the Conservatory—not in acting, but in making friends. Through the influence of some of these friends she was engaged, upon her graduation, by the Comédie Française—the foremost theater in Europe.

SARAH BERNHARDT

Her first appearance on the stage was a failure. The critical notices were extremely unfavorable. She took poison and hovered for several days between life and death. When she recovered, she explained to her shocked friends, "Life was useless; I wanted to see what death was like."

She was a great tragic actress everywhere, it seemed, except on the stage in these early years. She was morbid to the point of an artistic passion. She fell deeply in love with an undertaker's assistant but refused to marry him when he would not permit her to be present at an embalming. Between the hours of her rehearsals she visited the cemeteries of Paris and sat among the tombstones like a sister of the departed.

An untamed young woman with the temper of a tigress. In one of her quarrels she slapped the face of the oldest and most respected actress at the Comédie Française. And then she resigned, throwing her career to the winds rather than to beg forgiveness. She disappeared from Paris, and the next news her friends heard was that she was seen in Spain attending the bull fights and making love to a red-faced matador.

None of those who wished her well—or who wished her ill—could keep up with the life she was living. At eighteen she was the toast of every table in the cafés. She had a love affair with a prince of the French Empire and bore him a son. And still she was unable to find herself.

Her lover repudiated her together with her baby. She went from stage door to stage door with the child in her arms. She found employment at the Gymnase; she resigned in a fit of temper; she flirted at the Port St. Martin. She had entered into a liaison with a leading actor at the Odéon, the theater next in importance after the Comédie Française, and was offered a part in a new play. Once again her début was a dismal failure.

And no wonder. "She has the head of a virgin and the body of a broomstick," remarked Alexandre Dumas who was in the audience. He might have remarked more truthfully, "the head of a virgin and the body of a lightning rod"—a body that absorbed the electricity of the universe.

Twenty-two now, still a failure but no longer confused. She had a child and a passion to make good—and a golden voice. Painfully, scrupulously, she learned the technique of her art and gave her voice the chance it deserved. She strained every nerve and fiber of her delicate body to her will. And within two years she was famous.

V

SHE scored her first great success in François Coppée's *Le Passant,* a play which ran in Paris for more than a hundred nights. She played a command performance before the Emperor Napoleon himself at the Tuileries. And many of the critics who had been ranged against her were now eager to beat the drum in step with her rapid advance. They discovered that her slender figure and fuzzy golden hair no longer were a liability but a heaven-sent gift. They declared that her mannish hips were divinely appointed for the masculine role that she played. The young author of her play went into a rhapsody about her. "What can I say of Sarah so slight, so slim . . . of Sarah luckily unpossessed of the haunches and thighs which make the usual impersonation of male parts so unrealistic and, indeed, so offensive . . . of Sarah with all the suppleness, the lightness, the grace of a young man!"

And the critics, when they heard these words, nodded a fervent *Amen.* "You cannot praise her for knowing how to say verse," wrote one of them. "She is the Muse of poetry incarnate. Neither intelligence nor art has anything to do with the matter; she is guided by a secret instinct. She recites verse as the nightingale sings, as the wind sighs, as the water complains, as Lamartine used in the old days to recite verse."

And as for her pale features? "She is a bit of smoke, a breath of the mist—a fugitive vision of delicate features under a shower of hair and a cloud of lace."

And now a mass of legends began to grow up around "Our Sarah"—as the poets and the artists of Paris called her—though she was scarcely old enough to be legendary. She was not a woman at all, it was rumored, she was a boy masquerading in woman's clothes. A high minister of state had called upon her and was received in her *cabinet de toilette* where she happened to be taking a bath. She had given five hundred francs to a blind beggar because he resembled a former lover. She went around the streets challenging men to duels. She smoked cigars and drank strong drinks. These, and many similar fantasies were circulated about her in the salons and the streets.

Sarah reveled in this publicity—and tried to outdo her legends. In the life of an actress, the bizarre is the real. Not content with being called anemic, she painted her face a chalk white. Not content with being told by the doctors that she had but a very short time to live, she made herself a coffin of rosewood with silver handles and had herself photographed in it with her eyes closed and with her hands crossed. It was her way of proving to Death that she could outstare him. She placed the coffin by her bed so that it would be the very first thing to strike her eyes upon awakening; and she had it carried along with her wherever she went. Often she slept in it. When guests came, she served tea upon it.

A creature of contrary moods. To offset the frailness of her appearance, she surrounded herself with a number of ferocious animals. A wildcat, two lion cubs and a tiger cub often accompanied her to the theater and raved in her dressing room during the performance. A huge dog guarded her apartment and he howled like Cerebus at the gates of hell. And because people shouted their praises of her acting, she showed them that she could paint and model and write novels also, and with almost equal skill. She made portraits and busts of her friends and had her work exhibited at the Beaux Arts. She wrote a play which was a huge success, she wrote a novel which was not a huge failure, she studied medicine and she became highly proficient as an anatomist. She was one of those geniuses to whom "true recreation is in reality a change of work."

She worked and she loved and she conquered. The names of her lovers and her flatterers "read like a biographical index of the great Frenchmen of the nineteenth century." And the one critic who had held out most stubbornly against her acting was once invited into her dressing room and came out of it her adoring slave.

VI

SHE WAS NOW the leading actress at the Comédie Française. Within these "sacred walls," one was expected to interpret the classics of Racine and Corneille and never to speak above a hushed whisper before the statue of Molière. Sarah was temperamentally "as well adapted to the official atmosphere of the Comédie Française as Whistler would have been to the Royal Academy." Imagine Beethoven spending his life as first violinist in a symphony orchestra devoted to an all Haydn and Mozart program, and never daring to play a note of his own! A genius must make noises and sounds that the fastidious do not like. The directors of the Comédie Française did not like the kind of life Sarah Bernhardt was leading or the kind of publicity she got. But when the Comédie Française visited London, the British audiences went wild over Sarah's acting. It was for Sarah they called, not for the Comédie. On the opening night, driven into a state of hysteria by the tremendous ovation she received at her entrance, Sarah played her role of Phèdre like an "intoxicated goddess"; and when the curtain fell, she dropped to the floor in exhaustion and vomited blood. The next day, against the doctor's orders, she slipped out of bed and took a carriage for the theater. For that evening she was scheduled to appear in another play. She fainted three times in her dressing room. Half-drugged with opium, she went through her part in a semi-stupor, leaving out an entire scene in her excitement. But she played the rest of it so poignantly that the other actors discolored their grease paint "with the rivers of tears that they shed."

Off the stage she insisted upon taking her illegitimate son, Maurice, to the most exclusive parties given by the most exclusive set of London. And always she demanded to be introduced as "Mademoiselle Sarah Bernhardt and her son."

This was not according to the classical tradition. The management of the Comédie soundly berated her for her "indiscretion" —and she resigned.

"You are deserting," her friends said to her.

"You are mistaken," she replied. "I am only changing barracks."

She had tested the true strength of her powers and she dreamed of future possibilities of emotional tragedy far beyond the range of the Comédie. She would manage her own theater, select her own dramas, give her own interpretations, always experimenting, daring, shocking—and triumphing.

VII

SHE MADE A TRIP to America in order to introduce her art to the New World. And the inhabitants of the New World came in throngs to see this amazing Frenchwoman who had set the affairs of Europe spinning so dizzily that "mountains danced minuets."

The press, however, was ominous. The critics complained that her repertoire was filled with plays too indecent to be shown on the American stage. There was one especially—a piece by Alexandre Dumas fils—*La Dame aux Camélias*. It was the story of a consumptive *fille de joie*. "Shocking, positively shocking!"

When Sarah arrived in New York, her managers advised her not to play this piece. "It has a bad name?" she said. "Very well, I shall change its name. You may announce on the billboards that I am playing *Camille*."

The puritans had effectively timed their diatribes against this play. The theaters were packed at every performance. When the play reached Chicago, Sarah Bernhardt's manager wrote to the bishop: "Your Grace, whenever I visit your city I am accustomed to spend four hundred dollars in advertising. But as you have done the advertising for me, I send you two hundred dollars for your poor."

Camille was a sensation. The death scene of the *fille de joie* became a classic. No one had ever played a death scene like Sarah. And though most of the people in the audiences knew no French, they saw the pallor on the face of the actress, felt the pain of her fragile health—and wept bitter tears at her tragic death.

And many of them recalled a story they had read in the papers, how one night in Paris during a performance the call boy had rushed through the dressing room shouting "Bernhardt is dead! Bernhardt is dead!" And the manager and the players had discovered her in her dressing room—stretched out on a couch and clothed in white with her hands crossed—a red stain on her chin and four huge candles at her head and her feet. And then when the stage manager rang down the curtain, announced the tragedy to the audience and came back to the dressing room to give vent to his grief, Sarah sat up, kicked over the candles, and roared with impish laughter, "This is my greatest role!"

And so "this Queen of Attitude, this Princess of Gesture, this Lady of Energy" played on. At her final performance in New York, fifty thousand people came to the stage door to bid her farewell. And when she reached France again fifty thousand people came to the dock at Le Havre to bid her welcome.

In Paris a number of the critics continued to abuse their

enfant terrible. But an equally large number of the critics called themselves *Saradoteurs*—"worshipers who doted upon the Divine Sarah."

She leased a theater of her own and named it the *Sarah Bernhardt Theater.* Here she attained to heights unprecedented —both in popularity and in scandal. She had become *the* theater, *the* dramatic art, *the* institution of tragedy and comedy—and *the* reckless giver of herself to her equally reckless lovers. She toured Europe with eighty trunks of her personal finery, and she thrilled the people with the melodramas of Victorien Sardou. Nothing happened to her by halves. "She nearly died at Genoa; at St. Petersburg the public went mad about her, the students took the horses from her carriage, and paid outrageous sums for seats at her performances; at Kiev she was insulted, and at Odessa she was stoned." She made stolid Scandinavians faint at the grief she displayed on the stage. She drew praise from the Prince of Wales, an insult from the German government and tears from the Russian Czar. And when she returned to Paris, she wore the jewels from many a crowned head in Europe.

"Sarah? Ah, yes, she is the devil's best triumph." After her love affairs with the greatest men of Paris, she married the greatest rascal of France. He was Jules Paul Damala, as handsome and as unprincipled as Satan himself. "He had the manners of a gentleman and the mind of a chimpanzee." He was a morphine addict. For seven years of married life he gave Sarah "instead of a wedding ring, a cross to bear." And then, wasted away by his dissipations, he died.

But if this was an epic defeat in love, she scored one epic triumph. When she was over fifty, she entered upon her last great *affaire de cœur*—with Edmond Rostand—an experience which left a golden flush of memory behind it. When she first met Rostand, he was an obscure poet. She took him for long drives in her carriage, and he read to her his poetry and his plays. Their souls unfolded and met. And out of these meetings the

Rostand of gold and glory, of *L'Aiglon* and of *Cyrano de Bergerac* was born.

VIII

SARAH BERNHARDT played a thousand death scenes, but her strength as an artist always cheated death. She worked fourteen and fifteen hours a day while strong men in her company crumbled. She quoted as her motto the proverb, "The better is always the enemy of the good." She must live on and on, assuming more and more roles in the great gallery of human drama—young men and old women, sinners and saviors, Hamlet and Tosca, Theodora and Joan of Arc—always aiming at tomorrow's better after yesterday's good. And thus, to the amazement of her doctors, this sickly actress with the immortal soul went on living for seventy-nine years.

In her middle age she fell while playing Hamlet and phlebitis developed in one of her legs. In the years that followed, her leg shrank, and the resulting pain turned her every hour upon the stage into a martyrdom. The poison in her leg crept upward. And in 1915, when she was seventy-one, the doctors warned her that an amputation would be necessary. She submitted cheerfully to the ordeal. From then on she sat in a wheel chair to play her roles. But the glory of her voice and the magic of her art were not diminished by her limited range of acting. On the contrary, they assumed a greater tragic intensity than ever. Men's minds went back to the struggle of another titan, the great deaf music-maker whose suffering had given a similar impulse to the free spirit of the world.

In her wheel chair she was carried (1916) to the soldiers at the front. She entertained them in the trenches. And with tears for *La glorieuse Blessée—the Glorious Invalid*—they went inspired into battle.

When death found her at last in 1923, she was exploring a

new medium for her art. She had made a contract with an American moving picture producer. But she was too ill to leave her house; she played in her sitting room. And when she could no longer sit in a chair she whispered, "Film me in bed."

And then the final death scene. After a performance with which she was particularly satisfied, she was accustomed to remark, "*Le Dieu était là.*" And as we look back upon the grand performance of her life, shall we not also say, "God was there"?

ISADORA DUNCAN

Important Dates in Life of Isadora Duncan

1878—Born in San Francisco.

1895—Began her professional career as a dancer in New York.

1904—Established her first school for the dance in Berlin.

1913—Lost her two children in an accident in the Seine River.

1921—Invited by the Soviet Government to establish a school of the dance in Moscow.

1922—Married Sergei Essenine.

1927—Died in an automobile accident at Nice, France.

Isadora Duncan

Isadora Duncan

1878–1927

Aₙᵧ ᴡᴏᴍᴀɴ who would write the truth about her life would write a great book." But what woman ever wrote the truth about her life? No feminine Walt Whitman or Rousseau as yet has given us her *Confessions.* "For the great moments of joy or agony all women remain strangely silent." Yet perhaps there is no one truth and no one life that we live, but rather a headful and a heartful of visions. "There is the vision our friends have of us; the vision we have of ourselves; and the vision our lover has of us." There is no single personality. "Where can I find the woman of all my adventures? It seems to me there was not one, but hundreds—and my soul, soaring aloft, was not really affected by any of them."

She was born in San Francisco by the sea, where she received from the rhythm of the waves her first ideas for the movement of the dance—and her first temptation to rebel against a world that permitted the blasphemy of tenement houses side by side with the freedom of the sea.

For they were poor, this family into which Isadora was born. Her mother was a music teacher—an Irish Catholic who had turned atheist and who had begun to read Bob Ingersoll when her husband became unfaithful to her and caused a divorce. She was a mother with a soul full of beauty crushed in a hypocritical world. Her four little children were rebels even before they understood the meaning of the word *rebellion*.

Isadora was a rough and tough little brat. When she attended grammar school, she was sophisticated beyond her years. The waterfront was the scene of her fairy tales; the cursing, uncouth stevedores were her fairy princes. Her frankness was refreshing. One day, when her teacher asked the girls to write compositions on their lives, the entire class was in an uproar as Isadora got up to read *her* contribution:

"When I was five we had a cottage on 23rd Street. Failing to pay the rent, we could not remain there but moved to 17th Street, and in a short time, as funds were low, the landlord objected, so we moved to 22nd Street, where we were not allowed to live peacefully but were moved to 10th Street."

But there was a pretty dream that kept the child from falling. Isadora Duncan was a dancer. How she could dance! When she was only six, she collected all the babies of the neighborhood who were too young to walk and taught them, while they sat on the floor, to wave their arms. As she grew older, parents sent their children to her "school of dance"; and business became so profitable that she decided she might as well leave school— "which is only a waste of time when I can be making money."

What an amazing conglomeration of strange moods and magic the angels had patched together and called Isadora! Once her mother took her to a ballet teacher for dancing lessons. When he told her to stand on her toes, she asked, "Why?" "Because it is beautiful," he answered. "No, it is ugly and against nature!" She walked out of the room and never came back.

Restless as a savage, and unpredictable as a mermaid who dwelt at the bottom of the sea that stretched out of Frisco "to the end of the world." Hardly had she arrived at her teens when she nagged her mother into launching her upon a professional career. Scraping together all the money she could lay her hands on, Mother Duncan bought the train fare to Chicago—"the city of the theaters." Isadora went before the managers and danced in a Greek tunic. But the managers shook their heads. What sort of dancing was this, anyway? One of them, however, the director of the Masonic Temple Roof Garden, was somewhat impressed. He was looking for a dance number "with skirts and frills and kicks . . . Now you might do the Greek thing first, and then change to the frills and the kicks and it might be an interesting turn."

And so Isadora got her first job—the beginning of a round of routine living and disappointed seeking and hope and hunger and despair. If only someone would let her dance in *her* way. "Please, Mr. Wiggins, Please, Mr. Smithens, Please, Mr. Daly. This isn't just another dance . . . I have a great idea to put before you." Into office after office she came, bristling with her little Irish uptilted nose. Hers wasn't just an ordinary dance. "I have discovered *the* dance. I have discovered the art which has been lost for two thousand years. You are a great theater manager, but there is one thing lacking in your program which made the old Greek theater great, and this is the art of the dance—the tragic chorus . . . I bring you the idea that is going to revolutionize our entire epoch . . ."

Our entire epoch, Mr. Jones, nothing less! . . . City after city she visited, braved desk after desk, year after year, smile after smile of disbelief. "I shall lead the way until All America will be dancing to the music of Walt Whitman's singing, a hundred million Americans hand in hand . . ."

The managers chewed upon their cigars and shook their heads. Occasionally she would get a flicker of a response. "Well, I have a little part in a pantomime that I am putting on in New York in October . . ."

And then the final catastrophe. The hotel in which she and

her mother had checked all their belongings burned to the ground. Not a suitcase was left.

She found herself now in a situation very similar to that of her pioneer ancestors, the Duncans who had crossed the plains in a covered wagon. Nothing to keep them home, and a vision to lead them on. She secured passage in a cattle boat that was sailing from the New world to the Old. And to her friends who looked on with amazement she flung back the words, "I am going to my glory."

II

AT THE OUTSET, London gave her little to eat and not much of anywhere to sleep. But there was the National Gallery where she might feast her eyes. For days she stood before the *Venus and Adonis* of Correggio, munching her penny buns and watching the "motions" of the artist's strokes. Her brother Raymond, a lean ascetic wrapped in the lore as well as in the dress of ancient Greece, had come along with her to London, eager to share her experiences and her dreams. They were going to spin the world around over a period of two thousand years, these two, back to the reign of pagan beauty when the gods were not above making love to mortals, and mortals were not beneath understanding the love of the gods. Who were these two Americans—a couple of lunatics living out of time? Raymond buttonholed people who had come to mourn their dead in the graveyard at Chelsea and harangued them on Plato's philosophy of the soul. And Isadora tried to teach them that life was not a solemn procession but a dance.

After a time Isadora received invitations to dance in her Greek tunic at dinners and at lawn parties. Artists and actors who attended these parties declared that the Winged Victory of Samothrace had come back to life. One young Scotch poet flung away his Keats and knelt at her feet. Never in his life, he said, had he experienced such beauty.

[232]

a planet where angels dwelt. "He was in a state of exaltation from morning till night. Even with the first cup of coffee, his imagination caught fire and sparkled. An ordinary walk through the streets with him was like a promenade in Thebes of Ancient Egypt with a superior High Priest."

When her child was about to arrive, she went to live on the shore of the North Sea. Her house was perched on the sand dunes, surmounting a flight of a hundred stairs. And here her little golden-haired daughter Deirdre was born. And Isadora went on dancing over the hearts of men.

She sailed up the Nile with a millionaire lover who fathered her second child, Patrick. The wine of love was sweet to her in Egypt! But she passed on restlessly to other arms.

Nietzsche's super-woman of a world to come! Her art, her love, her religion, were her children, the two little offshoots of her being, the souls of her soul. As soon as they could walk, she taught them to dance; and when she accompanied them on the piano they danced like little birds in their white tunics. They had none of the conventional upbringing of other children. They were as natural, as unashamed as two sunbeams after a morning shower. They would be the leaders in the dance for all the little children, she said. For the hope of the world rested in little children. And around these children she would build a school based upon the sheer magic cult of the natural expression.

One afternoon the nurse took Deirdre and Patrick out for an automobile ride. Isadora kissed the window at the spot where her little girl only a few moments earlier had pressed her chubby nose. And then she stretched herself out on a couch to rest for her evening dance engagement. And suddenly somebody came into her room with a terrified face. "Your children are dead."

The sedan in which the chauffeur was driving the children had plunged into the River Seine. The nurse was found holding them to her breast as if pathetically trying to shield them from the rising water.

Hundreds of students gathered all the white flowers they could find and scattered them over the bushes in Isadora's garden. The children were carried home, dressed up in their finest clothes, with their golden locks combed and curled as if they were merely sleeping and would wake up with the sun. "They lay hand in hand like two smiling angels."

Isadora knelt. No tears now! "They never had a sorrow and we must not be sorrowful today. I want to be brave enough to make death beautiful—for all the other mothers who have lost their babies . . ."

But when they placed those little bodies in the crematorium, she knew that all life was a dream. For otherwise, who could ever survive its tragedies? She cut off her hair and cast it into the sea. Thereafter her dancing became even more beautiful. She danced with arms that cradled nothing. "Who will ever forget the gesture of the maternal arms that cradled nothing?"

To find a new purpose in living, Isadora went with Raymond to Albania where there were reports of great famine among the people. She helped him to organize a group of women who wove upon the seashore, and she taught them to sing in unison with their weaving in order to relieve the monotony of the work. They made a great number of beautiful couch covers and Raymond sold them in London. With the income from these sales, he bought food for the hungry weavers and their families.

Isadora returned to Paris just as the drums of the First World War began their deathly music.

The government took over her dancing school and transformed it into a hospital. She was very sick. They carried her down in a stretcher to show her what was being done. The plaques and the paintings that she had hung so triumphantly on the walls were taken down, to be replaced by Jesus on the Cross. "Dionysus had been completely crushed. This was the reign of Christ."

IV

THE WAR YEARS PASSED. A revolutionary government was established in Russia. When Isadora heard the news, she slipped into the red tunic in which she had frequently danced the *Marseillaise* and danced for the coming of the second dawn of the world.

In 1921, the Communist government invited her to come to Moscow and to open a school for dancing children. She accepted the invitation with wild enthusiasm. Here at last was the meaning of life. She was not interested in the politics of the new order, but she was tremendously interested in the opportunity for a new art. Now at last she would demonstrate to the world just what she had meant with her dancing. She had never aimed to create a diversion for the stage but a religion for the people. There was nothing narrow about her art. It was a method for building a better humanity—the highest intellect in the freest body. This had been the secret of the democracy in ancient Greece. She would make an Athens out of Moscow—an Athens out of the entire world! And she would work with children. She would never again feel the loss of Deirdre and of Patrick. She would teach the children of the workers and the peasants to express themselves beautifully, and they in turn would teach other children until one day all the children of mankind would dance to the hymn of Beethoven's Ninth Symphony into a reality of human brotherhood. As she rode to Moscow, the words kept singing in her mind—

"Be embraced in love, ye millions. Here's a kiss for all the world! . . ."

And Isadora, carried away with her new-found happiness, came before the Russian workers in her red tunic and danced the *Marche Slave*. With a sublime gesture she rose from her knees, straightened her back and broke the chains of humanity, as the workers cheered and sang the *Internationale*.

But the world was not quite ready for her art. The Russian

government was too busy feeding its workers to worry about their dancing. Her school for the creation of international beauty came to an untimely end.

Well, that was life. *C'est la vie!* Among the artists for whom she danced, she espied a golden head. She rushed over and knelt at the feet of Sergei Alexandrevitch Essenine. He was a leader among the young poets of the revolution. He played the balalaika divinely. He was a tall and powerfully built peasant and he couldn't understand a word of this woman's language. A magnetic woman in flaming red who seemed like Venus until you looked up into her face. It was a face lined "with years and tears." He was only twenty-seven, almost young enough to be her son. He was fascinated by her—and he despised her. But she was insistent. She learned Russian sentences to say to him—pretty love-words. Stupid, middle aged, genius-woman! "Ya gotova chevolat cledi tvoik nog," she said softly. "I worship the very ground you walk on."

"Go to the Devil!" he said.

She ran her fingers through his hair. She had great plans for him. She who had vowed that she would never marry any man married him. She made a will bequeathing her entire property to him. And he kicked her, struck her in the face, tore up the pictures of her children—and wrote the poetry of genius!

Isadora took him out of Russia. She dressed him in expensive clothes and caused a sensation all over Europe wherever she traveled with this "mad Russian bear."

They came to America. Isadora danced at Symphony Hall, in Boston, waved a red scarf over her head and shouted hysterically, "This is red. It is the color of life and vigor. You were once wild here. Don't let them tame you!" Whereupon several old ladies and gentlemen rose from their seats and hurried out, though the young students of Harvard remained to cheer.

And at all the press conferences Sergei shook his head vigorously. "Isadora, I am hungry—eat—eat!"

Back in Paris again, at the Hotel Crillon. Sergei, in the heat of reciting his poetry, threw the chairs out of the window, smashed the furniture, the mirrors and the doors, seized his supper guests by the neck and hurled them around the room. He was taken into custody. Isadora begged for him, explaining that he was a very sick man and that he suffered from epileptic fits. They released him on the promise that he would leave France immediately. The couple crossed into Germany. The following night Sergei sat in his hotel suite tenderly playing his balalaika as the innocent light of a blue heaven looked out from his eyes. Then suddenly he rose to his full massive height and went on another rampage of furniture smashing. He was placed in an insane asylum. Once more Isadora came on her knees to the authorities to beg for her beloved Sergei. She could not live without him. The beautiful boy was misunderstood, she explained. He was a dear delight—so sensitive, so passionate. She promised that she would control his moods.

They set him free; and before long he was brandishing a pistol and threatening to shoot her. Night after night she rushed from her bedroom and sought another room in order to save her life. And the following morning he would come and kneel before her —and she would stroke him tenderly.

On the way to Moscow Sergei smashed the windows of the train. He robbed his wife of her money and tossed handfuls of bills around in the cafés. He carried a suitcase with him constantly and he threatened to kill anyone who took it away from him. But one day he left it at home; Isadora opened it and found in it her dresses and her other belongings which she had been missing.

She knew that the world was growing disgusted with the spectacle of a middle-aged artist holding on desperately to her "genius hoodlum." Even her former devotees were ready to say, "Enough of Isadora Duncan, this modern Circe with her litter

[239]

of swine, enough of the henna dye that cannot hide the gray streaks in her hair!"

What was the meaning of this reckless disposal of the gift of her body given her by the gods? "In the midst of all this filth and this purity, this fleshly body filled with hell fire, and this fleshly body alight with heroism and beauty, where is the truth? God knows, or the devil knows—but I suspect they are both puzzled."

She fled into the interior of Russia to escape from her husband. He slashed his wrist, wrote a last great poem—in his blood—and hanged himself.

V

IN 1927 SHE WENT TO NICE and set up a studio on the seashore. She had been born by the water. Once she had said that all the great events of her life had taken place by the water. The end of a cycle was approaching.

She was almost fifty now. Sometimes at night she stood on the balcony and the invisible washing of the sea played soft music to the illusion that she was once more Isadora, the priestess who had emancipated all the women of the world, the genius at whose feet sat every poet and musician and sculptor of her generation. Yet even at such moments the price of her triumph was too much for her to bear. Yes, she was still a beautiful lady when the spirit moved her to be beautiful.

And thus she sat one evening—movingly, painfully beautiful. A friend had brought a little boy, her three-year-old son, to the table. The child, pointing to Isadora, said suddenly, "What is the matter with the beautiful lady?"

She jumped up from her chair and vanished into the garden to conceal her emotion.

The next morning she took aside a very close companion. Her lips were white as she spoke. "If you have the slightest affection for me, *find me a way out,* Mary. I cannot live, I cannot pretend any longer in a world filled with golden-haired children!"

And that evening—it wasn't much different from any other evening—she was preparing to go out for a ride in a new sport roadster that she was planning to buy. "We shall get this auto, Mary; and after a wonderful trip through the vineyards—yes, I must go through the vineyards once more . . ." She wrapped her red silk scarf around her neck—that scarf in which she had danced so often to the song of the liberation of mankind. "Good-bye," she called to Mary as she settled in the car. "Good-bye, my friends, I am going to my glory."

As the car started, Mary saw the fringes of Isadora's scarf trailing carelessly on the ground. And then the car stopped suddenly. The fringes of the scarf had caught around the axle of the rear wheel. Isadora's head was pulled sharply over the side of the automobile. When they cut the scarf from her neck the head fell forward. A single rotation of the wheel had strangled her. The hand of God had been merciful and swift.

They brought her warm body into her studio and wrapped it in her dancing tunic and stood in silence—half waiting for her to rise and to perform the miracle of her art before them once again. For they were little children in faith—these pagan followers of hers. And when they saw the flames of her funeral pyre consume her body, they whispered, "Good-bye, Isadora, and *bon voyage* to Olympus . . . How the great dead poets will thrill at your entrance!"

SCHUMANN-HEINK

Important Dates in Life of Ernestine Schumann-Heink

1861—Born in Lieben, near Prague.

1878—Became a member of the Dresden Opera Company.

1882—Married Ernst Heink.

1896—Gained a worldwide reputation at Bayreuth in Wagnerian roles.

1898—Made her American début in Chicago.

1898–1904—Reached the height of her career with the Metropolitan Opera Company.

1917–18—Sent five sons to the war.

1932—Made her farewell appearance at the Metropolitan Opera Company.

1936—Signed a moving picture contract at the age of seventy-five; died in Hollywood, California.

Her most famous operatic roles include:

Carmen; The Witch (in *Hansel und Gretel*); Orpheus; Fricka (in *Die Walküre*); Erde (in *Das Rheingold*); Ortrud (in *Lohengrin*).

Schumann=Heink

Ernestine Schumann-Heink

1861–1936

IT WAS while Ernestine was studying the mass at the convent in Cracow that Mother Bernadine discovered she had a beautiful voice. She was very much excited. Nothing like this had ever happened in her house of God before. She sent for Ernestine's mother.

"I know it will sound peculiar to you, Frau Roessler," said Mother Bernadine to the wife of the Austrian army officer who was blessed with too many babies and too few guldschen. "But I ask you not to neglect this little child of yours. God has given her a voice. She will be a superb actress or a great singer."

"But we have no money—nothing. We move from barrack to barrack when my husband gets his orders. We are alone in the world. How can we do anything for her?"

"Surely something will happen. Where God has given such a talent there will always be a way."

Later at home Papa Roessler's face grew terrible when he heard about the conversation. What was all this nonsense? The daughter of Hans Roessler of His Majesty's troops to become an actress, a bad woman? "I will never be able to face the men in the regiment!"

"But, Hans, not all singers are bad women," ventured his wife timidly. She was Italian born. And singing was not so dreadful to her. "Adelina Patti is a singer. And look how the whole world is at her feet."

So it was a new day for this little Austrian girl who had been brought up to hear only the clanking of the spurs and the oaths of the soldiers. They bought Tini Roessler a piano for one dollar in Austrian money. Ach, how old it must have been! The strings were cracked. The hammers were loose. Tini tied the broken parts together with a piece of twine, sealed them with wax, and somehow music came.

Papa Roessler and his family were always on the move, wherever army orders took them. They had left Lieben—where Tini was born in 1861—for Cracow, and now they came to Gratz. And one day mother was going to have another baby. She was hungry. She had a new life to feed.

"Tini," she looked up from the bed and her eyes sparkled, "I would so like a piece of Swiss cheese to eat. But how can we afford it? That is a luxury for rich folks."

"I will go and get it, mother."

But when Madam the Grocer found that Tini had not the money to pay, she roared, "Be off!" And the little girl's eyes filled with tears.

"Please, Madam, my mother is sick. And she is going to have another baby and she wants that cheese now."

"No, you can't have it. Off with you!"

"Please, Madam, if you give me the cheese I will sing and dance for you. I will sing a folk tune of Hungary and dance a folk dance. And you may call all your friends and neighbors to sit on the stairs and watch me."

And when the irresistible little beggar saw the old woman's

[246]

face light up at the suggestion—"But please, Madam, may I bring the cheese home to my mother first?"

"No, you little devil! If I gave you the cheese you wouldn't come back to dance. You must dance first . . ."

After this episode, Tini performed frequently for the common folk—and for the great society people, too. She curtsied so prettily that everybody gave her whatever she asked. It was a fine thing, this curtsy. All the little girls of the Austrian army officers learned the etiquette of the court so that they might at any time be ready to meet the Emperor and the Queen. But learning these manners had not been so much fun as playing with the horses in the stalls of the barracks.

Or singing to people. Even the opera stars who passed through Gratz heard about the little girl with the homely mouth and the pretty voice. One of these stars, the great Materna, heard her sing and spoke sternly to her mother. "Her voice is good enough, to be sure, but she would make an impossible appearance. She is short and stumpy and undernourished." And then, turning to Tini—"Don't cry, child. You will get along somehow, for you have a great big heart."

Once, after many singing lessons, came a day that Tini would never forget. She stood on the platform dressed in a black frock made over from one of her mother's old dresses, a red rose in her hair, and sang her part in the chorus of Beethoven's *Ninth Symphony*. And for her share in the performance she received six dollars in Austrian money. Mighty spirit of Beethoven. Poor little Tini. What a glorious pair they made that day! Two dollars she gave to her mother. With the rest she bought a big cage for her canary and the first pair of white curtains ever to adorn the windows of her mother's parlor.

II

AT FIFTEEN, despite the prophecy of Materna, Tini became an opera singer. The Director of the Royal Opera at Dresden was charmed by her voice, yet he signed her at a ridiculously low salary. And he gave her only minor roles. She boarded with the widow of the organist who had played at the State Cathedral. She lived on sausages and beer, "to make her strong." In addition to her duties at the opera she sang in the church, at the vespers to which only a few old ladies came—"and they were mostly deaf." But other ears, perhaps, were listening to the development of her beautiful contralto voice—the ears of the kings and the queens of old who lay in their vaults underneath the nave. Their bodies were preserved at freezing temperatures for the glory of the state. And the chill penetrated to the air of the upper church and froze Tini and all the other choir folk as they sang the mass. Tini was mightily impressed by the pageantry of the kings and the queens—those above ground as well as those below. And once, when she was about to sing the mass as the royal couple entered the church and began their procession down the aisle, the little girl stopped in awe and forgot her pitch. Then she caught up with the other singers, in a loud clear voice, singing the wrong notes. The aged conductor struck her over the shoulder with his baton. "You damn little goose," he whispered hoarsely as the tears rolled down his face. He was a very old man. He didn't know but that each note he conducted might be his last. What right had youth to ruin this farewell song of old age!

Youth was rash to the point of tragedy. At eighteen, Tini carried on an entire season's flirtation with a handsome young grenadier across the footlights of the opera stage. But then her eyes turned from brass buttons to the simple manners of the secretary of the opera company. And though her contract expressly disallowed it, she married this secretary—Paul Heink.

She lost her job. He lost his. Then babies began to come.

When three children had been born, Paul Heink got sick of the adventure and left her. The rest of the world was little concerned with her singing and her babies. From stage to stage she went begging for a chance. And the director of the Hamburg Opera Company hired her contralto voice for ten dollars a month. On this she was to live with three children!

But in the little German world of music there were two sensitive superfolk who discovered her. At the great Brahms Festival she sang before the composer himself. And when it was over, Brahms stormed the breakers of applause and clambered up to the platform with the conductor Von Bulow to kiss her hand. When Von Bulow looked into her face, he knew that this woman had not eaten a full meal for months. Casually, as if it couldn't mean a thing to a great singer, he invited her home to dinner. And at the end of the dinner he said, "You can go home to your children and take something for them, too. Now what is your favorite dish?"

Her eyes wrinkled up suspiciously. Was it quite proper to say? "Sauerkraut! Sauerkraut mit Schweinefleisch!" she stammered.

He cleared his throat. "Now listen, Madam Heink. You are to come to me twice a week for dinner. Eat as much as you want. And there will always be plenty for you to take back to your children."

Then the fourth baby came. She paid the midwife two and a half dollars for her services.

Meanwhile Von Bulow had been called to other engagements; and in the midst of a busy career he forgot the little singer whose life he had saved. And the world of music forgot along with him. It was as if she had never sung at the Hamburg Festival at all.

Her lot was pitiable. Her husband had incurred a mountain of debts which the German law compelled a wife to pay. But she could not meet them. The sheriff took away her furniture.

And one day in November she decided she could stand life no longer. She took her baby in her arms, gathered her other children, and set out for the railway tracks. She had learned what time the train would come. It would all be over in an instant. The wind sent a shiver through her frame. The children, cold and bewildered at the look in their mother's eyes, began to cry. The whistle sounded. She bent over the children, pulled them close to her, and the tiny hand of her little August froze her. Little Lotta lifted her face up to her mother's and cried, "Mama, I love you. I love you. Take me home!" It was as if the train had already struck her. She turned back.

Then she came into the office of Herr Pollini, the director of the Hamburg Opera, as if she were not a woman but a flame. "Herr Direktor, when I asked for a chance at a first contralto part, you laughed and said I would make a good comédienne. When I asked for a chance at life you ridiculed me almost to death. But let me tell you this: I have come back to life. I shall be the first contralto of your opera. I shall be the first contralto of Germany. I shall be the first contralto of the world!"

III

FOR A WHILE LONGER she burned turf in the oven to keep her children warm and sat all day on benches in the park waiting for appointments. And then success came. The prima donna of the Hamburg Opera had given way to a temperamental outburst just before a performance of Carmen. She refused to sing.

The manager turned in his desperation to Madam Heink. "Can you sing the role without a rehearsal?" he asked.

"I'll sing it if I die on the stage," she replied.

She had no costume. Members of the cast collected odds and ends in which to dress her up. One gave her a veil; another, a skirt; still another, beads and a comb to wear in her hair. She was a patchwork of things too large and too small. Her shoes pinched her feet; when she walked, she winced. No opera story ever written was more fantastic than this reality. But when she commenced to sing, all the incongruities about her dress and her person were forgotten. The audience realized but one thing—that here at last a perfect voice had been fitted to a perfect part.

She was signed to a ten year contract and she settled down to learn the minutiae of her art. She cast into the rubbish heap all the rules of acting and of stage technique and did things her own way. "Ah, du lieber Gott," she pleaded whenever her managers tried to point out to her the "right way" to act. "Don't tell me any more—leave me alone, please. I must do it my own way, or else I am no good."

Her managers fumed at her—and were spellbound. "You are no good, but you are a genius all the same."

She married again, this time to an actor, Carl Schumann. They had met at a New Year's party. He gave her a pair of white gloves for his wedding present. "These gloves are unsoiled, Tini, and thus will I keep you and hold you in my heart until my last hour."

She went to Bayreuth, the musical shrine of Richard Wagner, and sang her roles in *Tristan, Das Rheingold, Lohengrin,* as they had never been sung before. For the German composer had written music of triumph through pain that was the very music for the soul of this stout little Austrian Frau. More plaudits were showered upon her—and more babies came.

When her baby Ferdinand was born, she received a contract for an opera engagement at Leipzig. She tore herself away from her infant, made the trip to Leipzig and commenced rehearsals for the performance of *Lohengrin.* Suddenly she began to suffer the pains of a nursing mother. She had not reckoned with nature. Her breasts were full; they tortured her. In rehearsal an actor accidentally hit her in the chest and she screamed aloud with agony. A chorus woman who heard how desperately she needed her baby came and told of an agonizing pain in her own heart.

For she herself had a child two months old, and she was too weak to nurse it. "I cannot afford a wet-nurse, and my baby is dying of slow starvation." The poor woman's voice trembled on the verge of tears. "Frau Schumann-Heink, would you—perhaps——"

"Why, of course, mein liebchen! Bring the baby to the theater, and I will nurse her right after I get through singing. And bring her every day. I will do everything I can to save her."

The opera, too, was saved. Every three hours she fed the child. She never forgot the look in the mother's face. Years later, when she sang again in the theater at Leipzig, a gray-haired lady brought a young girl of sixteen to her dressing room. "Here she is, Madam Schumann-Heink. My daughter—the starving little baby you nursed in this very theater years ago. Do you remember?" The girl wept as the great singer took her in her arms.

In 1898, Frau Schumann-Heink came to America. It was the fulfillment of a dream that had dominated her for many years. When Mr. Grau, the manager of the Metropolitan Opera House, wired her to come on contract she took passage with her husband for her American début.

When her ship arrived in New York, Mr. Grau greeted her—and paled. Confound this woman! She was always with child at the wrong time. "Madam Schumann-Heink, this is terrible! I am afraid you will never be able to fulfill your contract with the coming of a new baby."

"Nonsense," she replied. "What do you know about babies? I have had them many a time. I shall sing regardless. You will see how I shall sing!" This big good-natured woman was a law unto herself.

But when she walked upon the stage in Chicago, the entire cast stood breathless because of that little life that was only a month away from making its own début. Could she sing and kneel as Orturd in *Lohengrin?* They didn't realize the strength and the big stout heart of an Austrian mother. She carried the whole world within her as she sang. The audience shrieked and stamped hysterically. Twenty times the curtain rose and fell. Then she made for her dressing room, broke down and sobbed like a little girl. People rushed in with flowers and telegrams. Grau was shouting and dancing like a maniac. "Heinke, you are a wonder! You are a wonder!" he kept on saying. "Baby or no baby, you *are* a wonder, Heinke!"

It was the greatest night of her life. It was a Yankee night. When her baby came, her eighth, the cheers were still in her ears. What could she name the baby but George Washington Schumann? The German consul paid her a visit, clicking his heels. "You cannot call this baby George Washington," he declared. "That is against the German law."

"You old fool," her husband retorted, "it is not against the *American* law. We are in America now. *George Washington Schumann it shall be.*"

IV

"I LIKE AMERICA . . . I'm naturally a regular old tramp—just like my dear father in that way—a soldier. A soldier of fortune. That is what every artist is . . . I like change and adventure."

In London she went to parties in Regent Park, played baccarat with the Prince of Wales. She sang for the aged Queen Victoria who took her face in her little old hands and kissed it. But after every season abroad she came back to the land of her youngest son. In Europe there were dynasties of kings to betray the age of a woman. "I was born under King So-and-so." But a woman in a kingless country was only as old as the present moment. At one time she felt that she was growing too "dated" in her operatic roles and so she plunged into light opera and musical comedy. Her friends were outraged at this "terrible comedown." But what was so dreadful when the heart was in your singing? Even when the heart bled? One night, while she was preparing to sing in Boston, she got a wire that her husband was dead. She swung ever so slightly as she read the news—and then went on with her song.

But a song could not prevent the world from going into flames. In 1914 there was a mutual outburst of murder on the part of men who once had loved the selfsame music. The oldest son of Madam Schumann-Heink went off to fight the war for the Kaiser; her four other boys took arms in the trenches opposite. The white-haired little mother, who with her divided sons was the very symbol of the tragedy of Mother Nature, went on singing.

News came to her that her oldest son, August, had been killed in action. And she went on singing.

She came to the soldiers in the army camps and the hospitals, bringing a song to their parched senses. Once she had sung to cheering houses, to audiences that rose in a hurricane of applause. And now she sang Brahms' lullaby to boys who lay silent and suffering, who had no arms to applaud with, and only eyes to show that they were her audience. She sang *Holy Night* to men who had been only boys the morning before the battle. And when she finished, she trembled before the mightiest gift she had ever received. For these stranger-boys called her "mother." They were her George Washington Schumanns everywhere. And the song they most frequently requested was the *Rosary,* a song of divine love. For they were all lovers.

I tell each bead unto the end—
And there a cross is hung!
O memories that bless and burn,
O barren gain and bitter loss.
I kiss each bead
    And strive at last to learn,
To kiss the cross, sweetheart,
To kiss the cross.

[254]

V

WHEN THE WAR WAS OVER, Madam Schumann-Heink sang on.
The American people turned her into a goddess of their household. And one new medium especially lent itself to her voice—
the radio. Over national hook-ups she sang on many important
occasions. She became the "official *Amen-maker* of each Christmas Eve and every Armistice Day." She sang and talked to audiences in her funny accent, talked garrulously and lovingly of
many small things. And every audience belonged to her. "Many
another prima donna has successfully mothered a large family,"
wrote a journalist of the early nineteen-twenties. "But she has
gone further. She has mothered audiences, mothered towns and
cities, mothered the American Expeditionary Force, and now
she mothers the American Legion."

"Mother Schumann-Heink" was not only emotionally but
physically expansive. Every pound of lovability in her had its
corresponding pound of flesh. And America took this adorable
and stout little woman, "from the top of her kindly old head
down to her mannish shoes," to its heart. As she sang the *Star-
Spangled Banner* in her quaint foreign accent, Americans removed their hats and wept. It was for *this* that humanity had
been fighting and dying these five thousand years—for the right
of all men to dare the anthem of freedom even though many of
them had been brought up in circumstances in which they knew
only imperfectly its language. A magnificent bargain! The American people taught to Madam Schumann-Heink the secret of
their democracy. And the singer taught to the American people
the secret of her art. And both these secrets were revealed to
have sprung from the selfsame source. For the common man
doing the common deed can be a great artist of the soul. And
the great artist who is to sing or to paint for eternity must reach
the soul of the common man. The spirit of the good singer is
little different from the spirit of the good citizen. Both must be

[255]

ready to die for their idea. Madam Schumann-Heink said to all young students of the voice—or was it Pericles speaking to a school of young orators?—"I touch my hearers only then when I myself feel. No misery that comes to us in life is lost, for it turns to our good. In his study the performer may laugh, weep and shudder; but when he appears before the public, 'the many-headed terrible,' his self-command must be complete. He studies in uncertainty, but he expresses himself with certainty. All that he has thought out, all the emotions that have been aroused in him and analyzed by him will never be lost. The performer must have such a perfect command that he can be aroused from his bed at midnight and electrify the public with his voice." An artist is a soldier of fortune, but a soldier of duty as well. God gave him genius to wear as a uniform in the service of his fellowmen.

The years got heavy for Schumann-Heink, but she who had borne eight children could bear eighty years if need be. At sixty-five she embarked on a twenty-thousand-mile "farewell tour." And when she had finished singing her good-byes at so tremendous an effort, she kept on singing as if nothing had happened. At seventy she told her friends, "I have come at last to youth!" Before the world could protest her defiance of the very laws of nature, she began a vaudeville tour traveling over the continent in a bus. What a comedown from Grand Opera! What an upsurge from grand old age! Bluntly she asked her critics—in her broken English—whether there was not a worldwide depression? Her concert receipts had dwindled with the stock market crash. She needed money. And so she had decided to tour with Roxy and His Gang, and the devil himself would not stop her from doing four vaudeville performances a day. Yes, she would keep on singing those heart-catching songs as long as there was breath left in those stalwart lungs. Until she lost her voice she would go on singing. "I want to die singing—not on the stage, not in a manner to create a disturbance, but quietly with a song

[256]

on my lips." A robust drinking song, perhaps. For was she not the daughter of her soldier father—even at seventy?

She broke both her ankles, put on stoutly-laced shoes and went on. Her song threatened to outlast life itself. No other opera singer had kept her voice so long. Her voice had tied two generations together, from the gay nineties to the gray thirties. She seemed to have learned the secret of some lost chord that sounded on eternally outside the concert hall of time. The manager of a large moving picture company in 1935, in his search for a successor to Marie Dressler, signed this "starlet" of seventy-five to make pictures. And she set to work with as much enthusiasm as though she expected to live forever. And people throughout the United States half expected to hear that rich contralto voice until time itself should be forgotten.

But one day she suffered a hemorrhage of the throat. They took her to a Hollywood hospital. The beloved little "Heinke" was ready to make her début in the Opera House of Valhalla.

JANE ADDAMS

Important Dates in Life of Jane Addams

1860—Born at Cedarville, Illinois.

1881—Graduated at Rockford Female Seminary.

1889—Established Hull House in Chicago.

1915—Presided at the International League of Women at the Hague. Became president of Women's International League for Peace and Freedom.

1931—Shared, with Nicholas Murray Butler, the Nobel Peace Prize.

1935—Died.

Among her more important books are the following:

1902—*Democracy and Social Ethics.*

1907—*Newer Ideals of Peace.*

1909—*The Spirit of Youth.*

1910—*Twenty Years at Hull House.*

1912—*A New Conscience.*

1916—*The Long Road of Woman's Memory.*

1930—*Second Twenty Years at Hull House.*

Jane Addams

Jane Addams

1860–1935

IN 1881, JANE ADDAMS entered the Women's Medical College
in Philadelphia. The following year, however, she was obliged to
give up her scientific course. A painful curvature of the spine had
laid her low. The doctor prescribed an extended trip to Europe
as a necessary relaxation after her rigorous work in the laboratory.
This trip was destined to transform a still-born physician into a
successful philosopher.

It was in the slum district of London that the urge first came
to her to devote her life to the practice of social philosophy. One
midnight she was sitting on the top of a sight-seeing omnibus
that made its way slowly through the putrid garbage and the
human derelicts of the East End "lower depths." A huckster's
truck had stopped at the curbstone. A rabble of men and women
were crowding around it—tattered rags, haggard faces, raucous
cries—haggling for the handful of vegetables that the huckster
was auctioning off. The decayed leftovers of his day's business to
the decayed leftovers of the human family. Lurid haze of the gas
lamps, nauseating odor of death. A cabbage unfit for human
consumption was tossed into the hands of a bidder who held up

the "extravagant" sum of tuppence. The "lucky possessor of the prize" took the cabbage to the curbstone and began to devour it, filthy and worm-eaten and raw, while his less fortunate companions held up their hands to bid for the less expensive remnants. "The final impression," writes Miss Addams, "was not of ragged, tawdry clothing nor of pinched and sallow faces, but of myriads of hands, empty, pathetic, nerveless and workworn, showing white in the uncertain light of the street, and clutching forward for food which was already unfit to eat."

Throughout her subsequent stay in London, Jane Addams "went about the city almost furtively, afraid to look down narrow streets and alleys lest they disclose again this hideous human need and misery." A new course in her education had begun. A daughter of the rich, she had beheld suffering from the top of an omnibus. A sister of the poor, she would climb down from her height in order that she might alleviate some of this suffering. On that midnight tour of London, Jane Addams had joined the "universal fellowship" of mankind.

II

When Jane was three and a half years old, she came home one afternoon from her play and found a dark flag hoisted above the gate posts of her front yard. "Why did you put that flag up there?" she asked.

"A great man has died, child. The greatest man in the world."

"What was his name?"

"Abraham Lincoln."

On another occasion when her father was sad and she asked him the reason for it, he told her that Joseph Mazzini, an ardent lover of mankind, had just died. Years later when she wrote of her childhood, Jane Addams observed: "I was filled with pride that I knew a man who held converse with great minds."

Her Quaker father was all in all to her—her mother had died

when Jane was two years old. He was a remarkable man, this state senator and prosperous miller of Cedarville, Illinois. Scrupulously honest himself, he had the utmost faith in the honesty of his neighbors. He never locked the front door of his house. Jane was sorry she had been born a girl. She was so anxious to grow up to be a great man, just like her father. She tried in every way to imitate him—even to the extent of rubbing the crushed grain in the mill in order that she might acquire his flattened miller's thumb. If ever she told him a falsehood, she couldn't go to sleep at night until she slipped out of her room and went down the dark stairway "to confess at his bedside."

He was so good and big, and she was so naughty and small. "Dear God, why didn't you give him the kind of a child he really deserves?" When strangers came to the Sunday School, she prayed that they wouldn't associate "that handsome man with this homely kid." On the way to church she deliberately walked with her uncle, who looked less distinguished than her father and was therefore more suitable company for her own insignificant little self.

Yet one day her father dissipated this feeling of inferiority on her part. It was on the main street of a neighboring city. She had come there with her uncle to do some shopping—a crooked, homely, shy little thing. Suddenly a tall, distinguished gentleman in a high silk hat stepped out of a bank. "Good Lord," she thought, all a-tremble, "I hope he doesn't recognize me in front of all these swell people!"

But he did. Removing his silk hat and swinging it wide, he made a courtly bow to his daughter. "How do you do, my dear?"

Jane could hardly speak for embarrassment. "Aren't you ashamed of me, father?" she managed to blurt out.

"Why, you foolish child, I'm proud of you!"

III

So HER FATHER was proud of her! Well, she would try—oh so very hard!—to make herself *worthy* of his pride. She read the Lives of Plutarch—for every one of these lives that she could report on, he gave her five cents; and she studied the lives of the signers of the Declaration of Independence—for every one of *these* lives that she could report on, he gave her *ten* cents. But of all the lives, she believed, her father's was the greatest. Throughout his legislative career, she tells us, nobody ever offered him a bribe, "because bad men were instinctively afraid of him."

At seventeen, Jane Addams entered Rockford College. And here she learned to worship two other heroes beside her father— the sage of Concord and the Carpenter of Galilee. So strong was her adoration for Emerson that "in a state of ecstatic energy" she polished the shoes of one of his mere disciples who delivered a lecture at the college.

The essays of Emerson introduced her to the service of beauty. The parables of Jesus converted her to the beauty of service. Every Sunday morning she read a chapter of the New Testament in the original Greek. *Here* was a life to emulate! She would dedicate herself, like her Master, to "the soothing of the afflicted and the healing of the sick."

But her lesson was not yet fully learned. She wanted to take up a "superior" profession, to become a doctor, to lend a helping hand from above. It was not until her sight-seeing tour of the London slum that she glimpsed the first true vision of her career. The golden words of Emerson, the Golden Rule of Jesus, pointed to the equal dignity of all the children of men. Descend from the heights of your vanity and take your place among your fellows. Enlist as a soldier in the common ranks of sorrow.

Her vision took gradual shape until it became crystallized into a definite resolve. This happened on a day when she was visiting a bullfight at Madrid. The sight of the slaughter and the brutal applause aroused within her a wave of resentment. Altogether too much of suffering was due to human cruelty. She must do something to put an end to this cruelty. At last she had found a concrete job for herself—to build a "cathedral of humanity," a practical school of moral readjustment.

She had set herself a difficult task—a *terrifying* task. But she went bravely ahead. "Always do," she said, "what you are afraid to do." And so, inspired by her vision, she returned to Chicago eager to undertake her new work in spite of her fear. The metropolis of the midwest had grown from eight thousand in 1844 to one million in 1889. And seven hundred and fifty thousand of them were foreign-born. Chicago was a world in miniature—Englishmen, Germans, Jews, Negroes, Russians, Poles, Irishmen, Italians, Frenchmen, Scandinavians, Bohemians, Swiss—these were only a few of the many nationalities that had been swept together by the winds of chance into a single community. Here were the human factors for the working out of the problem of Practical Democracy. These immigrants had brought with them the misunderstandings and the prejudices of a hundred countries. But they had also brought the hopes and the dreams of those countries. If Jane Addams could teach them to discard their prejudices and to unite their dreams, a new day would dawn in America—a day of justice and beauty and vigor and joy such as the world had never seen.

This, in brief, was her vision. Her life's work was to humanize and harmonize American society, and by the American example to harmonize and humanize the society of the world.

IV

SHE CREATED a new philosophy—the philosophy of social service. What this world needs, she said, is not an "uplift" of the immigrants by the Americans, or of the lower classes by the higher classes, but a mutual interdependence between alien and native and between class and class. The rich and the poor alike, she felt, had much to gain from their contact with one another. The rich were in need of greater sympathies; the poor, of greater comforts.

In order to establish this abstract theory upon a foundation of concrete fact, she rented a small house on Halsted Street—the Chicago desert of industrial sandstorms and material want. She called this little oasis of hers the *Hull House,* after the name of its architect and former occupant. A pleasant, homelike place, with wide halls, open fireplaces and a piazza on three sides. She furnished the rooms with "luxurious simplicity"—handsome tables, inviting couches, bookcases and pictures and bric-à-brac she had picked up in Europe—everything, in short, that a wealthy person would want for a private home, and then she threw open the doors and extended a gracious welcome to the public. "All ye that are hungry, come in and eat. All ye that are weary, come in and rest."

At first the foreign population in the surrounding district—"a whirlpool of filthy and rotten tenements, foul stables, dilapidated outhouses, dives, saloons, flies, vermin and children"—looked with suspicion upon this "strange American woman" who had moved into this "strange swell house" in their midst. What did she want of them with her invitations? They weren't used to this sort of thing from the "better" classes. There must be some trick behind that smile of hers. Best to stay away from that house.

A few daring souls, however, ventured into the house and found, to their astonishment, a human being like themselves. This Lady of Halsted Street was no "slummer" but a friendly neighbor. They spread word about the miracle, and little by little the "visits" to the Hull House became more frequent. One day a Greek woman rushed in with a sick baby in her arms. Her husband was away at work. She had no money for medicine or for doctors. Miss Addams secured a doctor and bought the medicine —and the child was saved. On another occasion an Italian bride of fifteen ran away from her husband to the Hull House because he had abused her for having lost her wedding ring. Miss Addams summoned the husband, gave the couple a friendly talk and the price of a new wedding ring, and husband and wife went off happily hand in hand.

Before long, the Lady of Halsted Street had become the unofficial counsellor of the entire district. "This rich lady is almost as nice as a poor woman." No service in behalf of her neighbors was too humble for her to perform. She not only *superintended* the work in the house, but lent a ready hand—and what was even more important, a willing heart—in the *doing* of the work. She opened a day nursery for the babies of mothers who worked in the factories. In this nursery she fed and amused and cared for the children at the daily rate of five cents per child. "This, you understand, is no charity. You are paying good money for the service." For the older children she started a kindergarten—also at five cents a day—where they were not only fed and amused, but educated as well.

As for the fathers and the mothers of these children, Miss Addams studied their needs and found that they suffered from a twofold hunger—they were starved materially and aesthetically. And so she provided Hull House with a soup kitchen and an art gallery. And—in spite of the sneers of her wealthy friends at her "Quixotic" ideas—she was not surprised to find that her art gallery was more popular than her soup kitchen. It was not for bread alone that the European refugees had come to America.

V

THE "SUBMERGED TENTH" of Chicago paid Jane Addams the highest honor. They accepted her into their "exclusive" proletarian society. She was one of them, the genuine article, a Good Neighbor.

Slowly the little homestead on Halsted Street grew into a big community center. The idea of the Good Neighbor policy spread to other cities. Similar settlements of International Americanism sprang up throughout the country. Houses of Friendship. Play rooms and work rooms and study rooms—crucibles for the softening of the human heart into a more sympathetic understanding. "If only the various races could understand each other, there would be no need for hatred or war." Jane Addams undertook the "daring" project of interpreting the races to one another. And this led to an amusing but highly satisfactory incident. One evening the Irish women invited the Italian women to a reception. "But the Italian women," writes Miss Addams, "were almost Oriental in their habits. They stayed at home and sent their husbands . . . The Social Extension Committee of the Irish women entered the drawing room to find it occupied by rows of Italian workingmen. They were quite ready to be 'socially extended,' but plainly puzzled as to what it was all about." Fortunately the Italian men had a lively sense of humor. They proceeded to take the place of their wives in the entertainment of their Irish hostesses. "Untiring pairs of them danced the tarantella, their fascinating national dance, they sang Neapolitan songs, one of them performed some of those wonderful sleight-of-hand tricks . . . and all of them politely ate the 'quaint' Irish refreshments." The entertainment was a huge success. The Irish and the Italians were mutually delighted to find that "these strangers are just like other people." They thanked Miss Addams for having "cured" them of their "sick prejudices" against one another.

Jane Addams was the American pioneer in melting the differences of a hundred nations into a single democratic ideal. And now that the foundations of her "dream-cathedral of interracial understanding" had been laid, she went on to the next stage of her building. She wanted to see a happier race of children and a more peaceful race of men. And so she began to work for the abolition of child labor and for the establishment of universal peace.

[268]

In the eighteen-nineties, child labor was one of the blots upon
our civilization. The imposing structure of American prosperity
had been grounded partially upon the backs of little children. In
the industrial centers the children were overworked and underpaid
to an appalling degree. Seven-year-olds were in some instances
driven fourteen hours a day at four cents an hour. In the needle
trades, the children were often set to work at the age of four or
five, pulling out the basting threads from the garments which
their parents were sewing. Many children were maimed and not
a few killed by the machines at which they were compelled to
work before they were old enough or strong enough to handle
them.

Jane Addams had a motherly instinct for children. She made
their cause her own cause. In spite of her numerous other duties,
she undertook a searching investigation into the problems of child
labor. Indeed, she became America's foremost authority on the
subject. Calling to her standard the various women's and workers'
organizations in Illinois, she engineered the enactment of a state
law (1903) forbidding "the employment of children under sixteen years before seven in the morning or after seven at night,
and the employment of children under fourteen after six at
night." This "Jane Addams Measure" was a good beginning in
the right direction. It became a model for similar measures in
other states. "If you want to prevent the evils of child labor,"
wrote the Boston *Journal of Education,* "get a copy of the law in
your state and send it to Jane Addams. She will tell you, better
than anybody else in the country, if it is wise."

Jane Addams, in her wisdom, planned not only to take the
children out of the factories but to keep them out of the streets.
"In one short block," a contemporary investigator had observed,
"I found seventy-five children playing in the gutter." Miss Addams undertook to remove them out of the gutters and into the
playgrounds. Thanks to the maternal pity of the childless "Saint
Jane," the children of Chicago to this day enjoy one of the most

extensive and best managed playground systems in the United States.

Her sympathies, "warm as the sunlight, wide as the world," were always on the side of "the eager and the thwarted"—the children whose opportunity for education and whose capacity for happiness had become prematurely stunted. In her profound and tender book, *The Spirit of Youth*, she calls attention to the divine fire that lies smoldering in the heart of every child. "We may either smother this divine fire, or we may feed it. We may either stand stupidly staring as it sinks into a murky fire of crime . . . or we may tend it into a lambent flame with power to make clean and bright our dingy streets." And in thousands of cases she personally tended the divine fire into a lambent flame. Children of many nationalities came into Hull House. Some of them passed under her guiding hand through the universities into the professions. A greater number of them went into the ranks of business or labor. But nearly all of them became transmuted through the magic of her personality into better and happier and more understanding Americans.

Understanding Americans—this was the ultimate object of her life. Peace through understanding. The natives of many countries were migrating to America to become mutually acquainted. And here they learned to know and to admire one another. *And to cooperate with one another.* Though they couldn't follow the language of one another's tongues, they could interpret the language of one another's hearts. They realized that their Old-World intolerances and hatreds and misrepresentations and fears were nothing but the bugaboos of foolish children. Russians, Frenchmen, Italians, Jews, Britons, Poles, Norwegians, Lithuanians, Czechs—all of them had the selfsame desire, the selfsame common yearning to feel the warm clasp of brotherhood between man and man. Jane Addams demonstrated the fact that in America a hundred quarrelsome nations could be united into one friendly family. Why couldn't she teach this vital lesson to the nations of Europe, of the entire world? She proceeded to initiate this new teaching. She became one of America's most passionate advocates of international good will. It seemed at times a hopeless task, but she never lost heart. Not even in 1914, when she saw the world engulfed in hatred. Nor in the following years, when she saw the collapse of civilization and the resurgence of barbaric dictatorships and fascist threats. For she had the patience of the true philosopher. She knew that the way to human understanding is precipitous and painful and slow. But she also knew that under the proper guidance the world would learn the lesson in the end. For she was sustained by that undying faith in the "continuity and interdependence of mankind."

In order to share her undying faith with her countrymen, she delivered a series of lectures against the barbarity of the military aggressors and their financial retainers. One of her friends described her as she looked on the platform: "A smallish, dark-faced woman, gentle of manner and soft of voice . . . She is dressed in a tailor-made suit of grayish blue . . . She is slightly stooped as she stands with her hands clasped behind her in a way touchingly childish, looking out at her audience . . . Her face is sad, though the eyes are luminous, and the lips adapt themselves readily to smiles." A frail and pallid wisp of a woman, insignificant in size, tremendous in magnetic power. And still modest to a fault. At one of her lectures the chairman introduced her as "the first citizen of Chicago, the first citizen of America, the first citizen of the world!" When she stood up to speak, she raised her hand to silence the applause. And then with a bashful smile, "I'm sorry, but your chairman must have meant somebody else."

VI

FOR A TIME during the (first) World War she stood almost alone. For she had foreseen, and she had dared to proclaim, that our entry into the war would lead to no permanent peace. They stigmatized her as being pro-German. She was, of course, nothing of the kind. She was merely pro-human. And so she was "spiritually exiled" from her fellows for the sin of loving them too well. This spiritual loneliness was to her like an imprisonment. For she was by nature a woman who could not exist in solitude. Her very life needed the sustenance of social contact. She felt like an alien in her own country. Her very friends began to spy upon her as if she were a criminal.

But she took her blows, and went on proclaiming the new international ethics. "New ethics," she said in one of her speeches during the war, "are unpopular ethics." And in courting this unpopularity, she felt herself enlisted in a crusade no less sacred than the crusade of the enlisted men. The brave soldiers in the trenches were ready to die for war. The frail soldier in the Hull House was ready to suffer for peace. Theirs was the courage of an ordeal shared in comradeship. Hers was the heroism of a martyrdom endured in loneliness. Of the two kinds of sacrifice, which was the hardest?

When the war was over, she felt that her crusade was only begun. She had organized, before the war, an American Women's Peace Party. In the whirlwind of the war, this movement had been torn apart. But with the return of calm weather the threads had been gathered up again, and Jane Addams proceeded to weave them into a new and larger pattern. The American Women's Peace Party joined the Women's International League for Peace and Freedom, and Jane Addams became the president and guiding spirit of this league. "The dictators of the world will make you fight," she said, "but the women of the world will make you free." Half of her prophecy has come tragically true. But the other half, she was convinced, would at a not-too-distant date come *gloriously* true. In 1931 she shared, with Nicholas Murray Butler, the Nobel Prize for Peace. She donated her entire share—about sixteen thousand dollars—to the Women's International League. "The real cause of war," she said in making the donation, "is misunderstanding. Let this money be spent in the cause of international understanding." The understanding that the nations can live at peace if only they will unite to get rid of their individual aggressors.

This thought was like a refrain that ran throughout the symphony of her life. The children of the human family have been kept too long apart. The selfishness of their leaders has too long imposed upon their ignorance. They must be brought together, they must be educated, they must learn to know one another. "It is time," she said, "that we got better acquainted."

VII

IN THE SPRING OF 1935, she felt a sudden pain in the side. The doctors, suspecting a serious infection, advised immediate surgery. When the ambulance arrived to take her to the hospital, she begged her doctors to wait a few minutes. "I'd like to finish the novel I'm reading before I go. There are only a few pages left." And then, smiling through her pain, she added, "I'd hate to die without knowing how the plot came out."

"Nonsense! You're going to live!"

But when they operated on her, they found a malignant tumor. Four days later she died.

As she lay in state, her "family"—fifty thousand native and immigrant Americans—came to bid her Godspeed. And many of them wept, and not a few prayed, as they passed her coffin. For they were about to put away from their presence the all-embracing Mother of Men. As one of her "boys," a Greek workingman, expressed it, "Her no just one people, her no just one religion. Her all peoples, all religions."

And some of them thought they saw the faint, shy flicker of a smile on her face. "I'm sorry, but this good man must have meant somebody else."

EVANGELINE BOOTH

Important Dates in Life of Evangeline Booth

1865—Born in England.
1878—Joined the Salvation Army in London.
1904—Became leader of the Salvation Army in the United States.
1917—Sent the "lassies" to minister to the soldiers at the front.
1934—Chosen Commander-in-Chief of the Salvation Army of the World.
1939—Retired to her home in Hartsdale, N.Y.

Evangeline Booth

Evangeline Booth
1865–

SHE HAD MANY PETS to feed and play with. Nelson the dog, and the rabbits and the silk worm. And there was Papa, the best playmate of all. Papa was a busy man. People said he worked "forty-eight hours of the twenty-four." He was developing some scheme for the emancipation of mankind. But when he was home, he sang and whistled all sorts of tunes—when he wasn't bothered by his dyspepsia. Papa never took the stairs at a walk, like other folk. He surmounted them "in a single bound." A superb athlete —and tender as a woman. And so understanding! "Gossip to me a bit, children," he would say even if the most important visitor in the world were waiting outside his study to see him. And then Eva would tell him of the horrible thing that had happened that day. It was about Bramwell, that devil of a brother who wanted to be a surgeon. Once he had dissected the body of a mouse right in front of her. And now he had taken her doll and cut it open. When she saw the sawdust run out she began to cry. And Bramwell taunted her. "Silly, did you expect to have an operation without blood?"

There was one little creature strictly loyal to Eva. It was Nelson the dog, a retriever. Papa had named him after the great naval hero. But one day Nelson got himself into a very unheroic plight. He bit the arm of the parlor maid. And then he disappeared from his old corner and Eva could not find him. Papa took her to the city and showed her the amusements and tried his best to comfort her. On the way home he told his little girl marvelous stories about Welsh ponies. But where was Nelson? Eva would not be comforted. Then a present came for her—all wrapped up. And when she opened it she screamed. It was a beautiful rug made out of faithful Nelson. And Papa, to quiet her hysteria, ordered it thrown away.

Eva was the seventh of the Booth little immigrants from heaven. The snow was piled high when she arrived on Christmas Day, 1865. In the year of her birth, the Reverend William Booth made the gravest decision of his life. Having quarreled with the Methodists as to the best method for the saving of souls, he resigned from his pulpit and left his church.

His home became the headquarters for the "new church." It was in the exciting atmosphere of great ideas and of great deeds that Eva grew up. "We Booths are a queer people," William Booth had joked. And somehow Eva knew that they were a different people. Very often her father came home at night with his face a sea of blood. For the new folk he preached to had never been to church and didn't care for God. The heroism of those hours of preaching took hold of Eva. She arranged the dolls and the brooms of the kitchen and the cushions of the parlor into a congregation and then she climbed upon the table and preached to them. These strange souls, too, had never been to God. What a glorious thing it was to sing a hymn for them and to become a Salvationist! That was what her father called himself.

Salvationism was a new kind of spirit for which you suffered pain. Her brother Bramwell had given up his idea of being a surgeon and had followed his father into the streets. Then Ballington and Emma and Catherine and Marian followed. They wore red ribbons and sang hymns and shook tambourines. What sort of magic was it? She ran over to her mother and put her head in her lap, crying with breathless excitement. "Please, Mama, *I want to live the life.*" And her mother patted her head and said, "We shall see, my dear."

Well, if Bramwell and the older folk were putting broken people together again, there was no reason why *she* couldn't do likewise. She tossed her red hair and put a sign in her basement: "Dolls to mend." And she called upon all the little children in her neighborhood to bring their rag and wooden people who had lost their eyes or their legs or their noses, and she would make them as good as new.

It was her first crusade.

II

WHEN William Booth left his church, he wandered through a "wilderness of the spirit." And out of this wilderness he fashioned an army of the Christian Mission to preach among the "submerged tenth" of London society. He had in mind the work of the evangelists and the prophets who had sought to convert "radically bad men" into radically good men. He moved into a little shack for an office and organized soup kitchens for the poor of Whitechapel. For "we cannot feed an empty stomach on religion alone." And then, since he was convinced that the only way in which he could lastingly save a chronic drunkard was by giving him work—by transforming him from the moment of his conversion into a seeker and a saver of another chronic drunkard—he recruited his preachers from the defeated and the damned that he had rescued everywhere, and he whipped them into an army for the rescue of their fellowmen. "We shall take our preachers from the ale-taps and the skittle alleys and the public houses." He knew that the "half-starved, half-brutalized men and women he worked with, who would refuse to go to the ordinary places of worship, would be pleased like children by parades and uniforms." He knew that the roll of drums would succeed where the church bells had failed. He realized that the humblest kitchen maid adored the British Tommy. And so he modeled his church organization after the British army.

For his troubles he received nothing but nationwide abuse. He asked the wealthy for donations, and during the first year only nine thousand dollars were subscribed. He asked the poor merely to follow, and many of them pelted him with garbage and stones. Every conversion was consummated at the expense of his blood. The magistrates broke up his meetings and the street-corner hoodlums broke his bones. Again and again he was dragged off to jail. The proprietors of the taverns, enraged at his crusade against drink, employed all the legislative machinery of the nation to hound him out of England. The residents of the exclusive residential sections expressed their "mortification" at the army of ragged beggars who marched boldly through their streets, waving flags and beating drums to preach salvation. Who was this public disturber of the nation's harmony, with his rabble of guttersnipes and his jangle of hallelujahs? Was he a madman or a conspirator?

The intelligentsia of the nation were shocked by "the naked tears and the swaying and the praying" of this William Booth, the ringing of his tambourines and the exaggerated sentimentality of his "conversions"—all this "claptrap," in short, which they looked upon as a "terrible blow against the dignity of the human mind."

But William Booth was unperturbed. No general cares to win a campaign by default. And this general loved the feel—and the publicity—of a fight. Whenever his public meetings were broken up by the clubs of the police, he lifted himself off the ground and shouted excitedly to his battered, badgered little band, "Now is the time to have our photographs taken for the morning papers!"

III

WHEN Evangeline entered her teens, her moment had arrived. She shook the tambourine and carried her fiery red hair like a banner into the London slums. She dressed in the rags of the slum people, sold packets of matches and flowers in Piccadilly Circus just like all the other flower girls. And when she had passed her self-imposed courses in misery, she was able to deal more expertly with the miserable. She stayed with the sick and sobered up the drunk and brought food into the meanest larders. A siege of fever had almost laid her low. For a time she felt as if her scarlet hair was a burning flame. But she got well. Before long her father raised her to the rank of captain in the Salvation Army. The toughs of the East End of London had banded themselves together in order to protect her. On one occasion a policeman came upon her as she was preaching, tried to arrest her and seized her roughly by the arm. But her "bodyguard" beat the officer senseless to the ground. Eva saved his life, cheered him back to health in the hospital and won a "salvation policeman." Until he died he sent her letters in his large scrawl, signed— "Your officer."

She marched her followers into Torquay, the exclusive sea resort on the Devon coast, in the belief that no one was too rich to be saved. But the society folk did not want the Salvation Army on their premises. They instituted legal proceedings against her. Eva took the case into Parliament and fought successfully for her right to preach in public.

One day she appeared at the office of a coal mine and declared that she would like to go down into the shaft and speak to the miners. The superintendent looked amazed. "Why, even strong men hesitate to make the descent, my dear young lady."

But she insisted. She was lowered in a basket. At a crucial moment the connection broke and she was almost killed.

The "white angel," as she was called, feared neither danger

nor ridicule. Once, when she spoke at a meeting of "bums," an impressive looking man "with the face of a lion" slipped into the audience without revealing his identity. He was John Bright, the great reformer who preferred to solve the problems of the poor through politics rather than through evangelism. He had come to the meeting to scoff. Yet the high purpose in the speaker's voice held him spellbound. Here indeed was a crusader who bore the name of the first woman worthily—Eve, the *mother of men!*

When she was twenty-three, William Booth appointed Eva to the command of the entire "Army" in London. Fortune was at last favoring the Salvationists. Many Englishmen who disliked the hallelujahs had nevertheless come to realize that these Salvationists were aiming to feed three million folk who were not "so much *born* into the world as *damned* into it." They noticed that while Parliament was debating about the best measures for the feeding of the hungry, the Salvation Army was setting up soup kitchens. They began to see at last, walking in the uniform of William Booth, a great humanitarian. And they poured money into his coffers.

In the meantime, a number of the Salvationists had migrated to the New World. Eva sailed to Canada to lead the army there. When a host of "down-and-outers" rushed into the Klondike to seek for gold in 1898, she organized a nursing corps to go along with them and to share their hardships. She went among the docks of the fishermen in Newfoundland and made life easier for them. When refugees fled from the atrocities in Armenia and some of them landed in Toronto, Eva was waiting for them.

She crossed the Canadian border in 1904 to lead the army of Salvationists in the United States—a mighty organization that had grown out of a few casual meetings in a Philadelphia stable. At first the people she had come to save did not "cotton" to her. When she spoke at Cooper Union, she was obliged to enter by the fire escape since a large crowd had gathered at the door to prevent her from appearing.

But she stayed to succeed. There was so much work to do in this New World. Wherever humanity ventured to walk, it left a trail of mud. In the slums of America she had found the bitter bread of sorrow—leavened with the hope of a new world order. "To visit a slum in America is to come into contact with the passions and the vehemence and all the rough crude genius for human brotherhood."

Eva set about to refashion this raw material into real men. She established a number of societies—some of them with whimsical enough names—for men are but children and must be humored out of mischief. For prisoners she established the *Brighter-Day League;* for unmarried mothers, the *Out-of-Love League*. She created a *Suicide Bureau* with the object of saving the lives of persons who were planning self-destruction. Every one of her ideas took concrete form. "This world is full of people who . . . expound dogmas," she said. "My father had no objection to these people. He was always ready to make good use of their brains and their money and their influence . . . But," she added, "it is our special call to deal with life as an emergency. It is all very well for the botanist to peer at a nettle through a microscope. But nettles have stings. They have to be grasped and we never hesitate to grasp the nettle . . . You see, there are very many men to be saved . . . The vital step is to save them here and now, not by legislation or poetry for the future."

Under this inspired leadership to save men *here and now,* thousands of Americans joined the service of the Salvation Army. The officer of the highest rank received under thirty dollars a week. Those enrolled in the ranks were unable to smoke or to drink or to take part in any of the commonest amusements. Yet they were held together by a common sympathy in one of the most exciting of sports. "People spend huge sums of money on the breeding of horses, cattle and dogs, but the Salvation Army is an army of sportsmen who place the highest bets on the race that lost human souls will run. There are men who enthuse over

[*283*]

the culture of flowers and the collection of pottery and bronzes, but the Salvation Army are connoisseurs in the collection and the redemption of broken human lives."

There is nothing silly or childish in the belief that a human being can be changed. "There is no doubt as to the reality of life-changing. Countless people of all ages and races and religions have found this release to be a sound psychological fact . . . With moral and often with physical health regained, our mended derelicts rejoice in a new liberty . . ."

And in America especially did the psychology of salvation receive a sympathetic understanding. For the citizens of the democracy knew that laws alone, a bill of rights alone, cannot save mankind. Thomas Jefferson had pointed out the divine fact that all men have the right to be free. And Eva Booth was devoting her life to see that all men *accepted* their right to be free.

IV

WHEN WAR CAME TO AMERICA in 1917, Eva Booth took away the peacetime bonnets of her "lassies" and sent them to the Front in tin hats.

> *Tin hat for a halo!*
> *Ah, she wears it well.*
> *Making pies for homesick lads*
> *Sure is "beating hell."*

They went through shell fire and showed that they could share hell to serve a cup of coffee. Each doughboy kept his rendezvous of destiny with the ministration of a woman by his side. For a woman's true place was by the side of her man when the world was aflame. The "lassies" kept up a constant liaison between lonely sons and lonely mothers. And when the war was over, Woodrow Wilson pinned the Distinguished Service Medal on Eva Booth.

[*284*]

His war was over; but for her there was no end of the fighting, no such thing as an armistice. When a woman has a passion for mankind, it doesn't burn itself easily out. There were men hungry in India. She organized relief. There were men crushed in an earthquake in Japan. Again she organized relief. She traveled to England, Norway, Denmark, Sweden and France to see the other branches of the great army which her father had created and of which her brother Bramwell Booth was now the commander-in-chief.

She was getting to be quite old now. Sixty—yet her hair was still a defiant red. That was because of the blood-tingling life she lived. Do not be deceived by the slender girlish figure, the white blue-veined hands, the delicately shaded complexion. She was a hard encasement for a gentle soul. She never found the horse she was unable to ride. Her athletic prowess had become a legend to her neighbors. Every morning she rode her horse *Goldenlocks* down the highway past a cemetery for dogs as punctually as the church bells struck the hour. She took jack-knife dives into Lake George clothed neck to ankle. Once she swam four miles with a broken ankle in a plaster cast. A tough, tender-heart! An angel of mercy who could bear nails in her flesh if necessary. And she was a poet too. In the moods of the night she wrote hymns for the Army. She composed tunes for the Army on her harp with the spirit of a medieval jongleur. A refreshing woman for the cynical and myopic nineteen-twenties. She beheld the sun as the flame of life when many other people mistook it for a five-dollar goldpiece.

And in the next decade, when the world was compressed into night, it was with the energy of a crusader facing a new dawn that she answered the summons to take over the universal leadership of the Army. Back she sailed to London, where she had served the first long watch against misery and poverty and disease.

Finally, in 1939, she resigned her leadership of the army and retired to her home in New York. And again war came to the world. But the General of the fighting Army of Salvation has not lost her faith that the men of good will are destined to hold the reshaping of the world in their hands. She is unafraid of a fight. Her own army has shown the way. "Do not abolish the fighting instinct in man. But let him attack his *real* enemies. Mobilize him for well-being. And the day will come when his militarism will be transformed into millennium."

HELEN KELLER

Important Dates in Life of Helen Keller

1880—Born at Tuscumbia, Ala.

1882—Deprived of sight and hearing and speech through severe illness.

1887—Got Anne Mansfield Sullivan as her teacher.

1890—First learned to speak.

1896—Entered Cambridge School for Young Ladies.

1900—Entered Radcliffe College.

1904—Graduated with honors. Entered upon a lifelong career of writing and lecturing.

1936—Lost, through death, her "dearest friend and teacher," Anne Sullivan.

Following is a partial list of her books:

1902—*The Story of My Life.*

1903—*Optimism.*

1910—*The World I Live In.*

1927—*My Religion.*

1929—*Midstream.*

1938—*Helen Keller's Journal.*

Helen Keller

Helen Keller

1880—

Peter finley dunne and Mark Twain were discussing the blindness of Helen Keller. "God, how dull it must be for her," exclaimed the author of *Mr. Dooley*. "Every day the same, and every night the same as the day!"

"You're damned wrong there," retorted Mark Twain. "Blindness is an exciting business, I tell you. If you don't believe it, get up some dark night on the wrong side of your bed when the house is on fire and try to find the door."

Helen Keller, because of her handicap, has enjoyed the excitement of trying to find the door out of the darkness—not only for herself but for the rest of mankind. Hers is the cause of the blind leading the blind, and of the seeing as well, to a new vision of life.

II

At her birth she was normal, like other children. When she was twenty months old, however, she was stricken with an illness —the doctors called it "an acute congestion of the brain"—which deprived her of her sight and her hearing and consequently of

[*289*]

her speech. Her parents looked pityingly upon her. Another of those human creatures condemned to the existence of an animal. How could she ever be expected to have *sense* if she was deprived of two-fifths of her *senses?* People who were merely blind, or merely deaf-mute, could be taught somehow to communicate with the rest of the world. But this child who was blind and deaf and mute—what hope was there ever for *her?*

A pathetic little animal who could neither understand nor make herself understood. Instinctively she felt that she was different from the rest of the world, and this feeling made her furious. She kicked and she screamed and she scratched at the people who tried to approach her. Unable to play like other children, she amused herself by tearing their clothes and snipping their hair with a scissors. A pitiable nuisance. There was no way of teaching her to behave. One day she locked her mother in the pantry, and she laughed as she felt the vibration of her mother's pounding against the door.

A nuisance and a danger. She had a baby doll and a baby sister. She loved her doll, because she was allowed to play with it. But she didn't love her baby sister, because she wasn't allowed to play with *it*. Once she found the baby sleeping in the cradle which belonged to the doll. In a fit of temper she overturned the cradle, but her mother fortunately caught the baby as it fell to the floor.

A danger not only to others but to herself. Accidentally spilling a glass of water on her apron, she spread it out to dry before the smoldering fireplace. When the apron failed to dry quickly enough, she drew nearer and threw it over the live coals. In an instant her clothes were ablaze. Her old nurse barely managed to save her life by throwing a blanket over her. "Poor thing," said her relatives, "it might have been more merciful if she had burned to death."

And then there dawned a miraculous day when a teacher came to her and made her a member of the living world.

III

It was thanks to Alexander Graham Bell, inventor of the telephone, that Helen's parents were able to get the "miracle teacher" for their child. Mr. Bell, who had a tender feeling for the "imperfect specimens of the potter's clay," had suggested that Mr. Keller write to the Perkins Institute for the Blind with reference to Helen's problem. As a result of Mr. Keller's letter, the director of the Institute recommended Miss Anne Mansfield Sullivan as a suitable teacher for the six-year-old Helen.

Anne Sullivan, a graduate of the Perkins Institute, was one of those rare geniuses who flower out of the muck of poverty and disease. Her father was a ne'er-do-well drunkard, her brother had died of tuberculosis, and she herself had been threatened with total blindness up to the age of eighteen, when a successful operation had partially cured her. At twenty, when she became Helen's teacher, she had recovered enough of her vision to read for the child and to lead her into a new world.

But how to begin? How to transform thoughts into words when the child had no conception of human language? Anne Sullivan found a way. The morning after she arrived, she gave Helen a doll—an object with which the stricken child was most familiar. And then, using the code for the blind, she slowly spelled out with her fingers into Helen's hand the word *d-o-l-l*. This finger play, to Helen, was a fascinating game. Flushed with excitement, she clumsily imitated the motions, *d-o-l-l*. Then she ran downstairs to her mother and traced those funny motions into *her* hand. "At that time," writes Miss Keller in *The Story of My Life*, "I did not know that I was spelling a word or even that words existed; I was simply making my fingers go in monkey-like imitation." Little by little, however, Miss Sullivan got her to realize that these motions had a meaning. *They pointed out a thing*. Something she played with. Something for which she had once thrown her baby sister out of her cradle. And there were other motions that pointed out other things. *D-o-g* meant something with a fuzzy snout that romped around you. *C-u-p* meant something out of which you drank. *H-a-t* meant something you put on your head when your mother took you out visiting. What a wonderful game! What a wonderful world! It was so full of so many things. *And everything had a name!*

One day she learned a new set of words—*mother, father, sister.* So that's what they were called. She had known them all her life without knowing it. And *teacher.* The name of that lovely new playmate of hers. Come, let's keep on playing the game. It's such fun! Give me more names, more, more. The child's hunger for knowledge was insatiable, and Miss Sullivan fed it with a resourcefulness that was amazing. In the springtime, when the daisies and the buttercups arrived and the birds and the squirrels awoke to new life, her teacher gave her blind little scholar an "insight" into the secrets of nature. And, "as my knowledge of things grew, I felt more and more the delight of the world I was in."

And then Miss Sullivan opened up for her a new delightful world—the world of books. She taught the child to read by supplying her with slips of cardboard on which various words had been printed in raised letters. New things, new names, new ideas. Stories. Poems. Pretty thoughts, pretty rhymes. She couldn't hear those rhymes, but she could feel with her fingers the same sorts of letters at the ends of the lines. Like the pattern of pretty trimmings on her Sunday dress. After all, you don't have to hear and you don't have to see the beautiful things of the world. You get to know them anyhow. You sort of *feel* your way to them.

Why, even those who can see and hear—Anne Sullivan had told her—must *feel* their way toward lots of things. *Hope,* for instance, or *joy,* or *love.*

"Now take love, Helen. Nobody can see it or hear it or taste it or smell it or touch it. Yet it's there just the same, strong and beautiful and real. How do you know? You can just *feel* it, that's how you know."

"Yes, Anne, *I* can feel it. I love *you*."

And thus the soul of Helen unfolded gradually until one day— miracle of miracles!—she learned to speak. The process was long and laborious and at times seemingly hopeless. The method, briefly, was as follows: Her teacher pronounced certain sounds while Helen passed her fingers over her teacher's tongue and lips and throat as these sounds were being pronounced. Then, passing her fingers over her own organs of speech, Helen tried to imitate the sounds by imitating the positions of these organs. After a seemingly endless succession of failures, the child—she was ten years old at the time—finally succeeded in articulating the letters of the alphabet. And then came the great moment of her life when she stammered out her first connected sentence—"It is warm."

The barrier between herself and the rest of the world had at last broken down. She was—almost—like other people! Her preliminary training had rescued her from the prison of her isolated helplessness. And now she was ready to enter with her peers into the competitive race of higher education.

IV

IN 1896, ACCOMPANIED BY HER TEACHER, she entered the Cambridge (Massachusetts) School for Young Ladies in preparation for Radcliffe College. Miss Sullivan attended the classes with her, took the necessary notes and then interpreted them to Helen in the code language for the blind. Her examinations Helen took at home under the supervision of the principal who had learned the "manual alphabet" and who spelled out the questions into her hand. She answered the questions on a typewriter by means of the touch system. "She'll never make it," said her teachers at the start. But she made it, and within a comparatively short time. Only a year after her admission to the Cambridge School, she passed her preliminary examinations for Radcliffe—and received "honors" in English and in German. Two years later she passed the final examinations and entered Radcliffe College— still inseparable from her "beloved" Anne Sullivan.

And now she was no longer aware of her handicaps. Together with the rest of the students she was ready to plunge eagerly into the hidden world of knowledge. "In the wonderland of Mind I felt as free as the next." She studied Shakespeare under Professor Kittredge and English Composition under Professor Copeland —"men who were able to give new sight to the blind." It was Charles Townsend Copeland—known affectionately to his students as "Copey"—who discovered her genius as a writer. "You have something of your own to say, Miss Keller, and you have a manner of your own in saying it." He suggested that she expand some of her classroom compositions into a story of her life. She followed the suggestion and gave to the world one of the rarest of human documents—the struggle of a soul, hedged in by excessive limitations, to penetrate an unlimited universe. And the universe, as she found it in her undergraduate days and throughout her later life, was a magical place of "large loves and heavenly charities." Blindness, she declares, is nothing; and deafness, nothing. We are all blind and deaf to the eternal things. But nature is kind to us all in her very unkindness. She has endowed all of us, possessors of five puny senses at most, with an infinite sixth sense—"a sense which sees, hears, feels, all in one."

The Story of My Life was published in *Ladies' Home Journal*, and later in book form. In the meantime, Helen Keller had been graduated from Radcliffe—*cum laude.* With the money she received from the sale of her manuscript, she settled down with Anne Sullivan on a farm in Wrentham, Massachusetts, for a life of writing and contemplation. A silent, soothing, yet exciting world. Rambles into the woodland—Anne Sullivan had strung a wire from tree to tree, so that Helen could go walking all alone without being lost. Excursions with her friends in her rowboat on the lake—"it is fun to try to steer by the scent of watergrasses and lilies, and of bushes that grow on the shore." Canoeing in the moonlight—"I cannot, it is true, see the moon behind the pines, but I can fancy that I feel the shimmer of her garments as I trail my hand in the water." Imagining the world as it really is—"has anyone ever known the *real* world?" Translating the sensations of sight into the sensations of touch—"often I had felt petals showered upon me by a passing breeze, and so I could imagine the sunset as a vast rose garden from which the petals had been shaken and were drifting through the sky." And, most joyous experience of them all, reading books—"literature is my Utopia." Anne supplied her with all the classics printed in Braille, and her sensitive fingers were kept constantly busy "looking" into the hearts of the masters. No need to pity Helen Keller on her Wrentham farm, with Anne Sullivan for her guardian and the entire world for her company.

And then a third person joined their rich and exciting world. John Macy, one of her English instructors at Radcliffe. He married Anne Sullivan and came to live with them at Wrentham. "I cannot enumerate the helpful kindnesses with which he smoothed my paths . . . Once, when I was tired with the manual labor of my copying, he sat up all night and typed forty pages of my manuscript, so that they might reach the press in time." A new variation in the old triangle of two women and a man. A triangle not of passion and jealousy and revenge, but of faith and charity and love.

V

FOR A BRIEF SPRINGTIME OF ECSTASY, Helen Keller was herself to experience the love of a woman for a man. During a brief vacation of Anne Sullivan and John Macy, a young man had come to her as her secretary. Love laughs at locksmiths—and at the makers of all other sorts of barriers. The young man proposed to Helen; and Helen, in a moment of yearning forgetfulness, accepted him. "For a brief space I danced in and out of the gates of Heaven, wrapped up in a web of bright imaginings." But she rapidly awoke to the reality. Physical love, marriage, the joys and the responsibilities of motherhood—these things were not for her. She must remain content in this world of her own, surrounded by her dreams and her books.

And her friends. It has been granted to few to enjoy so many and such abiding friendships as were Helen Keller's. Among those who gave her of their very hearts—to mention only a handful—were the philanthropists H. H. Rogers and Andrew Carnegie and Otto Kahn, who tided her over many a dismal bog when her finances were low; Mark Twain, that sad man of laughter who always used to tell her that she saw better than most people—"the world, Helen, is full of unseeing eyes, vacant, staring, soulless eyes"; Frank Doubleday, her publisher "whose kindness to me has been the kindness not only of a friend but of a father"; Eugene Debs, "that neglected St. Francis of the twentieth century"; and Alexander Graham Bell, of whom she wrote at the time of his death—"Although life has never seemed the same since we learned . . . that Dr. Bell was dead, yet the mist of tears is resplendent with the part of himself that lives on in me."

Her life was saddened by the departure of her friends. But she went on with her work of teaching both the seeing and the blind. She traveled across the country on a lecture tour—she had learned to speak with sufficient clearness to make herself understood on the platform—and she was hailed everywhere as a "miraculous freak of nature." She was amused at the picture that she got of herself through the newspapers. "I learned for the first time that I was *born* blind, deaf and dumb, that I educated myself, that I could distinguish colors, hear telephone messages . . . that I was never sad, never discouraged, never pessimistic, that I applied myself with celestial energy to being happy . . . We supplied (the newspapers) with the facts when we were asked for them; but we never knew what became of these facts." What the stunt-seeking public failed to recognize about Helen Keller was merely this—that she was a human being with somewhat more than her share of mortal affliction and decidedly more than her share of immortal genius. The gods had given her less sight but more vision than the ordinary.

Her vision enabled her to see into the future of mankind. She believed that the salvation of humanity would come through an intelligent application of Socialism—food for the hungry, shelter for the homeless, education for the ignorant, peace among the nations, and justice for all. "There is in the world today too much thoughtlessness and too little joy." If the greedy were able to *think* better, the needy would be able to *live* better. In her contemplation of human progress, she said, she was neither too sanguine nor too despondent. "Like the poet Henry van Dyke" —she wrote—"I am not an optimist; there's too much evil in the world and in me. Nor am I a pessimist; there is too much good in the world and in God. So I am just a meliorist, believing that He wills to make the world better, and trying to do my bit to help and wishing that it were more."

And so, like a sundial—"I record only the serene hours of life"—she lived in her beautiful world and tried to do her bit to help make it more beautiful. And when the shadows fell across her path, she brushed away her tears and waited patiently for the next bright day. One of the darkest shadows of her life fell when Anne Sullivan died (1936). It was as if a part of her own soul had died. "I suppose," observes Dr. Richard C. Cabot, "that such an extraordinary partnership of two human souls has never existed before upon this earth." For a time, Helen Keller was like a lost creature. But finally she shook off her despondency and with the help of her new secretary, Miss Polly Thompson, she went on with her work. Went on interpreting through her sensitive mind the world which she "saw" through her sensitive fingers. And how vividly she could see with those fingers of hers! One day she visited the studio of the sculptress, Malvina Hoffman. Among the statuary that she studied, she came upon the figure of a man. She felt the folds of the cloak, the rope girdle, the sandals on the feet. "A monk," she said. Then she went on and felt a wolf pressing its head to the man's side, a rabbit resting in his arms, a bird nestled in the fold of his cowl. She traced her fingers back to the man's face. It was raised toward the sky. "A lover of God and a friend of the animals . . ." And then, "I see! It is St. Francis!"

Like St. Francis of Assisi, Helen Keller is convinced that the end of the road toward which she is so patiently groping is but the beginning of a more beautiful road. "I cannot understand the poor faith that fears to look into the eyes of death." For beyond lies the city of the sun where she knows that she will meet again her departed friends. A confirmed Swedenborgian, she declares that after her death she will for the first time be *truly* able to see. And so, "with steadfast thought I follow sight beyond all seeing, until my soul stands up in spiritual light and cries, 'Life and death are one!' "

MADAME CHIANG KAI-SHEK

Important Dates in Life of Madame Chiang Kai-shek

1899—Born in Shanghai.

1908—Came with her sisters to America.

1913–17—Attended Wellesley College.

1927—Married Generalissimo Chiang Kai-shek.

1934—Launched, with her husband, the New Life Movement for the regeneration of China.

1936—Secured the release of her husband who had been kidnaped by Chinese bandits.

1937–42—Helped her husband in leading the fight of the Chinese people for their independence.

Madame Chiang Kai=shek

Madame Chiang Kai-shek

1899—

THE SOONGS were a hustling family in the South of China. The entire coast of the United States was dotted with the tea rooms and the restaurants of adventurous Chinese like them. They were the restless pioneering tradesmen—the dynamic class of every civilization. They were the bridge through which the east and the west met—the carriers of the twentieth century seed of internationalism.

In 1872 the Soong family sent out one of their number, a nine-year-old lad, to learn the tea and the silk business in his uncle's shop at Boston. It was a glorious opportunity, not given to many sons of China, to acquire the business habits—and the success habits—of the United States. Soong Yao-ju came to Boston, worked in his uncle's shop—and soon discovered that he was unhappy about the whole affair. Perhaps, as he took his walks along the Boston harbor, the sea awakened in him an instinct for poetry that the hypnosis of business had long put to sleep in the rest of the family. The restlessness of the sea waves made him long for things unattainable in the little silk shop, stirred him with a vague, indefinable longing that can lead either to destruction or to greatness.

But for the present, Yao-ju kept accounts and learned to become an efficient business machine. And then, at thirteen, he could stand it no longer. He rushed down to the harbor and stowed aboard a ship that was putting out to sea. Like the dreamer that he was, he didn't know exactly where the ship was going; but his instinct told him that the sea air was good for him.

And then matters took a radical turn. He put ashore at North Carolina, was converted from the religion of his ancestors to Christianity, and changed his name to Charles Jones Soong. He was adopted into the home of a rich textile manufacturer and was brought up as a wealthy American son. He received a thorough education at a preparatory school and at the Methodist Trinity College. And then he studied divinity at Vanderbilt University and became a full fledged Methodist pastor. He decided to go back to China as a missionary and to bring the good news of the Gospel to the sons and the daughters of Confucius.

But the young man was still uneasy. He returned to Shanghai and found that in this city of go-getting aggressiveness, western fashion, he had scarcely the heart to preach the message of a Christian patience and spiritual concentration, exactly as it had been preached two thousand years ago. For a time he devoted himself to the importation of foreign machinery for flour mills and cotton factories. And then he went into the interior and saw the deplorable conditions of the coolies and the peasants by the hundreds of millions—and he found again the vision of adventure for which he had run away. He joined the underground movement of those who were laboring to overthrow the corrupt dynasty of the Manchu Emperors who had kept the colossus of China in a swoon of opiate impotence for many years. He became the close collaborator of Doctor Sun Yat-sen, the leader of the fight for a Chinese republic. He founded a publishing house ostensibly to print Bibles in his missionary work, but secretly to issue pamphlets designed to stir the people up against the monarchy. In his mission—Christ's mission—of a preacher turned revolutionist, he was finding his salvation.

As a political agitator, however, he was not outstanding. He did more for the revolution in his private capacity as a husband and father than ever he was to realize. He married a Methodist like himself and brought up four children in the Christian faith. And three of these children changed the destiny of China.

II

THEY had charming names, these three girls. Eling, which means "Kindly Life"; Chingling, "Glorious Life"; and Mayling, "Beautiful Life." But Charlie Soong's neighbors in Shanghai pitied him. Of what use are *girls* to a father—and *three* of them? Truly, Soong was blessed with much misfortune. And when he observed that he was planning to send his daughters to America for an education, the conservative Chinese were gravely shocked. *Girls to be educated like boys?* A hundred generations of ancestors would hear of this and call down upon Soong the wrath of the mighty gods of China. Even Soong's friends were sorely puzzled when they heard him declare, "The emancipation of women will be the first step toward the freedom of China."

Mayling was the youngest of the Soong daughters, not more than nine when she accompanied her sisters to America. Eling and Chingling entered Wesleyan College, in Georgia; and Mayling, by special arrangement, lived on the campus with the daughter of the college president. She was a rough little tomboy; she had been brought up in her brother's clothes. However, it was her immense eyes and the extraordinary beauty in them that justified her name—"Beautiful Life."

She was never afraid of a fight. She had a quick, passionate temper, and quarreled hotly. Once an older person walked into the room where she was disputing with her little friend, and said, "Mayling, are you not ashamed to carry on like this?" And Mayling replied with a blush, "Oh, Mrs. Ainsworth, I rather enjoy it!"

When she was ten, her inclinations were literary. She had read every word of Dickens. She spoke an elegant English with a Georgian accent like her father's. She was an American with a pride in America. She spent one summer in a Northern school; and when the history teacher asked her to describe Sherman's march through Georgia, the little girl from Shanghai replied, "Pardon me, I am a Southerner, and that subject is very painful to me. May I omit it?"

In the meantime, great events had taken place in China. The miracle had happened. In 1911 the dynasty of the Manchu Emperors had been overthrown by the party of Doctor Sun Yat-sen. Like a rotten tree the monarchy had fallen before the swift blow of the revolutionary axe. The rebel troops had occupied Wuchang, and Hankow, Nanking and Shanghai, in short order. The success of the revolution had caught even Doctor Sun Yat-sen unprepared. He was traveling in America trying to raise funds. But he rushed back to China and became the President of the Chinese Republic. Mayling's sister Chingling, trembling with excitement, wrote an article about the new Republic in her college paper, the *Wesleyan:* "It is one of the greatest events of the twentieth century, the greatest event since Waterloo . . . Five months ago our wildest dream could not have been for a Republic . . . The Revolution has established in China Liberty and Equality, those two inalienable rights of the individual which have caused the loss of so many noble and heroic lives. But there is still Fraternity to be acquired. Dean Cranshawe, of Colgate University, said in one of his lectures that Fraternity is the yet unrealized ideal of humanity, that Liberty has no safe foundation except human brotherhood, and that real Equality can never be anything but a dream until men feel towards each other as brothers. And it may be for China, the oldest of the nations, to point the way to this Fraternity . . ."

III

As SOON AS they completed their education, Eling and Chingling went home to take part in the great adventure, and Mayling was left alone in America. She entered Wellesley College and made a brilliant record. She astonished and delighted her classmates with her quaint Southern accent, her American-Chinese manners, her variety of talents. She graduated with the highest academic distinction. And then she returned to China at the age of nineteen, after an American sojourn of ten years—a period during which "I have been all over the United States, in practically every single State." She had left Shanghai as a child and now she was returning as a woman to undergo a process of readjustment which would not be easy. Among other things, she even had to relearn her mother tongue. A stranger in the strange land of her birth.

And indeed it was a strange China to which she was returning. Matters had taken a tragic turn for those aflame with a vision. The reactionary clique had overthrown the liberal government; and Sun Yat-sen, together with Mayling's father (who was now the treasurer of the Chinese Railway Commission), had been forced for a time to flee to Japan.

But at that moment of bitter defeat, the amazing Soong family had pledged itself by marriage to the foremost men who were fighting for the new China. Eling married a wealthy young liberal, Doctor Kung, descendant of China's leading financiers. Chingling, who had become Doctor Sun Yat-sen's secretary, flaunted the traditions of conservative China by announcing her engagement to this middle-aged philosopher who already had children by a first wife. A second wife in China was looked upon almost as an outcast. But Chingling showed the courage of her emancipation by marrying the man whose burning ideal she shared.

And now Mayling alone had no husband. Doctor Sun and his government had already succeeded in returning to the Southern Provinces before she came home to Shanghai. From the quiet luxury of the college campus she found herself suddenly plunged into the stormiest period of her people's history. China had entertained the dream of a united Republic, and had emerged from this dream a country divided and bleeding. The Northern Provinces had been seized and ravaged by the war lords who had marched against Doctor Sun. The nation was going through the first stages of a civil war.

At her mother's house in Shanghai, Mayling met the military adviser and supporter of Doctor Sun—the irrepressible Chiang Kai-shek. In 1912 he had studied the art of war at a Japanese military school. He had been drawn to the revolutionary cause and had led an army in a successful campaign against the Manchu dynasty.

And now suddenly he was fired with another ideal. For his eyes had met Mayling's. And Mayling's eyes had met his. He came to her mother to ask for the hand of "Beautiful Life"— and he was bluntly refused. He was a divorced man. It was rumored that he was a philanderer. "There were at least two women in Canton to whom he should have been married." Moreover, he was not a Christian.

In despair young Chiang went to his friend, Doctor Sun, for advice. "Wait a while," counseled the older man. And Chiang, even at that age, proved himself a master strategist. Impulsive and audacious by nature, he played a waiting game—he waited almost ten years. And when he had become one of the foremost personalities in the Asiatic world, he gained his prize.

IV

IT WAS ON DECEMBER 1, 1927, that the "strong man" of China was married to Mayling. The blunt right arm of the Flower Kingdom had found its heart. Doctor Sun had died, and Chiang was appointed commander-in-chief of the nationalist Chinese armies. The "fathers of the Chinese Republic" had realized that in a world of bandits and aggressors, of dictatorial ambitions and imperialistic wars, the dreams of the great Chinese philosopher were worth only the size and the equipment and the morale of Generalissimo Chiang's armies.

Chiang was a forthright soldier who owed his reliability to a few simple moral and social ideals which he had derived from his contact with Doctor Sun. Thus far, the sacredness of his mission had scarcely touched him. But when he took his wife, he entered upon an entirely new phase of the spiritual world. Love had made a shrewd and momentous choice. Companionship with Mayling had transformed him from a great soldier into a great man.

And his country was sadly in need of his greatness. Doctor Sun's dream of a united China was as far from realization as ever. A group of communists, in defiance of Chiang, had seized the Northern Provinces and had established their government at Hankow. But in defiance of this government and in spite of the peril, Madame Chiang went with her husband from the modern city of Shanghai, on the sea coast, to the little "hamlet" of Nanking, in the interior, to set about building a capital for the new China that must one day be the China for all.

Even in the land of a people thousands of years old there is a new beginning and a new adventure—an ever recurrent urge to pioneer—and this must be the secret of its deathlessness. Nanking was a dirty little village. Its houses were icy barns. Its streets were so narrow that two vehicles could not pass abreast. Yet it was from here that the builders hoped to extend the work and to set the spirit radiating for a reborn China. And Madame Chiang joined heartily in the work of her husband. With the stuff of national destiny in her hands, she summoned all the courage and the philosophy of her twenty-nine years. She established schools for the children of the revolutionists who had died in battle. For the *new* China must be the *young* China. "These children, it seemed to me," she wrote some years later, "would be the most valuable material if they were molded right, as they all had revolutionary blood in their veins." And so she put into practice her long cherished ideals of education. "My children were taught to use their hands and their bodies and to reason out why such and such a thing should be done in such and such a way." She put into the heads of these citizens of the future the instinct of *learning* by *doing*.

And she put into the head of her husband, the Generalissimo Chiang Kai-shek, the instinct of *doing* by *learning*. In long walks, in the quiet intimate communication of their hearts, she inspired Chiang with her dreams. Under her influence, and because of a promise he had made to her mother, he studied the New Testament and became a Christian. Through her he learned the ideals of Western—and especially of American—ethics. Under her guidance he came into contact with the political philosophy of Thomas Jefferson and with the social mysticism of Abraham Lincoln.

But theirs was a marriage of reciprocity. Madame Chiang was her husband's teacher—and his follower. She gave him of her mind, and she partook of his courage. When the communists in the North became aggressive and the Generalissimo marched his armies into combat, she accompanied him, "living wherever they could find quarters, in thatched huts and railroad stations and farmhouses." She saw for the first time, in the hinterland of China, the pitiable living conditions of the millions of coolies, and the more she saw of the filth and the ignorance and the degradation, the more she became determined to clean it all up—figuratively as well as literally. She inspired her husband with plans for a crusade of morality and cleanliness among the Chinese masses—a campaign against "ignorance, dirt, carelessness, unsuitable dwellings, the corruption that has for so long cost so much in human suffering." The Chinese had perpetuated during all the modern centuries their ancient superstitions. She was determined that they should perpetuate only their ancient virtues—courtesy, responsibility, honesty, good will. She enlisted the aid of all the missionaries in China, experts in evangelism, to help her emancipate the Chinese masses. The campaign was called the *New Life Movement.*

And as if to sweep away a hundred centuries, she traveled with her husband by plane into portions of China rarely visited by the government officials. They penetrated mountain fastnesses and robber strongholds and came to villages whose inhabitants had been out of touch with the center of China for a thousand years. The members of the government at Nanking were shocked. This sort of hobnobbing with the riff-raff was quite un-Chinese. "Presidents and generals simply never went to such places." And without even a strong bodyguard! How dared they! They would surely be assassinated.

But Madame and the Generalissimo were determined. It was no small task that they had set for themselves. Overnight they were trying to bring the nation up to the habits of the twentieth century. And what could be a better example for the superstition-ridden people than for their leaders to walk unarmed and unafraid in their midst? Wherever they went, they studied the local industries of the people, the opportunities for political and economic reforms. They asked questions of "petty officials, even passers-by." Madame Chiang met the leading women of the various communities and encouraged them to step out of their homes, to take an interest and a direction in public affairs, to assume a social responsibility. And in several places they enabled the women to open clinics for the treatment of their opium patients.

On one occasion the Generalissimo nearly paid with his life for his confidence in the people. As he entered the Northern Provinces unarmed, he was seized and kidnaped by a group of rebel generals sympathetic to the communists. His few attendants were massacred. All China awoke one morning to learn that the government in the person of Chiang was held prisoner in a small room in Sian. It was a position of extreme danger. But the Generalissimo faced it with a fearless dignity. He refused to take food from his captors. He ordered them to shoot him instantly if they were in rebellion, or to release him instantly if they still recognized him as their lawful head—in which latter case he would bring them to civil trial.

In the meantime, the news of his capture had electrified the world. Panic had swept over Nanking, China's capital city. The only one who remained calm was Madame Chiang Kai-shek. She spoke to the people over the radio and told them to hold their peace. When the government offered to send an army to Sian, she warned against bloodshed. She wired to the leader of the rebels who were holding her husband a message in which she pointed out "the disastrous effects that your action will have upon the unity of the nation"; and she expressed her belief that "you mean no harm to the country or to the Generalissimo by your imprudent and impetuous action . . . and therefore you ought to retrieve yourself before it is too late." Then she took a plane together with her brother, T. V. Soong, and an American friend, and flew straight to Sian in order to negotiate with her husband's captors for his release. Before she arrived in the rebel stronghold, she handed a pistol to her American friend and ordered him to shoot her if she were to be seized by the rebel troops.

Charmed by her daring, the captors allowed her to come into the presence of her husband. He looked up from the bed where he was confined. "Why have you come here?" he asked in alarm.

"I have come to see you," she answered with the nonchalance of a schoolgirl.

The eyes of the Generalissimo filled with tears. Only that morning he had opened his Bible at the sentence, "Jehovah will now do a new thing: He will make a woman protect a man."

The kidnapers had lost heart for the adventure. And on Christmas Day—thanks to Mayling's diplomacy—the Generalissimo was released, unharmed.

V

AND then came the evil little men who in their madness believed they could crush the work that Madame Chiang and her husband were doing for China. The Japanese sent their legions into North China, and forced Chiang's governors out of Manchuria. They swept into the interior of China and swaggered their pistols at the customs officials and blackmailed and browbeat and bled China for billions of dollars. And then, on July 28, 1937, they let loose their entire horde of hatred upon the people of Madame Chiang. They failed to realize, these brigands with their ships and their tanks and their planes, that their clumsy weapons were striking against phantoms—wraiths that lured them into ambush on lonely roads, specters that led them to death through hunger and disease and attrition, shadows whose true substance was an idea that stood woundless and deathless in a hail of shrapnel and taunted them again and again to come on to their destruction . . .

Madame Chiang associated herself with China's air force. Though she got plane-sick easily and was obliged on long trips to lie on the floor with smelling salts to her nose, she flew more miles than anyone else in China who was not a pilot. She rallied the men. She looked over them as a mother. She knew every plane and every pilot. "Whenever they took off, she was down at the field to watch." She climbed a hill in the midst of a hail of bombs to observe and check the fighting, and she met all the returning pilots with accurate accounts of what they had accomplished.

As the Chinese armies slowly retreated into the interior, leaving all their large industrial cities on the coast to the enemy, she helped to organize semi-mobile industries that were manned by refugees. The machinery for each industrial unit was light and could be transported farther and farther inland, close to the unexploited raw materials, so that the Chinese war production moved on foot with the fortunes of the armies and the people.

Today Madame Chiang is fighting the greatest battle of her life. "I am not a mystic. I am not a visionary. I believe in the world seen, not in the world unseen." But the implications and the possibilities of the ideals for which she is fighting are greater perhaps than those entertained by any mystic philosopher of the past.

Sad irony. Madame Sun, who during the civil war had joined the communists, came finally back to her. What she anticipated as a reunion in the hour of greatest joy has become a reconciliation in the hour of deepest tragedy. China has been united at last—not, however, by the powers of humanity, but by the forces of barbarism. The Chinese have been compelled to move their capital around in lively fashion—from Nanking to Hankow, from Hankow to Chungking. There in Chungking, their last great stronghold, they have blasted caves in the rocks and sent their population underground into the shelter of the earth. There they are fighting at this hour. The dream of Doctor Sun Yat-sen is no longer visionary. It has been transformed into the hard and practical blood-tested, fire-tested fortress of rock. And in that shape it will remain "until the besieged people of China and of the world shall step once more into the light."

And then? Madame Chiang prophetically outlines the place

of a free China in a free world: "We are determined that there shall be no more exploitation of China . . . the ruthless and shameless exploitation of our country by the West in the past and the hard-dying illusion that the best way to win our hearts is to kick us in the ribs." No nation and no individual, she insists, must be allowed "to wax rich" at the expense of other nations or individuals. All inordinate incomes must be whittled down, by progressive taxation, to a point that will be healthy both for the rich individual and for his poorer neighbors. For "the excess of wealth should belong to humanity . . . There must be equality among all peoples and races . . . peace and harmony for the nations; clothing, food and housing for the individuals." Adhering to the principles of Doctor Sun Yat-sen, China must become an integral part in the social democratic realignment of the nations. "We have won our place in the front rank by our prolonged and unyielding resistance to violence. We shall keep it by playing a major part in building a better world."